The Art of Writing Fiction

MARY BURCHARD ORVIS

New York

PRENTICE-HALL, INC.

1948

PRINTED IN THE UNITED STATES OF AMERICA

To

My G.I. Students

Preface

WRITERS are not only born, they must also be made. And they must do the making themselves. The task is arduous; all the hints and helps they may receive will not make it an easy one. "Inspiration does indeed come at the outset to every writer," says Edith Wharton, "but it comes most often as an infant, helpless, stumbling, inarticulate, to be taught and guided; and the beginner, during this time of training his gift, is as likely to misuse it as a young parent is to make mistakes in teaching his child."

This book seeks to give writers help in making the most of their gifts and to give beginners help in avoiding wasted effort, misdirected energy, and discouragement. Never before have so many people had exciting and interesting experience to communicate. Indeed, every former G.I. is a potential author. All too often, however, the subject of narration, whether explored in books or classes, does not take up the many related matters—the very "geography" of writing—which make the writer master of his province. The story may "get itself told," but the experience is not communicated.

By emphasizing the simple and even incidental, out of which moving and often complex fiction arises, this book attempts to encourage the beginner and free him from inhibiting ideas about plot. It also attempts to direct his attention away from the imitative and sterile and into the creative and sincere, which offer the only chance for real satisfaction. It underlines insight into experience as primary, and skill and technique as necessary but nevertheless secondary. Finally, it tries to show, by means of extensive quotation from the best writers of our time, the subjects best suited to narration and the devices available to achieve the desired effects.

Even the writer who looks only to financial rewards will, it is hoped, find this book helpful. Inasmuch as the slicks which constitute his goal require a high degree of dexterity, he must acquire a high degree of technical proficiency, and we endeavor to show him the way. To the experimenter and innovator in the art of writing fiction, an immense territory—in scope, technique, and style—is open today, but this free range is itself an obstacle to beginners. For them indecision and want of discipline almost coincide, and for them we have attempted to set up our major signposts at the start of the road, whether their final aim is the run of the goldmine slicks or the satisfying acclaim that does eventually come to the serious and important writer.

The author makes no pretense to originality. The contribution, if there is one, lies in combining various important matters, in relating them to each other, in synthesizing discussion of subject matter, attitudes, principles, and techniques.

She acknowledges a great indebtedness to the many writers of literary criticism upon whom she has drawn, both consciously and unconsciously. She is especially aware of the influence of the prefaces of Henry James, contained in *The Art of the Novel*, and is also indebted to Professors Joseph Warren Beach and Herbert Muller and to Alfred Kazin, whose books have helped form her judgments. Above all, she is grateful to the many authors and publishers who have responded so generously to appeals for the privilege of using illustrative passages.

M. B. O.

Contents

Establishing Creative Attitudes

WHAT must one do to become a writer? What does it take? The answer is that, like other arts, fiction writing takes a good deal. It takes a rich personal development, with the widest possible background of education and experience. It takes concentrated, intensive thought. The writer must have something to say. Creative writers often seem, it is true, to live in the ivory tower, and they may do so as far as certain practical aspects of life are concerned; but more often they have with them in their tower a knowledge of the best that has been thought and written. They have standards gained by disciplines and established avenues of intellectual growth.

"One must *be* something in order to *do* anything," Goethe wrote; and Thomas Mann reminds us that Goethe said that he could not read without feeling a compulsion to produce works similar to the great things he read; "he brings home to all artists the fact that it is necessary for them to keep in constant contact with masterpieces, so that the creative spirit can be maintained at its height and prevented from relapsing ('*Zurückschwanken*'). The words express a sense of peril with which even he, the greatest, is familiar. It displays the modesty, the constant striving, learning, adaptation, imitation even, which does not dread losing its particular identity, but proceeds on its way with blithe confidence in the power of assimilation to which he refers. . . ." [1] If Mann, who is one of the greatest writers of his time, if not the greatest, feels that way about "what it takes to be a writer," certainly the rest of us should be aware of the necessity for self-development as a basis of good writing.

What we write can rise no higher than its source has risen. The good writer, the serious writer, is a person who has enough development to see life seriously and "see it whole." More often than not, one finds him widely read and highly educated as a result. He may even have imitated the best. What then, having spoken of his familiarity with the work of others, do we mean by the phrase "creative writing"? We mean simply the attitude of openness toward life in all its aspects, combined with an effort to determine one's own view of it and to impose finally upon this view the mental and emotional disciplines which result in making it worth while for other people's consideration. Knowledge, observation, feeling—these are the keystones of a writing career. Combined with imagination and the power to recognize the general in the particular, these qualities go to make up that vague cluster of gifts that we call "artistic temperament." To attempt to define this temperament is to invite argument. It can hardly be defined, because its psychological elements are too little understood. It is perhaps more than anything else, a *way of looking at life* combined with a willingness to sacrifice much to the expression of one's vision. It is more than a willingness to sacrifice; it is a *compulsion* to get something out of one's system.

Good writing is born of deep feeling. It is a result of what Henry James called "some particular sharp impression or concussion." If, having this impression of a given moment, one has also the ability to see its larger aspects, its universal

[1] Thomas Mann, *Freud, Goethe, Wagner*, translated by Rita Matthias-Reil. New York: Alfred A. Knopf, Inc., 1937.

applications, its *symbolism*, he has important gifts indeed. The deep feeling alone is not enough. It is not enough if I am shocked by my husband's philanderings with his stenographer and wish to express my emotion in a story about this situation. It is not enough if I view it in an entirely personal way. I may write this story only if I can treat it with insight; and insight requires literally the ability to see beneath the surface, to see the deeper hidden meaning. And this in turn implies an ability to see things dispassionately, without the blinders of personalized emotion; it implies sympathy and understanding. The neurotic who can see only one side of any personal relationship and that side his own, is not very well equipped for the kind of objective view which is necessary for illumination. The principle of objectivity is important.

Is this paradox? We have said that the artist expresses his own individual point of view, his own vision of life. Now we say that he must learn to be dispassionate; to view life and his own work objectively. "An act of self-expression might better be called self-exposure," writes John Dewey in *Art as Experience*, "unless the activity is undertaken as a means to a consciously entertained consequence, and also with a passionate excitement about the subject-matter." This precept bids one be excited about his ideas, but at the same time it urges him to bring cool judgment to bear upon them. Mere feeling is not enough.

Nature, on the other hand, has made us all egocentric. Few of us are capable of judging our own feelings and attitudes, much less those of other people. The writer can only try to distinguish between his own private frustrations and the legitimate uses to which they may be put in writing. He must learn to evaluate his experience in terms of fiction. That involves facing himself and the things that he does not know, facing his own faulty background and trying, if need be, to overcome it. If he is sufficiently talented he may overcome it as Jesse Stuart did, by developing his insight and thus making it yield rich fictional material, his own very special "line." The very life that could have handicapped him by its lack of cultural opportunities became the life of his well-understood fictional characters, enabling him to make his real contribution to American literature.

Life presents us with the raw material. We can make of it what we wish. Henry James in his Prefaces[2] recalls a remark of Turgenieff's in regard to the origin of his "fictive picture."

It began for him almost always with the vision of some person or persons, who hovered before him, soliciting him, as the active or passive figure, interesting him and appealing to him just as they were and by what they were. He saw them, in that fashion, as *disponibles*, saw them subject to the chances, the complications of existence, and saw them vividly, but then had to find for them the right relations, those that would most bring them out; to imagine, to invent and select and piece together the situations most useful and favorable to the sense of the creatures themselves, the complications they would be most likely to produce and to feel.

"To arrive at these things is to arrive at my 'story,'" he [Turgenieff] said, "and that's the way I look for it. The result is that I'm often accused of not having 'story' enough. I seem to myself to have as much as I need—to show my people, to exhibit their relations with each other; for that is all my measure. If I watch them long enough I see them come together, I see them *placed*, I see them engaged in this or that act and in this or that difficulty. How they look and move and speak and behave, always in the setting I have found for them, is my account of them—of which I dare say, alas, *que cela manque souvent d'architecture*. But I would rather, I think, have too little architecture than too much—when there's danger of its interfering with my measure of the truth. . . . As for the origin of one's wind-blown germs themselves, who shall say, as you ask, where *they* come from? We have to go too far back, too far behind, to say. Isn't it all we can say that they come from every quarter of heaven, that they are *there* at almost any turn of the road? They accumulate,

[2] Henry James, *The Art of the Novel*, pages 42 and 43. New York: Charles Scribner's Sons, 1934.

and we are always picking them over, selecting among them. They are the breath of life—by which I mean that life, in its own way, breathes them upon us. . . ."

Life breathes the germs of stories upon us. All one need be is open, receptive, *aware*, conscious always of the implied drama of human relations. All one needs is to look about him, look within himself, reflect like a mirror what he actually sees. It is highly important for the beginner to realize that he must look to life for his material, writing from his own direct observation. If I have not met or associated intimately with millionaires, I can hardly expect to write convincingly of them; nor can I write convincingly of a peasant if I have not associated with peasants. If I am a shopgirl in a small town and have never traveled, not even through careful reading, I can hardly hope to create a living senorita in a lace shawl being wooed by a toreador twanging a guitar after a triumphant fight with a bull. If I do not know the senorita, her lover, or the civilization in which they live, they have little reality for me and still less for my reader.

The achievement of *reality*, let us emphasize, is the fiction writer's first and primary aim. A story is an account of certain people in a given action. If my characters live only vaguely in some corner of my imagination, I cannot make others see them. I cannot, in all probability, sustain the required illusion. There have, of course, been great creative imaginations that spoke allegorically of gods and goddesses, of heaven and inferno, of worlds that never were, of things that could not happen. Even Poe's *Tales of Mystery and Imagination* took a special kind of imagination, an imagination springing from a decidedly abnormal temperament, a mind suffering from the effects of drug, alcohol, and disease. Such writing is less common in the twentieth century, which has up to this time been greatly concerned with the depiction of reality. There is, however, a tendency today toward the strange and semi-real, the fantastic and allegorical. The interest in the highly symbolic writings of Kafka, in such a book as his moving *Metamorphosis*, in which a man turns into a cockroach, is of considerable significance. But, for the most part, readers want to have an illusion of the reality of the characters and events depicted.

This discussion of fiction writing is not intended for those whose special inspiration and rare imaginative gift need no help. It is for those beginners in the more generally trodden paths who can write best of things known first hand. The artist can embroider all he wants to and indeed he often weaves a rich carpet from a few threads; but those threads are most likely brought together from a more or less known world, closely observed.

The development of the power of close observation is very important. By camera-like observation of concrete, specific detail, one gathers the elements that serve to make fictional characters come alive. It is no use to describe a heroine who is only the composite of all heroines in the women's magazines; or to describe a Hollywood that one knows only from reading magazines; or to construct a plot which is merely an imitation of some *Saturday Evening Post* story giving the "lowdown" on a business or activity. Such "imaginative" writing is not imaginative at all in the true sense of the word. It is only imitative. The creative writer shuns imitation, except as he uses models for exercises. He shuns the composite heroine or plot; and lest he be contaminated, he shuns the popular magazines. His entire effort is to discover and reveal his own special vision of life.

The creative writer is an experimenter. He is not afraid to try new materials and new methods. He is not afraid to take the everyday things and put them together in *new combinations*, imposing a pattern of his own upon the welter of experience. He knows that if he doesn't give his own vision, he gives nothing. That vision is made up of *sensory impressions* —feeling, hearing, tasting, seeing, smelling; of *emotional experiences*, evoked by sensory impressions, by memory of people and their conduct; *of ideas* evolved in thinking philosophically about people and their lives. Good fiction is always the result of seeing the details of life; seeing them not as isolated details, but as a part of a larger whole. The little boy rolling his hoop in Jules Romains' passage quoted in the next chapter is not just a little boy; he is a symbol and therefore significant to all mankind.

People read in order to enrich their lives one way or another. Our reader may, it is true, be looking merely for escape from his immediate world, for the lightest and most transitory of entertainment; but he is more often, unconsciously perhaps, looking for something "better" than life. He wants greater richness and he is willing to enter imaginatively into the lives of others to get it. If he can, by any chance, recognize himself or his friends in the fictional world of his choice, he is pleased and says, "How true to life that is!" Many readers get their chief pleasure out of this sort of realism, the pleasure of *recognition*. To afford it is one of the aims of literature.

Thomas Mann's ironic portrayal of the eternal feminine in the scenes between Potiphar and his wife in *Joseph in Egypt* gives us this delightful sense of amused recognition; so also does James Joyce's wonderful description, toward the end of *Ulysses*, of the wandering thoughts of a woman lying in bed; so also Franz Werfel's account of the bickerings of the magnificently brave group of Armenians facing extermination in *The Forty Days of Musa Dagh*. All of these literary experiences give the reader a rich, ironic, two-edged sense of the humanity of human beings.

Recognition of the universality of sensory impressions also has its own particular validity. Marcel Proust's vivid descrip-

tion of the long train of recollections invoked by the taste
and smell of a little cake dipped in tea, in *Remembrance of
Things Past*, is the ultimate expression of the tremendously
important role played by associative processes arising from
re-experiencing a sensory impression which was originally
associated with a powerful emotion. The writer who can
catch the vividness of such experience and thus invoke a
similar sensory impression for his reader, gives that reader a
valuable experience. Thomas Wolfe, writing about his ride
on a night train from Albany to New York, evokes memories
of train plush, sound, smell, sight, consciousness, so brilliantly
as to give all train travel new meaning. Wolfe's actual personal experience has been so vividly communicated to his
reader as to give the reader a sense of universality. He becomes aware of the things that he has in common with other
men. This is indeed the art that "speaks" as Joseph Conrad
said in his Preface to *The Nigger of the Narcissus*,[3] "to our
capacity for delight and wonder, to the sense of mystery surrounding our lives, to our sense of pity, and beauty, and pain;
to the latent feeling of fellowship with all creation—and to
the subtle but invincible conviction of solidarity that knits
together the loneliness of innumerable hearts . . . which
binds together all humanity—the dead to the living and the
living to the unborn."

To be able to go out receptively, imaginatively, with great
interest and curiosity, to life and to people, is at once the
secret of real living and the secret of the creative temperament. The great writer often combines the trait of introspec-
tiveness with this power of penetrating into the very heart of
experience, even of submerging himself in the flood of sensory
impressions or in the labyrinth of human motivations and
conduct. "It is difficult to analyze the ultimate quality of an

[3] From *The Nigger of the Narcissus* by Joseph Conrad, copyright 1897, 1920
by Doubleday and Company, Inc.

artist's triumph," writes Frances Birrell in an essay on Marcel Proust and adds:

> Proust, it seems to me, had the extremely rare faculty of seeing his characters objectively and subjectively at the same moment. He can project himself so far into the mind of the persons he is describing that he seems to know more about them than they can ever know about themselves, and the reader feels, in the process, that he never even dimly knew himself before.

Proust wrings the utmost intensity out of such a sensory experience as the scent of the lilacs at his childhood home in Combray, the shifting of the sun's rays on the balcony, the play of light and shadow upon a cathedral façade; out of such emotional experience as the death of his grandmother, his mother's kiss at night, a dinner at the Verdurins, the piano playing of Swann's mistress. Because of this extremely sensitive outgoing quality which was combined in Proust with an insatiable curiosity about the inner lives and deeper motives of people with whom he came in contact, he was able to give to the world a series of books which reach the ultimate in revelation.

It is difficult, indeed, to understand, and much more difficult to make clear to others, the nature of this rare ability to see characters subjectively and objectively at the same time. It seems to involve the elements of sympathetic imagination and objectivity. Proust, for instance, relates with equal vividness and power the story of his grandmother's death and that of an evening in the snobbish society at the Verdurins, combining in both cases his profound powers of insight with deep emotion. But the emotion in some way becomes depersonalized, universalized, and thus of value to others. If it had remained purely personal, it might have been merely a neurotic outlet.

James T. Farrell gives his testimony on this point. When he was asked, for instance, if he wrote about his childhood because he hated his memories and wanted to get rid of them, he replied, "It is overstating to say 'hate.' I suppose that I am compensating to myself but I am not doing it out of anger, because in literature anger is a luxury that you can't afford. Anger throws your concept of character out of line, it destroys an honest and true conception."

Righteous indignation is another matter, of course. Anger about evil as it affects others, anger at social injustice or cruelty between individuals becomes a powerful, dynamic force. Dynamic anger has, moreover, to some extent been purified of the personal; or, to put it differently, the personal has been sublimated into an anger that may be socially valuable. Out of anger has come much great world literature.

The author will stand out between the lines in any case, whatever he does. He is necessarily revealed in the light of the things with which he is concerned. We can speak of the camera-like mind; but we must not carry our comparison too far, for actually the mind is highly selective. It is stimulated by a multitude of situations and people. The author must, like the painter, select from the welter of experience those impressions and ideas which arouse his interest and his enthusiasm. He is a man who has learned to filter his experience. The rays of the sun will not do it for him. And the more sincere he is in his effort to see clearly, to purge his soul of egoistic attitudes, the better his chance of becoming a good writer. He must also rid himself of self-consciousness.

"I must try and write simply, fully, freely, from my heart," says Katherine Mansfield. "*Quietly,* caring nothing for success or failure, but just going on. . . ." Miss Mansfield is perhaps the chief innovator of the modern quality story. This "English Chekhov," as she has been called, left a very complete record of her writing philosophy and experience in her letters and diaries, a record that can hardly be too highly recommended to the student who wishes to acquire a truly creative attitude. John Middleton Murry, Miss Mansfield's husband, pointed out in his Introduction to *The Life of Katherine Mansfield* [4] that "her life was a constant effort towards clarity, towards what William Blake called *Self-annihilation.*" She sought to "make firm her hold upon a kind of vision—the true vision of the Imagination" and in order to attain it she had to achieve "a complete abeyance of the Self." This inward necessity meant to be completely occupied, to the exclusion of all other feelings, by "an intense longing to serve my subject as well as I can." Mr. Murry adds that Mansfield had what Bagehot called "the experiencing nature," which is "but another name to distinguish those rare beings who are governed by an inward compulsion to expose themselves to Life. . . . They can take nothing, in this matter of life-experience, at second hand."

Katherine Mansfield saw in the little incident many revealing indications of character and symbolic truth; thus she was able to produce what James once termed a "picture aiming at those richly summarised and foreshortened effects—the opposite pole again from expansion inorganic and thin—that refer their terms of production, for which the magician has ever to don his best cap and gown, to the inner compartment of our box of tricks. From *them* comes the true grave close consistency in which parts hang together even as the interweavings of a tapestry." This very special talent of Mansfield's for catching the essence of the fleeting moment, combined with her remarkable ability "to throw off the covers that hide the expressiveness of experienced things" so that we see them freshly, vividly, in a new light, makes her very rewarding to the student of writing. Both her statements about writing and her stories themselves offer startling revelations to the novice. This is especially true for the sensitive and in-

---

[4] R. E. Mantz and J. M. Murry, *The Life of Katherine Mansfield*. London: Constable and Co., 1933.

telligent reader, the one capable of responding to the subtlety which implies more than it actually puts into words. Although her art is by no means easily imitated—it is too elusive, too finely and highly wrought—nevertheless the very simplicity of her basic material is provocative and encouraging, especially for those people who have mistakenly thought of fiction chiefly in terms of plot.

Reading Mansfield's stories, one realizes anew the potentialities of everyday material about us all. Mansfield's Miss Brill and her Ma Parker are everywhere, within our common experience. We too can learn to expand the incidental and fugitive contact into something universal and significant. We can do it if we develop our insight, our awareness, and our sense of form.

All good fiction has form, no matter how modern or surrealistic. Indeed the particular value of fiction over raw experience is that it imposes a pattern or a meaning upon life. Life is frustrating, chaotic, illogical, fantastic, and, more often than not, apparently meaningless; full of useless suffering, pain, tragedy. Yet man, as a rational and idealistic creature, craves order, plan, and satisfaction of individual potentialities. He may turn to religion, philosophy, poetry, or fiction for his answer to the riddle of life. If he turns to fiction, he wants some sort of organization, meaning, and pattern. It is the author's task to supply these values; to supply them, but not to falsify life itself. It is his task somehow to find Conrad's "fellowship" for him who is lonely, and that means Everyman.

The writer must see the relations of things; he must recognize cause and effect in human affairs and thus satisfy our sense of order or justice. We see other, fictional people struggling as we ourselves struggle, suffering as we ourselves suffer, and thus we find solace, that strange selfish solace implied in the phrase "misery loves company." There is no escape from struggle as long as we live: we struggle to be born, to maintain life, to mould it to our heart's desire. We can only hope to gain enough wisdom to carry on well our battle against nature, environment, man, and society; and against the by-no-means-puny conflicts within our own psychic being. The individual is naturally egocentric, and the environment is inhibiting and often hostile to his anti-social and even his legitimate urges. Thus it is that a man must always struggle, must always be engaged in conflict. Indeed, the very modern therapeutic treatment by psychoanalysis is aimed at the elucidation and elimination of conflicts within the psyche.

Perhaps the conflicts are often what make life interesting. They give it tang and tension. Real living is not just existing on a plane of sameness, peace, acquiescence. Real living is more than routine. It is made up of moments of electrification, recognition, shock. *Shock* is a true attribute of the aesthetic experience, even if it only affords recognition of a fact or truth. Shock intensifies living. It comes when man is up against the new and different and therefore begins to live more excitingly. He is suddenly lifted out of the everyday; and old, humdrum patterns of thought and conduct no longer serve. He must devise new ones. Out of this clash with the new situation comes Longinus' "much food for fresh reflection." Of this kind of crisis is fiction built. It is this that the author feels and feels intensely. It is what he writes about.

Fiction deals with consciousness and what happens there; primarily with crisis, necessity for difficult decision. What we call experience is many faceted; but when we use the word in any capacity whatever, we imply some kind of impact other than that of everyday routine. We actually save the word "experience" for those moments which constitute the peaks of life. Life is never in reality a mere record of minutes, hours, days, years; it is a record of the big moments, moments of tension, uncertainty, excitement; moments of living more fully and more beautifully. An experience brings new awareness, greater illumination, finer clarity.

Such moments come to all of us and such moments we all seek. No life is without them and that is why everyone has something to write about. Can I transmute such moments into experience that is significant for others? Can I make the reader live more intensely, more bravely, more beautifully, through my realization of what some big moment has meant to me? If I can, I can "write." Writing is not a forbidding enterprise viewed in this way. It is only, as James wrote, "an ado about something" which interests us deeply.

Katherine Mansfield could watch a fly struggling in an ink blot and make the fly a striking symbol of man's cruelty and his unawareness. She could watch a child on a bicycle under the electric light, or a child playing a piano, and make of the slight experience a story. Even her own ghastly "boiling, bubbling, cough" entered into the story of an old lady watching her grandson die of tuberculosis. These stories, first published here in the early nineteen-twenties, seemed only fragments to many readers; but they have, nevertheless, come to be recognized as stories in the modern sense, and they have given innumerable young writers an all-important feeling for the essence of the moment. It is this feeling, this awareness, this sensitiveness, this insight into things beneath the surface, this realization of the things that *could* happen, that makes literary imagination.

Most of us, for instance, have sat in parks next to other Miss Brills. What does Katherine Mansfield make of her Miss Brill? [5] Miss Brill, poor and alone, lives in a romantic world of the imagination. One fine day she takes her treasure, a battered fur neck-piece, from its mothballs and goes to sit

[5] Katherine Mansfield, "Miss Brill," from *The Garden Party and Other Stories*. New York: Alfred A. Knopf, Inc., 1923.

in the park where she likes to listen to other people's conversations. "She had become really quite expert, she thought, at listening as though she didn't listen, at sitting in on other people's lives just for a minute while they talked around her." Finally a young girl and boy come and sit down at her bench. "The hero and heroine, of course, just arrived from his father's yacht." Miss Brill prepared to listen happily.

"No, not now," said the girl. "Not here, I can't."
"But why? Because of that stupid old thing at the end there?" asked the boy. "Why does she come here at all—who wants her? Why doesn't she keep her silly old mug at home?"
"It's her fu-fur which is so funny," giggled the girl. "It's exactly like a fried whiting."

Miss Brill got up to go home and the author tells us:

On her way home she usually bought a slice of honey-cake at the baker's. It was her Sunday treat. Sometimes there was an almond in her slice, sometimes not. It made a great difference. . . .
But today she passed the baker's by, climbed the stairs, went into the little dark room—her room like a cupboard—and sat down on the red eiderdown. She sat there for a long time. The box that the fur came out of was on the bed. She unclasped the necklet quickly; quickly, without looking, laid it inside. But when she put the lid on she thought she heard something crying.

Ma Parker, an old charwoman, provided Mansfield with a similar theme: the basic loneliness of poor old women. It has been used repeatedly and doubtless will continue to be. Ma Parker has just lost her little grandson, the last person who belonged to her; and when she finally gives way to her grief after a day of caring for the rooms of her callous "young man," she has no place to go to cry in private. We leave her alone on the cold, windy corner.

Both of these stories are a bit sentimental for our taste today, and one could well wish that the last sentence had been omitted from "Miss Brill." They do serve, however, to illustrate the moving use to which slight material can be put.

A child's first encounter with death and older people's rather indifferent attitudes toward it make up the theme of Mansfield's more elusive and subtle story, "The Garden Party." [6] In this story a gardener has died the day of a party, and a highly sensitive little girl is much shocked that the party goes on as if nothing had happened. She herself later, however, also momentarily forgets the poor widow and her grief. "I'll remember it again after the party's over," she decides. She goes to the party and has a happy time, and then her father speaks of the gardener's death. Appalled, her mother asks her to take the left-over cakes to the widow. Laura goes, wondering why it is that she can't realize the death, and looks upon the young man "sleeping so soundly" with closed eyelids. Later when she gets home, her brother begs her not to cry. "Was it awful?"

"No," sobbed Laura. "It was simply marvelous. But, Laurie—" She stopped, she looked at her brother. "Isn't life," she stammered, "isn't life—" But what life was she couldn't explain. No matter. He quite understood.

"*Isn't* it, darling?" said Laurie.

Katherine Mansfield has brought her delicate perceptions to bear upon everyday materials in this story. There is no plot in the sense of complication, nothing could be simpler in structure, yet a clear and vivid picture is given, a consistent emotional tone is sustained, and the reader comes away with a strong sense that "life is that way." Mansfield has not yielded to any temptation to "round things off"; and if the characters are somewhat shadowy, they are, nevertheless, memorable. We live through the child's disillusioning experience with her and come to the conclusion that we always eventually come to in the presence of death: the realization of the superficiality of human reaction. Because of the subtle overtones that make it rich and beautiful, the story is difficult

[6] *Op. cit.*

to sum up, and, in attempting to do so, one realizes anew the futility of trying to convey in other words the meanings so perfectly conveyed in Mansfield's.

Her kind of writing is not quite as easy as it may seem, for all the simplicity of the material. It implies the greatest awareness of life, the greatest sensitivity to its many aspects and imports. "When I am writing of 'another,'" Mansfield says, "I want to lose myself in the soul of that other that I am not." This *oneness* with the material is essential for the author. It involves intense preoccupation with the characters involved, a sort of giving of the self. These qualities can, perhaps, be consciously developed if one is aware of the necessity of concentration; if one is aware that he must identify himself momentarily with his Miss Brills and Ma Parkers. One must feel "the impact of the troubled life, the affair which matters deeply for some person," for one of those who are, as James said, "intense perceivers of their predicament."

"What most of us lack in order to be artists is not the inceptive emotion, nor yet merely technical skill in execution. It is capacity to work a vague idea and emotion over into terms of some definite medium,"

wrote Dewey in his *Art as Experience*.[7]

The writer's task is to express the emotion, to try to see the meaning of the situation, to reveal its symbolism, the larger tendencies of which it is a part.

"Bare recognition is satisfied when a proper tag or label is attached. . . ." Dewey says further, "But an act of perception proceeds by waves that extend serially throughout the entire organism. . . . The perceived object or scene is emotionally pervaded throughout."

This phase of experience involves surrender. "Perception is an act of the going-out of energy in order to receive, not a withholding of energy. . . . We must summon energy and

[7] John Dewey, *Art as Experience*. Courtesy of G. P. Putnam's Sons, 1934.

pitch it at a responsive key in order to *take* in." Such is the aesthetic experience, for both writer and reader. And no less a thing than morality is involved in this kind of response to life and literature. It involves emotion as well as intellectual perception, passionate feeling. Dewey reminds us of Shelley's words: "The great secret of morality itself is a going out of our nature and the identification of ourselves with the beautiful which exists in thought, action, or a person, not our own."

Henry James phrased the same idea beautifully: "Try to be one of those people on whom nothing is lost." Experience, he believed, is never limited, never complete. "The power to guess the unseen from the seen, to trace the implication of things, to judge the whole piece by the pattern, the condition of feeling life in general so completely that you are well on your way to knowing any particular corner of it— this cluster of gifts may almost be said to constitute experience. . . ." [8]

The reader must strive for experience in this true sense, and the writer must certainly be able to capture it. To possess this kind of vision one must be sensitive—but sensitivity involves being open, alert, externalized; looking outward, speculating upon people in the dramatic and tragic relationships or the ironic or comic ones. To see others with this deep excitement, this curiosity, this sympathy, this passion, is to be lifted out of that self which inhibits and cramps most of us and to gain a larger vision.

This larger vision comes both to writer and to reader through the development of open-mindedness. Both must abandon prejudice and remember that one of the chief functions of art is, as Dewey says, precisely to "sap moralistic timidity that causes the mind to shy away from some materials" and thus limits experience.

[8] *The Art of Fiction.*

.2.

Ordinary Things in an Unusual Way

THE power to trace the implications of things, to give the material of everyday life that "certain colouring of the imagination whereby," Wordsworth says, "even the ordinary things are presented to the mind in an unusual way," is what distinguishes the gifted writer from his less creative brother.

Just how far it is possible for one to develop his imaginative powers no one can say. There is no formula. One can only strive to acquire habits of awareness, curiosity, attention to significant and revealing details, to feel, as James said, "the inordinate intellectual 'sport' of it: the how and the whence and the why these intenser lights of experience come into being and insist on shining." "To have felt one's subject right," he thought, was "luck." It meant finding "its center, the point of command of all the rest."

There is a phrase to remember, *the point of command*. It has to do with those all-important matters that freshmen study in English composition—unity and emphasis. The point of command is obviously the very heart of the matter, its core and its meaning.

Let us take, by way of illustration, a famous passage from Jules Romains' chapter in *Men of Good Will*[1] describing a small boy's long journey through the streets of Paris with his

[1] Jules Romains, *Men of Good Will*, Volume 1, Chapter 17, translated by Warre B. Wells. New York: Alfred A. Knopf, Inc., 1933.

hoop. Here is simple, incidental material; nothing could be simpler. But see what Romains brings out of it!

We are viewing the experience largely through the eyes of the boy, Louis Bastide.

The slope was very steep. Horses had to take it at a walk; and they pulled their loads up in jerks, straining for all they were worth and striking sparks out of the stones. One day little Louis had been there when a fire engine with magnificent horses arrived at a gallop and attacked the slope. A few yards up the hill, they had to slow down like everybody else.

So it was obviously very difficult to roll a hoop up such a slope. It needed plenty of enthusiasm and stout-heartedness at the beginning; and then a determination not to weaken, not to give way to your tiredness—to say nothing of great skill in handling your stick.

.   .   .   .

Its [the hoop's] dimensions had given him something to think about. But Louis expected to go on growing for some years yet; and he could not imagine that a hoop of which he got fond might some day cease to be dear to him and simply strike him as a child's trivial toy. His only reason for ever discarding it would be its getting too small for him. In choosing a rather big one, Louis was taking thought for the future.

He went down the stairs, with the hoop hanging from his shoulder. Once he was out in the street, he stood it in the middle of the sidewalk, very straight up, holding it lightly with the fingers of his left hand. Then he gave it a smart tap. The hoop rolled away. The end of the stick caught up with it at once, keeping it in the right direction; and after that Bastide and his hoop had run one after the other; rather like a child running after a dog that he has on a leash; and also rather like a rider who lets himself be carried along by his horse, but at the same time keeps on spurring and guiding him.

When you have played a long time with a hoop, as Louis Bastide had done, and you have had the luck to find one of which you are very fond, you come to realize that things are quite different from going out in the ordinary way. Try and run by yourself; you will be tired in a few minutes. With a hoop, you can keep tiredness at bay indefinitely. You feel as though you were holding on to something, almost as if you were being carried along. If you happen to feel tired for a moment, it seems as though the hoop imparted strength to you in a friendly kind of way.

Besides, you don't have to run fast all the time. If you know how to do it, you can go almost at a walking pace. The trouble is to keep the hoop from falling to the right or left; or clinging to the legs of a passer-by, who struggles like a rat in a trap; or lying down flat on the ground after going through extraordinary contortions. You must know how to use your stick, how to give the hoop very gentle taps, just as though you were stroking it and helping it on its way. Above all, in between your taps, you must keep control over any tendency of the hoop to waver, with the help of your stick, which must just graze the edge of it on one side or other all the time, keeping it on the move or changing its speed, with the end of the stick held ready to intervene quickly at any point where the hoop threatens to fall into a lurch.

This chapter illustrates the power of a creative imagination to expand everyday, episodic material into writing that is significant and revealing of larger things, a larger whole. Romains demonstrates here the closest observation of how horses act and how hoops roll, and at the same time indicates the character of the little Louis, whose foresight and practicality predict the man to come later in the long series of novels. The whole chapter is embroidered by a fine sense of humor, especially in the later portions where the boy pictures himself as a gallant horseman with a mission to accomplish, pushing ahead over the mountains blocked by snow. Coming to an especially dangerous crossing our boy now sees himself lying dead, the wreck of his beloved hoop near his body and the stick still clasped in his hand. The idea of his mother's despair frightens him even more than the idea of death!

Then after a particularly "delicate maneuver," rolling his hoop in the road and walking beside it on some steps, using his left hand for the stick, Louis came to the end of his long journey. And the boy wanted to

raise himself up faster, as though up there, on the cornice of the hill, were all the joy, all the games, all the adventures of the future. The very noise of Paris passed into his body, though he was not aware of listening to it. . . . Like all these noises, the hoop, too, bounded and mounted. The child of Paris, as he stopped to take breath, drank in a sound of destinies that came to him from everywhere.

With superb psychological insight and creative imagination Romains here has achieved a really powerful *symbolism:* the journey with the hoop is the journey of life itself; it is the journey of life, not just for Louis Bastide, but for all little boys in Paris and for all mankind.

Romains took an ordinary game of childhood in a bewildering city environment and imposed upon these materials an *artistic unity*, bringing order out of chaos, a pattern and a meaning out of the game and the boy's reactions. He had a point of command and his chapter became significant both as a unit in itself and as a part of a novel portraying the whole vast pageant of Parisian life over a period of many years. It is the simplest kind of narrative, but how artistically conceived and executed! How unforgettable!

The material of childhood experience constitutes one of the most inexhaustible wells for fictional material—for stories written not for children but about them. Such stories are usually almost plotless, certainly lacking in any elaborate complication; and they are, by virtue of the psychologically undeveloped character of the child, limited in dramatic possibility. Nevertheless they have their own special kind of interest for the adult mind, their own kind of charm and significance, their own power of subtle implication of the man to come who may be all of us. Such stories offer overtones of important relationships between parents and children and even between parents themselves. Such writing can be delicate and elusive. One sees it at its best in Marcel Proust; one sees it in very modern terms in Katherine Anne Porter, in Ernest Hemingway, and in Wallace Stegner.

An everyday family picnic in the mountains is Wallace Stegner's subject for a sensitive story. "Two Rivers" [2] deals with the relationship between father and son, son and mother. It lacks dramatic quality of the kind that many people expect

[2] *The Atlantic Monthly,* June 1942.

or used to expect in a short story; yet it holds a maximum of psychological insight, realism, humor, and universality. The characters' special awareness and sensitivity to the mysteries of time and memory lift the experience far above the humdrum, and our picnic is no longer "everyday" but a very special experience.

We meet our boy as he is awakened by his father's singing.

He didn't want to be joked with. Yesterday was too sore a spot in his mind. He had been avoiding his father ever since the morning before, and he was not yet ready to accept any joking or attempts to make up. Nobody had a right hitting a person for nothing, and you bet they weren't going to be friends. Let him whistle and sing out there, pretending nothing was the matter. The whole business yesterday was the matter, the Ford that wouldn't start was the matter, the whole lost Fourth of July was the matter, the missed parade, the missed fireworks, the missed ball game in Chinook were the matter. The cuff on the ear his father had given him when he got so mad at the Ford he had to have something to hit was the matter.

The boy dressed and went into the main room, still nursing his grievance, despite his father's cheerful greeting. During breakfast he responded to neither his father's nor his mother's efforts to cheer him. "I don't want to cheer up," he said, and his parents smiled at each other.

Later he heard the Ford "sputter and roar and then calm down into a steady mutter."

"It goes!" he said [to his mother].
"Sure it goes." She pulled both his ears, rocking his head. "Know what we're going to do?"
"What?"
"We're going to the mountains anyway."

.   .   .   .

The boy was out into the porch in three steps. With one shoe on and the other in his hand he hopped to the door. "When?" he said.
"Soon as you can get ready."
He was trying to run and tie his shoe-laces at the same time as he went out of the house. There in the Ford, smoking his pipe, with one leg over the door, his father sat. "What detained you?" he said. "I've been waiting a half hour. You must not want to go very bad."

"Aw!" the boy said. . . . "When did you get all this ready?"

His father grinned. "While you slept like a sluggard we worked like a buggard," he said. Then the boy knew that everything was perfect, nothing could go wrong. When his father started rhyming things he was in his very best mood, and not even breakdowns and flat tires could make him do more than puff and blow and play-act

He clambered into the front seat and felt the motor shaking under the floor-boards. "Hey, Ma!" he yelled. "Hurry up! We're all ready to go!"

Who would not want to go on reading this story after such a charming introduction! We want to know this family better. We like these tactful parents who know so well how to handle a child; we like the boy's swift change from resentment to happy excitement because we all know such reactions first hand. We love the ironic formality of the question. "What detained you?" and as we read on we see that, in a way, it sets the tone for the entire story. Later we see how good the reference to the father's rhymes is structurally, since the story ends with another delightful rhyme summing up the day's rather mystical experiences. The opening scene is ideal in that it achieves so many artistic aims in a few sentences.

Later we find a quite Proustian element of strangeness, an elusive remembrance of things past.

Somewhere, sometime . . . and there were mountains in it, and a stream, and a swing that he had fallen out of and cried, and he had mashed ripe blackberries in his hand and his mother had wiped them off, straightening his stiff fingers and wiping hard . . . His mind caught on that memory from a time before there was any memory, he rubbed his finger tips against his palm and slid a little down in his seat.

Finally they went home through the beautiful early mountain evening that was "almost solemn." In the front seat the boy stood looking back, and his eyes "went curiously out of focus" as they had earlier on his way up. Then he caught his father and his mother looking at each other, "the look they had sometimes when he had pleased them and made them proud of him." The father began to sing a crazy improvised song about Brucie and the river and some black bears that were juicy and the river that was cold and hot. His rhyme gave the final touch to a perfect day.

The boy looked up at his father, his laughter bubbling up, everything wonderful, the day a swell day, his mother clapping hands in time to his father's fool singing.

"Aw, for gosh sakes," he said, and ducked when his father pretended he was going to swat him one.

One of the great charms of this story is its realism, the delightful choice of detail, like the expression about the car that steamed and shook and couldn't "seem to keep anything on her stomach"; and "died with a last, lunging gasp." The contact with the snake: "it was a good feeling to have been along and to have shared something like that with his father. It was a trophy, a thing you would remember all your life, and you could tell about it." Mr. Stegner has here achieved the marriage of realism with mysticism. The out-of-focus look in the boy's eyes, for instance, is a realistic description of what happens when the human spirit wanders for a moment into another realm, into a kind of consciousness a bit beyond its usual realm, a consciousness arising from the very hidden depths of memory. It is the kind of thing that one may have seen in one's mystical friends. It is what Proust was talking about in his discussion of that sensory experience which leads men to "touch simultaneously epochs of their lives—with countless intervening days between—so widely separated from one another in Time."

It is typical of the richness of talent in writing that in one brief narrative describing a trip to the mountains the author has been able to give pleasure and enlargement of understanding on so many literary levels. The less tutored reader will revel in the humor and the use of familiar detail which recalls his own boyhood. The more developed reader will revel in the characterization as such, as an artistic achievement, and will find his imagination challenged by the mystical element. To attempt the somewhat difficult task of recounting this story is to appreciate anew its beautifully woven structure, so tight, so economical, yet so rich in implication and meaning.

A closer approach to the short story form was made by Ernest Hemingway in another father and son story called "Indian Camp." [3] The father here is also wise and understanding; the central core is a young boy's introduction to the terrors of birth, with a coordinate pattern, which seems to some people more important, of the suicide of the Indian father. Here again we find subtle elements of humor and insight.

Nick and his father go to take care of "an Indian lady" who is very sick, off across the lake. An old woman stands in the doorway holding a lamp.

Inside on a wooden bunk lay a young Indian woman. She had been trying to have her baby for two days. All the old women in the camp had been helping her. The men had moved off up the road to sit in the dark out of range of the noise she made. . . .

In the upper bunk lay her husband who had cut his foot.

"This lady is going to have a baby, Nick," he [Nick's father] said.
"I know," said Nick.
"You don't know," said his father. "Listen to me. What she is going through is called being in labor. The baby wants to be born and she wants it to be born. All her muscles are trying to get the baby born. That is what is happening when she screams."

We see the preparations for the birth and finally the baby is born. But "Nick did not watch." He looked away so as not to see what his father was doing. When it was all over the father was feeling "exalted and talkative as football players are in the dressingroom after a game." Then he looked

[3] From *In Our Time*. New York: Charles Scribner's Sons, 1930.

at the Indian in the bunk above (strangely silent) and found him dead. He had slit his throat.

"Take Nick out of the shanty, George," the doctor said.

There was no need of that. Nick standing in the door of the kitchen, had a good look into the upper bunk when his father, the lamp in one hand, tipped the Indian's head back.

.   .   .   .

"I'm terribly sorry I brought you along, Nickie," said his father, all his post-operative exhilaration gone. "It was an awful mess to put you through."

"Do ladies always have such a hard time having babies?" Nick asked.

"No, that was very, very exceptional."

"Why did he kill himself, Daddy?"

"I don't know, Nick. He couldn't stand things, I guess."

"Do many men kill themselves, Daddy?"

"Not very many, Nick."

"Do many women?"

"Hardly ever."

.   .   .   .

They were seated again in the boat, Nick in the stern, his father rowing. The sun was coming up over the hills. A bass jumped, making a circle in the water. Nick trailed his hand in the water. It felt warm in the sharp chill of the morning.

In the early morning on the lake sitting in the stern of the boat with his father rowing, he felt quite sure that he would never die.

In all three of the extracts from narratives about children we have seen affirmative values. There have been indications of happy and wholesome relationships, of family love, understanding and devotion, and we have felt that the child in each case would get a decent start in life.

Other stories dealing with children, however, emphasize the other side of the picture, and we see in Katherine Anne Porter's *Downward Path to Wisdom*, for instance, the actual making of a neurotic going on before our very eyes. This wonderful story is much too complexly woven to be suitable for analysis at this time or to permit of condensation, but the initiation of a little boy into the ugliness of grown-up life, the way in which he is taught to hate, not only Papa but *everyone*, constitutes a whole sermon in child psychology, at once moving and illuminating.

From the first scene in which a four-year-old in his parents' room hears them quarrel about him—"Bright-looking specimen, isn't he?" "I suppose you'll say it's my fault he is dumb as an ox"—to the last scene where he sees another terrible quarrel over him between his mother and his uncle, the child meets only evil, blundering, cruel people who turn his every act into something naughty and *tabu*. Through action which extends over several days the unhappy pattern is repeated until it becomes heart-breakingly clear that our little boy will grow up to be like the adults who have pressed him into their own wretched psychological mold.

One can scarcely open a contemporary anthology of short stories without finding interesting examples of the modern treatment of material about children. From Frances Eisenberg's penetrating little studies of case histories, often highly amusing as well as illuminating, to William Faulkner's account in "That Will Be Fine" of the debasement of a child through the appeal to his acquisitive instincts, there is a very wide range of treatment. If any two authors have taken the same point of command, certainly no two can be said to have evoked the same *emotional tone*. To study these stories is to become aware of the many *nuances*, the many facets of childhood material in a day and age when even the average reader has at least a smattering of knowledge concerning the factors that act, early in life, to determine human character. Incidental material here has the poignant implications of future tragedy, of the warped lives that might have been whole and happy. The writer who understands child psychology and who feels deeply has an inexhaustible source of moving material. In the Porter story, Stephen's fright at his grandma's smile—"There was something wrong with her smile"—and his heart's turning over within him as he "bleated like a lamb, 'Maaaaama' " and ran away from Uncle David and toward his mother, arouse in the reader the sort of pity and terror which are ineradicable. And Stephen is only one child out of a world of children pitifully helpless in the hands of those who are mistakenly called adults.

Henry James says in his Preface to *The American*, "A beautiful infatuation this, always, I think, the intensity of the creative effort to get into the skin of the creature; the act of personal possession of one being by another at its completest—and with the high enhancement, ever, that it is, by the same stroke, the effort of the artist to preserve for his subject that unity, and for his use of it (in other words for the interest he desires to excite) that effect of a *centre*, which most economise its value." [4]

The story of today, at its best, "gets under the skin," and deeply. The beginner's story, however, most often fails because it does not even approximate any such depth in treatment. Any experienced reader of manuscripts will certainly bear out the statement that many writers, perhaps the majority of them, fail because they have only scratched the surface of their material, whereas the sophisticated reader of today demands at least a "high enhancement" of the values touched upon. Yet the student has only to make an intensive study of the stories that are praised by competent critics, the stories that judges of contests select and that compilers of anthologies include, to see that they *do* get beneath the skin. The failure of a writer first to appreciate the deepest values of his subject matter and then to focus upon them with a powerful searchlight comes, more often than not, from a failure to

[4] *Op. cit.*, page 37.

mull over the story, to live it daily for a considerable period of time, to know its characters thoroughly, inside and out, and to extract from a given situation its utmost philosophical meaning.

Mona Van Duyn's story "The Bell," which won the *Kenyon Review* second prize for 1945,[5] is a highly satisfying illustration of the powerful exploration of subject-matter related to the everyday life of childhood. It is built around the establishment of a "conscience" in a little girl whose mother turns a friendship with a little boy into a powerful guilt feeling, a feeling so strong that we finally leave her in the grip of a terrifying dream which will, we feel sure, appear again and again to warp the pattern of her life. No subject-matter could be simpler, none truer or more revealing of the tragic error of training which places emphasis upon the wrong thing and molds the plastic child in the parents' unhealthy image.

We meet little Janie as she plays with her dolls and covertly listens to her mother quarreling with Grandma. The first sentence tells us that many things are *tabu* in this household, things "belonging to Mother." Then, sentence by sentence, Miss Van Duyn develops the picture: Grandma's German protest, "Ach, the Kleine—such a little one yet . . .," Grandma's voice "which was somehow protecting her from something"; the "scolding sound" of Mother's voice; the banging of pans in the kitchen indicating anger and domination; and then Mother's so angry, intense effort to awaken conscience, the conscience that is "a little bell in your head that rings when you've done something naughty." This "hard and unfriendly" bell is difficult for a literal-minded child to visualize and understand; and Janie wants to ask questions about it, but mother does not like questions, and it is clear that something is "wrong." Mother's one concession is that

[5] Mona Van Duyn, "The Bell," *The Kenyon Review*, Autumn 1945.

other people cannot hear the bell, and thus Janie is relieved of "a shame almost too deep to bear."

In the second part of the story Janie goes with her wholesome Dad to play at his gas station while he works on his books. Then comes a happy meeting with a little boy named Keith and later Keith's suggestion of a kiss which, in some way, becomes "more remote" in the back of the parked car to which they retire. Keith shows embarrassment but has with "great cleverness," Janie thinks, thought up another adventure, "an adventure more different and strange than any she had ever imagined to herself" but which produced "a strange wavering in her, a pushing backward and forward under her mind" that was "not a fear exactly" but "rather something that wanted to be left alone or was not ready yet." Naturally, quite without thought of any bell, Janie says, "No, I don't think I'd like to."

She goes happily home with Dad and, while she is in her pleasant warm bath, mother starts asking questions: has she remembered to put on her sweater when it got cool? Then it is that worry about whether she has been good or bad begins to "joggle her mind" and suddenly she remembers "the bell, the terrible watching bell in her head." She has forgotten to listen for it! And so she tells about meeting Keith, and Mother after an ominous silence asks, "Was Keith a nice little boy?"

Now Mother is on the scent and the child's doom is sealed, for the ensuing questions and Mother's and Grandmother's attitudes serve all too clearly to give the little girl a sense of there being something *wrong* with all men, even her father. That which was innocent is turned into something sinful, bringing on a dream which is psychoanalytically significant and very portentous for the future. We feel sure that the terrible bell will go on ringing for the rest of the child's life, warping all her relations with men, bringing her to God-

knows-what maladjustments. Miss Van Duyn has gone beneath the surface of everyday material here, revealing the
true and the terrible of a thousand case histories, with that
emotional impact which lifts fiction above the merely factual.

The Central Point of Command

HOW does the writer come by these effects? How does he go about the all-important business of producing that vivid emotional effect which is the aim of the short story?

First of all, by *feeling* his subject "right." After living with his story long enough to have explored its various possibilities, the writer should ultimately come to the core; the next step is to integrate the story elements—character, action, theme—into a controlled organic whole, to bring about a perfect realization of his goal, a *single vivid effect*.

It was Poe who gave classic utterance to one of the few valid formulas for fiction writing. It was Poe who put into effect those formulas so helpful even today when most old rigid forms have been discarded. It is exciting, too, to realize that those fantastic and unreal narratives which startled Europe toward the middle of the last century, those narratives so full of emotion and horror, were wrought by a man who worked them up, as James worked up his, through coldly intellectual processes. In his essay *The Philosophy of Composition*, Poe put his finger on the idea later developed as the "central core."

I say to myself, in the first place, "Of the innumerable effects, or impressions, of which the heart, the intellect, or (more generally) the soul is susceptible, what one shall I, on the present occasion, select? Having chosen a novel, first, and secondly a vivid effect, I consider which it can best be wrought by, incident or tone—whether by ordinary incidents and peculiar tone, or the converse, or by peculiarity both of incident and tone—afterward looking about me (or rather within) for such combinations of event, or tone, as shall best aid me in the construction of the effect.

The writer should have an effect in mind and that a *novel* or *vivid* one. These ideas are important. Poe has illustrated his thesis by his analysis of how he produced "The Raven." First (of all things!), he decided upon the length—about a hundred lines. (Such a method is very bad indeed for fiction writers.) Then he chose the exact tone, one of sadness, because he believed that the highest manifestation of beauty, "Beauty of whatever kind, in its supreme development, invariably excites the sensitive soul to tears." Then he decided that he would produce continuously "novel effects" by "*variation of the application* of the *refrain*—the *refrain* itself remaining, for the most part, unvaried." He would use one word for refrain, the character of which must for poetic reasons be "sonorous and susceptible of protracted emphasis. . . ." The vowel *o* and the consonant *r* would do this, the word "Nevermore."

Monotonous repetition involved another problem, the solution of which brought him to "a non reasoning creature capable of speech." Thus the raven. Returning to his idea of melancholy, he realized that the idea most melancholy to all men is Death. And when is death most melancholy? When it is related to beauty. Let it be Death, then, of a beautiful woman.

This idea of the death of a beautiful woman fascinated Poe, for reasons analytically interesting but not important here, and we find it appearing in "Ligeia," "Eleanora," "Berenice," "Morella," and "The Oval Portrait." All deal with death under strange and morbid circumstances. The same intellectual processes which entered into the writing of "The Raven" seem to have entered into these stories, which are more descriptions of mood than they are descriptions of people in action. Neither the characters nor the action have much reality for a modern mind, but the emotional effect is, despite this fact, vivid and unforgettable. The stories could spring only from a strange and morbidly sensuous emotion coupled with a melodramatic imagination. Nevertheless, Poe's conscious intellectualization of the processes of writing is helpful to any beginner who takes the trouble to note how he produced his effects.

To go through a Poe story underlining the words which help to establish the mood is to be impressed by the amount of repetition. Poe used the strange, bizarre details which are themselves startling; and such details are conducive to vividness of total impression, especially if reiterated. The student interested in writing for the mystery magazines will find it profitable to try an imitation of Poe. Serious writing of today, however, achieves its impression by less obvious means. William Faulkner, for instance, is almost alone in his power of arousing fear, horror, and terror of cruel and sadistic characters, but, while his characters are often "abnormal," they lie within the realm of the possible, of psychological belief. Faulkner's melodrama is the melodrama of life itself. The reader is not merely living through a nightmare, as with Poe; he is having a real and terrible experience. Faulkner is quite as memorable as Poe. No one can forget Popeye and the terrible things he does, in *Sanctuary*, nor the growing menace of the symbolic winds in "The Wild Palms" and the inevitability of the doom awaiting the Negress in "That Evening Sun."

Both Poe and Faulkner bring home the importance of the novel and portentous. Viewing the work of many unpublished writers one becomes aware that often they have avoided the really exciting kinds of subject-matter; they have shied away from what, perhaps, they regard as melodrama. Nor should the emphasis which this book puts upon everyday material mislead the reader into thinking that the strange and terrible are not legitimate in good writing. Indeed they are! They are just as much a part of life as the commonplace and everyday. They *are* everyday, as anyone knows who reads his newspapers. Even Henry James, with his emphasis upon the finespun, was quite aware of the power of the sinister, and when he set out to use it he succeeded in writing one of the most famous of ghost stories, "The Turn of the Screw." He speaks of the "hovering prowling blighting presences" of his "pair of abnormal agents" in his Preface:

The essence of the matter was the villainy of motive in the evoked predatory creatures; so that the result would be ignoble—by which I mean would be trivial—were this element of evil but feebly or inanely suggested.

The total effect of a short story consists of an emphasis upon a character trait, an incident and its revelation, or an action which has thematic significance; sometimes—but less often than one would think—upon the mere excitement of "plot." Whichever of these unities the writer selects, his first necessity is the *direction* of the reader's attention into the right channel. This direction gives, from start to finish, the reader approach to the work as a whole. By skillful manipulation of detail, with the utmost use of indirection, innuendo, and suggestion, the author reveals an experience which is colored by his outlook upon life, his vision, his wisdom and his insight. No two writers will communicate exactly the same thing in exactly the same way: there is always the special color given by the personality of the writer that is responsible for the final effect. The most important kind of unity is that of the *special quality* given the experience presented.

The matter of channeling attention is explained psychologically in an interesting little book called *A Psychological Approach to Literary Criticism,* by Maier and Reninger. The authors point out that artistic writing is primarily a matter of directing the reader's attention. They say that in order to communicate his experience the author must "set up certain concrete symbols, or substitute objects, which will act as stimuli, which will in turn produce in us approximately the same interpretation experienced by the artist. The individual receiving the stimuli from the artist in the form of concrete symbols, such as words (in literature) or colors and shadings and lines (in painting), must be capable of responding to these symbols in such a manner that he will catch the artist's experience." [1]

Using geometrical figures, the authors explain what an artist sees:

Step 1 represents an unformed mass of stimuli. These set up nerve impulses on the retina (in the case of the eye), and the end result is a visual experience—an object on a certain background. The object is the result of a specific grouping of part of the mass of sensations which are aroused by the stimuli; while the remainder of the mass of sensations fall back and become the background. What the artist sees, then, is determined by the nature of the grouping that his organism makes from the sensations, which are in turn determined by the stimuli that come to him from the outside world: this is his interpretation or *configuration* [2] (Step 2). If the artist wishes his interpretation to be experienced by other people, he must present them with a pattern of symbols (Step 3). Because of past conditioning these symbols will produce certain experiences in them. If the symbols function as intended, the experience will approximate that of the writer (Step 4).

The power of author-imposed direction is made clear in the illustration given in finding the hidden man in the puzzle picture.

We fail to find him at first because we get the ordinary grouping which does not include the hidden man. Finally, after trying to shift

[1] N. R. F. Maier and H. W. Reninger, *A Psychological Approach to Literary Criticism*. New York: D. Appleton-Century Company, Inc., 1933.

[2] Italics supplied—M. B. O.

various lines in order to eliminate the first grouping, we see him. We understand that we have missed him because certain elements in one organization make up his outline, while in a different organization they are leaves and parts of trees. What we naïvely call reality is thus a function of the way our organism groups or organizes the sensations. . . .

In perception, affection (likes and dislikes) plays a part. In scientific observation the affective elements are eliminated as much as possible by varying the conditions of the experiment and the attitude of the observer. Normally, however, our habitual likes and dislikes play a part in what we perceive; that is, there is a strong subjective element in our interpretations of experiences due to our past conditioning. It is this *subjective element* [3] which distinguishes an artist's configuration from a scientist's: the chief difference between a scientific treatise and Conrad's *Lord Jim* is the relative absence of the subjective element in the former and the relative abundance of it in the latter.

"The literary artist," the writers decide, "must arrange his symbols in such a way as to cause the reader to experience his interpretation. An artist, then, must not only experience a highly desirable interpretation, but he must be able also to communicate his grouping to others." Next, the authors make the vital point that "great discoveries are likely to result when unusual or unexpected directions have been taken in starting out upon a problem." The successful direction in art is not the common or obvious one, it is rather the result of an *unusual configuration*. Such a configuration is brought about for the reader through the successful organization of the writer's material in a special way. One of the finest examples of the use of direction in literature, Maier and Reninger point out, is to be found in Antony's speech over the body of Caesar, in Shakespeare's *Julius Caesar*.

Antony begins by paralleling the mob in his thinking, but as he applies one direction after another, imperceptibly, gradually, more and more he turns the direction of thinking, always so gradually as to be unnoticed, until finally he has reversed the original direction of

[3] Italics supplied—M. B. O.

the mob's thinking. The same words that originally flattered Brutus in the eyes of the mob become bitter reproach and a cry for the blood of Brutus.

Concluding their chapter on "What We Do When We Write," Maier and Reninger say:

Great writers are able to rid themselves of old directions, while mediocre authors cling to old and habitual ones. Using these old directions, writers achieve only second-hand interpretations, while the great writer, using an unusual direction, may achieve an original interpretation. . . .
Perhaps it is now even more clear why so much depends upon exact language patterns: a false word may produce a false direction, which in turn will weaken the entire configuration. Perhaps poetry is affected most directly by the use of a single false word, or by the inclusion of an exact word or phrase. When we realize that language is a substitute stimulus for actual situations, we recognize how finely it must be adjusted to achieve its end—a configuration in the mind of the reader which approximates that in the mind of the writer.

This interesting analysis should serve to make the reader doubly aware of the import of Poe's maxim that there shall be no single word in a story which does not serve the single effect, as well as the import of his emphasis upon the novel, the word "novel" as used by Poe meaning the new configuration.

It is a commonplace, even for the beginner, that there are only a few plots possible to the writer: it is what the writer does with his situations and plots that counts. It is also a commonplace to the manuscript reader that no two writers will emphasize exactly the same plot or the same values in the same way. There is always the subjective matter of the author's personal interpretation of the facts which he sees, of the slant, bias, or philosophical outlook that he brings to bear upon life.

One of the most interesting kinds of configuration is that which conveys the artist's *inner sense of reality*. This kind of narrative, more and more common since Katherine Mansfield's innovation, baffles and annoys the reader who is looking only for plot, since the emphasis is not so much upon action as upon vision. To many, however, vision is the main thing nowadays. Literary emphasis has changed our ideas of what constitutes a story, and it is only the unsophisticated and illiterate who still think of fiction in terms of complication, or plot, alone.

Before we attempt to investigate the difficult problems of plot, let us pause to dwell upon this matter of the writer's vision, that configuration which conveys his inner sense of reality. The student who is in a hurry to find a formula for writing fiction may resent what seems to him an overemphasis upon values, rather than upon methods or techniques, but he can ill afford to ignore the matter of values and vision, if he wants to be in tune with his time. There is no use at all in thinking nowadays of the O. Henry kind of thing as the ideal, the pattern to follow. The pattern story, the formula, is unmistakably dated as far as quality audiences are concerned.

Listen to Professor Joseph Warren Beach of the University of Minnesota:[4]

The new writers are as much concerned as the old ones with the psyche as the focus of life experience. Only, with their modern conceptions of the psyche, they grow more and more impatient of the quaint little patterns into which the old psychological novelists had tried to force this protean creature, and their disposition to ignore all sorts of things that go to make up human personality. And the new writers have felt the need to break up these conventional patterns. . . .

Instead of regularity of form, they show a tendency to what at first blush appears a freakish changefulness and unpredictability. . . .

Instead of uniformity and simplicity, they tend to diversity and complexity. . . .

Instead of concentration around a limited issue, they show an eccentric tendency, a tendency to fly off in many different directions. . . .

[4] Joseph Warren Beach, *The Twentieth Century Novel*. New York: D. Appleton-Century Company, Inc., 1932. Italics supplied—M. B. O.

A continuous action seems to them too unlike ordinary experience, with its freakish, accidental interruptions, its overleapings of time and circumstance. They feel that the sense of life is often best rendered by an abrupt passing from one series of events, one group of characters, one center of consciousness, to another.

Moreover, they don't particularly care about neatly finishing off a given action, following it through to the fall of the curtain. . . . they know the imagination has the faculty of filling up gaps in an action presented in fragments, of *getting the impression of an entire life* [5] from a mere hinting indication of the high moments. Again, they feel that the imagination is stimulated and rendered more active, is actually exhilarated, by broken bits of information, as the nerves are stimulated by the discontinuity of an electric current.

The idea of "getting the impression of an entire life" is highly important. The reader will do well to keep the phrase in mind. The story to be narrated is the specific incident or incidents which are symbolic of the character's *whole life* —better yet, of human life in general. The story is a kind of summing up.

Such a summing up, to take as example a portion of Virginia Woolf's *To the Lighthouse*, gives us an idea of what is meant by the sense of inner reality: [6]

Against her will she had come to the surface, and found herself half out of the picture, looking, a little dazedly, as if at unreal things, at Mr. Carmichael. He lay on his chair with his hands clasped above his paunch not reading, or sleeping, but basking like a creature gorged with existence. His book had fallen on to the grass.

She wanted to go straight up to him and say, "Mr. Carmichael!" Then he would look up benevolently as always, from his smoky vague green eyes. But one only woke people if one knew what one wanted to say to them. And she wanted to say, not one thing, but everything. Little words that broke up the thought and dismembered it said nothing. "About life, about death; about Mrs. Ramsey"—no, she thought, one could say nothing to nobody. The urgency of the moment always missed its mark. Words fluttered sideways and struck the object inches too low. Then one gave it up; then the idea sunk

[5] Italics supplied—M. B. O.
[6] New York: Harcourt, Brace and Company, Inc., 1931.

back again; then one became like most middle-aged people, cautious, furtive, with wrinkles between the eyes and a look of perpetual apprehension. For how could one express in words these emotions of the body? express that emptiness there? (She was looking at the drawing-room steps; they looked extraordinarily empty.) It was one's body feeling, not one's mind. The physical sensations that went with the bare look of the steps had become suddenly extremely unpleasant. To want and not to have, sent all up her body a hardness, a hollowness, a strain.

. . . .

She addressed old Mr. Carmichael again. What was it then? What did it mean? Could things thrust their hands up and grip one; could the blade cut; the fist grasp? Was there no safety? No learning by heart of the ways of the world? No guide, no shelter, but all was miracle, and leaping from the pinnacle of a tower into the air? Could it be, even for elderly people, that this was life?—startling, unexpected, unknown? For one moment she felt that if they both got up, here, now on the lawn, and demanded an explanation, why it was so short, why it was so inexplicable, said it with violence, as two fully equipped human beings from whom nothing should be hid might speak, then, beauty would roll itself up; the space would fill; those empty flourishes would form into shape; if they shouted loud enough Mrs. Ramsey would return. "Mrs. Ramsey!" she said aloud, "Mrs. Ramsey!" The tears ran down her face.

Virginia Woolf's criterion for a novel is, says David Daiches, "Is life like this?" There is no "art for art's sake" nonsense about Virginia Woolf, he adds. She recognizes the function of literature as that of illuminating experience for the reader. But where does one find experience and how is it to be illuminated? Mr. Daiches quotes Miss Woolf's *The Common Reader:* [7]

Examine for a moment an ordinary mind on an ordinary day. The mind receives a myriad impressions—trivial, fantastic, evanescent, or engraved with the sharpness of steel. From all sides they come, an incessant shower of innumerable atoms; and as they fall, as they shape themselves into the life of Monday or Tuesday, the accent falls dif-

[7] Virginia Woolf, *The Common Reader, First Series.* New York: Harcourt, Brace and Company, Inc., 1932.

ferently from of old; the moment of importance came not here but there; so that, if a writer were a free man and not a slave, if he could write what he chose, and not what he must, if he could base his work upon his own feeling and not upon convention, there would be no plot, no comedy, no tragedy, no love interest or catastrophe in the accepted style, and perhaps not a single button sewn on as the Bond Street tailors would have it. Life is not a series of gig lamps symmetrically arranged; life is a luminous halo, a semi-transparent envelope surrounding us from the beginning of consciousness to the end. Is it not the task of the novelist to convey this varying, this unknown and uncircumscribed spirit, whatever aberration or complexity it may display, with as little mixture of the alien and external as possible?

Miss Woolf has been talking, it is true, in terms of the novel. There are differences, of course, between the novel and the short story forms. But her point is valid for both, and the whole of modern experimental writing, as well as much literature that is more widely read, bears her out. It is for this very reason that one can no longer speak of "rules" about fiction writing; one can hardly lay down a single all-inclusive formula that has not been violated by some important writer —and successfully violated.

But if any formula is valid nowadays, it is the formula of unity of impression. Whatever the writer's sense of reality conveys, no matter how strong his sense of unreality and chaos even, whatever it is, it must convey a more or less unified *idea, emotion, tone.* Not only must it convey a single effect, but it must convey an effect that has its own *nuances.* Not a generalized emotion, but a *specific* one. The writing of today is distinguished by this careful selection of very specific nuances.

Would the reader be interested in a study of the emotional nuances achieved by Mansfield in three love stories, all extremely slight as to complication, all dealing with one general aspect of young love, yet each as different from the other in tone values as could be imagined?

In "Honeymoon" [8] two naïve young people are trying to be grown-up. First, we feel the bride's happy excitement:

"Isn't it extraordinary to think that here we are quite alone, away from everybody, with nobody to tell us when to go home, or to—to order us about except ourselves?"

. . . .

But now he caught hold of her hand, stuffed it into his pocket, pressed her fingers, and said, "I used to keep a white mouse in my pocket when I was a kid."

"Did you?" said Fanny, who was intensely interested in everything George had ever done. "Were you very fond of white mice?"

They finally reach the hotel and are beset by waiters "to cut them off from every possible kind of escape." George "looking most dreadfully bored, and Fanny, trying to look as though she'd spent years of life threading her way through strangers, followed after." Fanny is tremendously impressed by George. "What it was to be a man of the world!" But all she wants to do is to "sit down and look like everybody else."

When the waiter leaves, George sighs in relief and "if it hadn't been ridiculous Fanny might have imagined that he had been as frightened of the manager as she." She longed to squeeze George's hand, but instead, he squeezed hers and said, "Fanny, darling Fanny."

"Oh George!" says Fanny, and nothing matters except love. Then she asks George "something fearfully important."

"It's this." Fanny paused a moment, looked down, looked up again. "Do you really feel," she said softly, "that you really know me now? But really, really know *me*?"

It was too much for George. Know his Fanny? He gave a broad, childish grin. "I should jolly well think I do," he said emphatically. "Why, what's up?"

---

[8] From *The Dove's Nest and Other Stories*. New York: Alfred A. Knopf, Inc., 1923.

Fanny haltingly expresses her fears: Some people "misunderstand each other about the most important things of all." But George merely laughs and says, "Couldn't be done."

What vision has Mansfield given us here?—a sense of the young girl's lyrical emotion, her feeling of luck, her admiration for everything George does and for his knowledge of the world, and her fleeting anxiety that their happiness may not always last. And this feeling is contrasted with George's actual qualities, which the reader recognizes as naïve and childish, and with the implication that perhaps George may not be quite sensitive enough always to understand his Fanny. Overtones of blissful happiness, contrasts, implications for the future—these are the somewhat elusive values of this glimpse of life through Katherine Mansfield's eyes.

In "All Serene" the heroine is also awed by her happiness. She has been married for three years. Twice during the story shadows pass over her sky: once when she wonders about the handwriting on a morning letter addressed to her husband, and once when, at the end of the story, he has left for his office and she looks at the drawing room, which is suddenly severe and remote in the morning light, so severe that she doesn't like it. Then she runs upstairs to lean over the starry petunias which he has mentioned. ("You smell exactly like a petunia," he has said.)

This story has the same lyrical joy, the same awed admiration for the husband, the same wonder that such happiness could be, that we saw in "Honeymoon." But the tone is different. It implies a shade of doubt, the doubt revealed in a defensive dwelling on the petunia remark to offset the little cloud.

In "Bliss" the heroine is also in a state of intense happiness. Bertha has become aware that, like the pear tree now flowering so symbolically, her love is about to bloom fully at last; but at the moment of greatest anticipation, when she can hardly wait for her guests to leave so that she can express her feeling, she sees her husband bend over Miss Fulton and his lips say: "I adore you." Bertha runs over to the window and looks at the pear tree. "Oh, what is going to happen now," she cries. But the pear tree is, ironically, "as lovely as ever and as full of flower and as still." Here, through the heroine's consciousness, we come to a realization of the actuality of the husband's indifference and unfaithfulness, and also of her very special sense of her own situation, her own self as "full of flower" and "still." This famous story, of course, is more developed, and therefore more clear, though it has ambiguous overtones, than is "All Serene," which was never really finished. Each of the stories, however, has its own special tone, each leaves its own individual impression of the evanescent quality of young love.

David Daiches reminds us in his chapter on Katherine Mansfield in *The Novel and the Modern World*,[9] that "in this type of literature it is the actual form of the story which gives symbolic value to the incidents." We find it extremely difficult to express "even the idea behind it," and he adds pertinently, "It is a commonplace of criticism that what a work of literature says can only be adequately expressed by the work itself."

The young writer will find a careful study of Mansfield, elusive as she often is, of immense value in developing his sense of the infinite number of values to be obtained from literary material. Katherine Mansfield can indeed show him how to follow Henry James' advice "to play the small handful of values really for all they were worth." She opens up to any student new visions of what writing can be, of how much it can *convey*. She teaches, above all, the importance of viewing the material intently for its less obvious values and meanings.

[9] Chicago: The University of Chicago Press, 1940.

"If," says Daiches, "by our way of writing we can persuade others to see as we see, to view as a symbol what they otherwise would regard merely as a stray fact, our literary work is sensitive, as Katherine Mansfield's is sensitive." Then he adds his own literary creed:

Whatever science or philosophy may be, literature is a presentation of facts—real or imagined—which implies at the same time, through the method of presentation or simply by the choice of the facts presented, or by both, an interpretation of those facts. This—to put the matter at its crudest—is what distinguishes a story from a mere record of events; what distinguishes a tragedy from an account of unpleasant happenings. . . . There is always interpretation, and often where there seems to be none the interpretation is most profound and most original.

Daiches believes that the personal sense of truth, "literature of vision," has come to replace "the formulas of a civilization," that Katherine Mansfield's work is not literature of plot at all, and that, therefore, Aristotle's principles of the drama [10] do not hold in considering it.

[10] Discussed in Chapter 12.

.4.

Conflict

THE most important element is conflict. Conflict dramatic is the root of suspense, and most readers expect it to bring them that feeling of rising excitement which makes a good play. Suspense is the element which makes one want to go on with the story, which makes one want to know, as James said, "what will happen, who will suffer, who not suffer, what tune be determined, what crisis created, what issue found." But James himself referred to plot as "nefarious." Plot *is* nefarious when it leads to banal imitation or to the artificial and insincere. But if complications grow out of real conflict and are handled in accordance with the laws of probability or inevitability, the reader feels the story's validity and reacts to it.

And what kind of conflict has reality? Conflict arising out of fundamental and elemental human passions; conflict springing from situations that arouse fear, pity, and terror, those situations which the newspaperman considers full of "human interest," those in which something important is at stake. Perhaps the threatened value is security, love, self-respect, or a career. Perhaps it is an ideal or a way of life or a freedom. Whatever the stake, it must be important.

When characters are in a situation that demands some kind of action and they do not know what to do about it, or when they are confronted by serious obstacles or clashes of interest, love, or duty, then, in all probability, we have suitable material for making a plot. The kind of situation from which our usual instinctive responses do not automatically deliver us, as Walter B. Pitkin pointed out, is the interesting one. The situation which gives the "automatic" response is not interesting. Our hero should have real grounds for his confusion, or, as James called it, his "bewilderment."

A man in an unusual situation, a man meeting the usual in an interesting way, or an unusual man in a usual situation—any one of these combinations challenges our interest. It promises a *new configuration*. Nothing is too strange or bizarre for modern fiction which recognizes that life itself is strange, paradoxical, and ironic, as witness Kafka's novel about the man who turns into a cockroach! Life is even unbelievable in some of its phases. Why indeed do we bear its vicissitudes, its disappointments, its defeats of our dearest and most legitimate plans, if, as Edwin Arlington Robinson said, "after all that we have lived and thought, All comes to naught?" The amount of struggle and conflict in most lives, "the shafts and agonies" in a world without a meaning do, indeed, give the philosopher pause; and they give the poet and the writer their subject-matter.

Tension and conflict are at the biological basis of life. If the lowest animals must struggle, how much more, then, must man, who has developed an intellect to give him purposes and ideals, who demands a meaning from life! Again, how much more the member of a highly organized society, which has established traditions about how he is to conduct himself in the matters most vital to him! How much more still must he struggle if he is emotionally high-keyed or sensitive and does not run easily with the herd! The highly sensitive man, the man who is a little different, or who feels himself different—this is the man who easily falls victim to severe and often devastating conflict.

It is the writer's business to see and to try to understand as much as he possibly can of the struggle going on about him;

to catch its excitement and to recognize the eternal fact that all the world is a stage whereon we have our little day and speak our parts and go our way. To this task he must bring some conception of form, and it will perhaps help him to recognize that drama has the broad outlines of an action with, as Aristotle said, a beginning, a middle, and an end. "A well constructed plot, therefore, must neither begin nor end at haphazard." It must have organic form and wholeness, this "imitation of an action and of life." Pitkin has called a short story "a narrative drama producing a single effect," and has emphasized the fact that plot is "a climactic series of events each of which both determines and is determined by the characters involved." His definition is, of course, but an extension of Aristotle's idea of close unity of character and action. Good craftsmanship rules out unrelated happenings such as occur in slap-stick comedy. It emphasizes cause and effect: that which starts off the action and which has within it the seeds of the conclusion. The ideal story has a tight, close-knit, highly integrated structure based on a main thread of action, the action being rooted in the conflict.

The nature of conflict will become clear to anyone who listens to "The Court of Human Relations" on the radio. He who can get under the sugar-sweet tenderness of radio techniques will see the kind of situations and problems that gets people into such acute predicaments that they will ask outsiders for help. The speakers nearly always reveal the intensity of their struggle by the breathless way in which they state their problems, by the way they hesitate and stammer, with faltering voices or chaotically rushing words. Actual people talking about their distress are revealing. They often seem unaware of the true nature of their difficulties, especially of their own faults, errors, and responsibilities for the trouble. Sometimes the listener can easily diagnose the evil; at other times the causes are too complex, or the actual elements of poverty, ill-health, or dependent relatives are insuperable. Sometimes there is no solution: the talkers have been caught in one of life's cruel traps.

It is one of the functions, perhaps the chief function, of fiction to show the making of traps, to show how life sets the trap or how the character makes his own trap and becomes hopelessly caught in it. Often those who are most enmeshed are the finest, the most sensitive, the most unselfish, the most idealistic. Their very goodness traps them. Aristotle's good man who meets a tragic fate by an error of judgment or some little flaw is the one who most deeply arouses our sense of pity. He is a man perhaps like ourselves— not too good, not too bad—victimized by circumstances arising either from his own inner conflicts or from without.

One of the simplest kinds of struggle is that arising from man's relations with nature—with the cold, the heat, the wind, sand, waters, or mountains, with danger from starvation or thirst or animals. Jack London wrote of primitive natural conflicts in the far north between men and animals and cold, of a man who froze to death because he made the mistake of starting out when it was forty degrees below zero, when his dog "knew better," and of using his last match to start a fire under the snow-laden limbs of a tree, with the result that the snow melted and fell on his fire. Joseph Conrad wrote more profoundly of struggles with the "tumult of the sea," "the immense matted" jungle, and the "imponderable" universe. Nowadays, men are writing of struggle with the very air and atmospheric elements. These primitive battles between man and his physical universe are often written about in simple stories intended primarily for boys. They are written about more artistically and more philosophically for mature readers, as, for instance, in Saint Exupéry's *Wind, Sand, and Stars*.

More complex is the struggle between man and other human beings. Here we find man in conflict with members of his family and with members of the outside world. He quarrels with some other man for a woman, a job, prestige, or money. He fights against the conventions and laws of an organized society which hampers and restricts him and puts him in jail or even takes his life; or he battles for an idea.

Many vital struggles come from economic situations which the historians of this century have gone to pains to reveal as determining forces in man's destiny. Steinbeck's novel *The Grapes of Wrath*, discussed at some length in Chapter 11, is the story of the losing battle of the "Okies" with a ruthless and cruel system made up of absentee landlordism, seasonal employment, and ineffective systems of transportation for goods. But this struggle began, for them, even earlier, with nature's failure during the years of the drought. The Joads were thus the victims of both nature's failure and society's. They were at the mercy of vast forces which they barely glimpsed. Men are constantly at the mercy of such forces in a world that is complex in its economic organization, and one wonders why more writers do not address themselves to such struggle. Think of the many aspects of the labor conflicts going on all about us! Of the family conflicts over union memberships, union sacrifices! Are magazine editors afraid of such material?

Nor is family life any less complex. Far reaching changes have been going on. Sociologists, indeed, tell us that there is not much left of the family in a civilization which has taken most of the housework out of the hands of the woman and either left her useless and futile or sent her into industry. Children roam the streets while their mothers work. Social life goes on outside the home in clubs, restaurants, and at the movies, and the automobile keeps all the members of the family constantly on the move. All these aspects of the emancipation of women, combined with scientific advance, have had their effect on morals. Things are now considered so-cially correct that were *tabu* even twenty-five years ago. Social change brings with it elements of stress and strain. A greater latitude and a resulting uncertainty appear where once the path was narrow but clear and to depart from it meant certain retribution. Sex sanctions themselves have come in for wide variation. The polls of student opinion oc-casionally taken now in universities are startling to anyone who went to college in the days when sex relationships for "co-eds" were unknown, or nearly unknown.

Women's magazines often deal with the conflicts arising between members of a family through their different con-cepts of what is good or bad conduct. Far too often, however, they fail to probe far enough beneath the surface. But many stories appearing in the "little" magazines or the quality mag-azines have dealt, as we have indicated earlier, with deeper matters, with interesting phases of father and son relation-ships, for instance.

A great deal of attention is being given today to the many critical situations of childhood, as any reader of current an-thologies will see. One of the most subtle treatments is that of Carson McCullers in the beautifully wrought novel, *A Member of the Wedding*, where a little girl who has always been lonely and on the outside of things becomes obsessively eager to wear a bridesmaid's dress and join the honeymoon. Many of the sophisticated stories of recent years have had their source in the growing awareness of the importance of childhood experience in determining the life-pattern. Francis Eisenberg has written very amusing and quite frankly psy-chological stories about the conditioning of children; Kath-erine Anne Porter wrote very seriously about it in her "Downward Path to Wisdom," which clearly forecasts a life of neurotic hostility.

Equally numerous are stories dealing with the many aspects

of racial conflict. This writing is tremendously important in a world that has not yet rid itself of fascism. Two of the important novels of the last three years have been about Negroes: Lillian Smith's *Strange Fruit*, which dealt very frankly and honestly with prevailing social attitudes and *tabus*, and Richard Wright's autobiographical novel *Black Boy*, which has great emotional power and significance. Short stories about the injustice and cruelty of white men to Negroes are to be found in practically every anthology. "I Forgot Where I Was," for instance, by Elizabeth Enright, appeared first in *Harper's Bazaar* and later in *The O. Henry Memorial Award Prize Stories for 1946*. The little girl, Fenella, a northern Negro, goes south with her mother and there first becomes terrifyingly aware of the "whole face behind the mask" of racial cruelty. Her mother tries in vain to comfort her with promises of Grandma's "cutest little house," her chickens, rooster, old-fashioned music-box, long skirts to dress up in, and a cat with two new kittens to name. But none of this changed "the newly emerging queerness of the world," and Fenella's mother could only rock her and kiss her and know "that the things she had to offer in the way of comfort weren't good enough, or even any good. But they were all she had at her disposal: only these kisses, only these words about kittens and trifles, and a clean new handkerchief to blow on."

Stories of Jewish persecution are as old as the Bible and as new as occupied Germany. One of the most striking, printed early in the war, was called "Address Unknown" by Kressman Taylor and showed, through letters, the gradual turning of a well-meaning German into a Jew hater. It concluded with the return of a letter stamped with the sinister postmark which implied the worst of the common terror. It was to become a familiar story. Newer versions of anti-semitism are occupying writers today to such an extent that one has come to expect two or three such stories in every new anthology.

"The Imaginary Jew," a story by John Berryman which originally appeared in *The Kenyon Review* and has been included in the O. Henry Memorial collection for 1946, brings out the fact that the fascist links liberalism with Jewishness. Mr. Berryman's "Jew" is a young Gentile who ventures in a park discussion to defend Franklin D. Roosevelt and the New Deal. The Jew-baiter turns upon him and calls him a Jew. Denial serves no purpose, and finally the tormentor says, "I don't give a damn what you are. You talk like a Jew." Mr. Berryman's hero, who is the narrator, concludes later: "My persecutors were right: I was a Jew. The imaginary Jew I was was as real as the imaginary Jew hunted down, on other nights and days, in a real Jew." This story is given additional significance by the fact revealed earlier in the narrative, that the hero has many Jewish friends, has, indeed, "a special sympathy and liking for Jews—which became my fate, so that I trembled when I heard one abused in talk." We have "no term" to describe the condition, he says, thinking of social life "as that from which political life issues like a somatic dream." This story is rich in social and psychological overtones and intimations. It will be illuminating for many other people who have identified themselves with Jews and who have taken upon themselves the burden of guilt for Gentile sadism. The struggle here, of course, is that of the Gentile liberal and humanitarian against the forces of fascism which make Jews scapegoats. "Fascist America was at stake."

Another interesting aspect of this struggle comes out in Arthur Miller's *Focus*, a very original piece of work. Here, again, a Gentile is accused of being a Jew, but this Gentile has thoughtlessly subscribed to anti-semitism. Suddenly, to his horror, when he is forced to put on glasses, he sees that he looks like a Jew. Very soon, his Christian-Front neighbors are turning against him. He goes to a Christian Front meeting in order to prove his anti-semitism and is run out; and finally he is attacked brutally near his home. When he seeks justice, the officer of the law asks him, "How many of you people are there on that street?" and Newman finally, "wetting his lips," says,

"There are the Finkelsteins on the corner . . ."
"Just them and yourself?" the policeman interrupted.
"Yes. Just them and myself," Mr. Newman said.

And saying it, Mr. Newman felt "as though he were setting down a weight which, for some reason, he had been carrying and carrying." The weight was the realization of guilt. The solution here was again in accepting the role of Jewishness. Yet the two stories are different in practically all respects, the Berryman story being the richer, the more illuminating, for all its brevity.

Irwin Shaw's "An Act of Faith," originally appearing in *The New Yorker* and also published in the 1946 O. Henry Memorial collection, is built around Seeger's realization, through a letter written by his father at home in America, of what anti-semitism has done to his brother, back from the war, unbalanced and worrying about what anti-semitism will do to his family, "weeping when the newspapers reported that a hundred Jews were killed in Tripoli." Also, the father is frightened by the little evidences of hostility toward himself from his faculty colleagues. Seeger thinks of all the "million other stories" belittling Jews—the gun he took from a German may come in handy back home. Finally, he turns to his two comrades, who have been trying to get him to sell the gun so that the three can have a good time in Paris, and asks them what they think of Jews. Their replies, masterpieces of humor and tactful reassurance, are infinitely satisfying, and Seeger decides that he will, perhaps, have to rely upon them at home even more than he did in battle. He promises to sell the gun, saying, "What could I use it for in America?" That challenging question is superb. It is the ironic conclusion to a perfectly integrated story.

One of the most moving of recent stories of cruelty to Jews is "The Girl Without a Name," by Alan R. Marcus, in the *Atlantic Monthly* for November 1946. In occupied Germany, as the author says in speaking of his story, "broken, homeless, unwanted survivors live on in a martyrdom after the war which was supposed to have been fought, among other things, to accomplish their liberation." The terrified collapse of Sophie, whose mind is seriously affected by her former life in a concentration camp, is unforgettable. Her hold upon reality and life is dependent upon her older friend Anna. Anna, one day, having been given a small sum of money by an American soldier, goes forth to buy cloth for a blue skirt for Sophie. But the German fascist does not want to sell to her, even though she has, at the cost of frightening effort, secured from the American officer in charge of the zone the necessary "permission" to buy. Slowly, scene by scene, this conflict is built up to its climax where Anna, who has become obsessed with the idea of getting the material for the skirt, clutches the cloth and runs out of the store. She is, of course, taken to jail. When, after a night of frantic anxiety about Sophie, she is finally released and rushes home, she finds that the child has died of sheer terror at being left alone. The story ends with the finely ironic description of the little groups of Jews who went to the cemetery. After the prayer, they

turned, and began to file hesitantly out again onto the street. Cohesively, keeping close together, the eleven liberated allies moved down the street, threading their way through the populous ranks of the beaten, subjugated enemy.

This story, by virtue of its rising, terrifying inevitability and of the helplessness of the little refugees, is extremely moving, the most moving of all the stories here discussed. It will be a long time before the reader can forget the two young girls who meet disaster at the hands of the "subjugated enemy."

If we have dwelt long upon the varieties of conflict growing out of "racial" attitudes, it is because these conflicts are important today. They are so important that they dwarf many other struggles. Nor does their importance lie only in the fact that injustice is being done on a vast scale; it lies quite as much in the effect of hatred upon the hater—which is something sinister and corrosive. As John Berryman concluded, "Every murderer strikes the mirror, the lash of the torturer falls on the mirror and cuts the real image, and the real and the imaginary blood flow down together."

Another class of conflicts with which the writers of today are concerned is the psychic or inner struggle, where the character is torn by warring elements within himself. Great narrative has frequently been concerned with man's dualism, with his constant struggle with the forces of "good" and "evil," with his "higher" and his "lower" nature. Man, "higher than the beasts," has had a great deal to live up to, torn between his natural impulses and the socially created *tabus* which have given him a sense of guilt or sin. With the development of the science of psychology and of psychoanalysis, modern man is more and more aware of psychic conflict, and today we find much of the most penetrating and sophisticated narrative concerned with the often unconscious ambivalences, tensions, and conflicts arising within the individual who is not, as a rule, as integrated as he likes to imagine. This subject matter is available to any writer according to his degree of insight. We often have to struggle with our more obvious conflicts and with our sense of opposing duties to the different members of our family: between our love for and our hostility to father, mother, brother, sister, and, eventually, friend, lover, husband, wife and child. All lives have dramatic internal conflict going on conflicts arising from the eternal dualities between desire and conscience. Modern psychology tells us that the sources of these psychic conflicts are more or less the same, arising from the early family and social relationships. But their manifestations and intensities are often individual and different. Marcel Proust reveals the overwhelming power of his mother fixation in a many-volumed novel about a neurotic who hates the object of his "love"; and D. H. Lawrence shows a variation of the same general pattern in his *Sons and Lovers*, where the mother image comes between the man and the object of his sexual interest. The treatments in these novels are entirely different and lead the heroes into entirely different lines of action, but the roots in both cases are the mother fixation.

The psychoanalyst and the clinical psychologist probe these conflicts, which are often entirely hidden from the sufferer himself. They probe for the Oedipus complex in practically every case of neurosis. This complex has ruined countless lives through making relationships with men and women of the opposite sex difficult or impossible. Freudian theory relates this complex to attitudes of getting and taking, of rivalry and jealousy, of hostility and competitiveness, and even of conscious or unconscious homosexuality, in apparently non-sexual relationships. The range of unconscious tensions is wide and productive of much suffering and maladjustment.

Drives arising from unconscious conflicts can become highly compulsive and, if the compulsion is strong enough, can force their possessor into conduct which we think of as supremely tragic: alcoholism, arson, rape, murder, insanity, or suicide. Writers have always been interested in obsessive conditions, but formerly they lacked the techniques which modern psychology has devised for the exploration of the drives behind conduct. The fact that they achieved characterization that is sound and that can be analyzed in terms of modern knowledge is, of course, evidence that those who have insight can know human nature without knowing how it gets that way.

Sophocles had a strong hunch and produced *Oedipus Rex*. Petronius had a strong hunch and gave us *The Satyricon;* Boccaccio had a strong hunch and wrote the so-modern stories of *The Decameron*. And Shakespeare, writing before the advent of psychology, is completely sound from all modern points of view. He was much aware of the ramifications of the guilt sense, the mother complex, and the tortures of ambivalence and spiritual conflict. Dostoevsky was a superb and modern analyst, and so was Hawthorne, living in puritan Salem. Great writers have always seen important aspects of the individual's struggle with himself, though they may not have had scientific knowledge to understand it or its causes. We shall go into this subject further in Chapter 10.

A scientific age would naturally insist upon causes, and it is therefore to be expected that we should find in the fiction of today more and more studies based on the kind of facts to be found in a social worker's book of case histories. Analytically sound stories about children are, as we have indicated, told in anthology after anthology and in the literary magazines. Perhaps this interest will eventually seep into the women's magazines which advertise themselves so complacently as handling subject matter of prime importance to home-makers and child-raisers. The older writers did not have the interest in children which crowds much of the best fiction of today, but this kind of subject matter has now become tremendously exciting to us, and it calls for deep probing. The great weakness of many writers, those whose works are published as well as those who have been unsuccessful so far, lies in the fact that they only skim over the lives that they attempt to depict, failing not because they do not know how to tell a story, but because they do not go beneath the very obvious surface considerations. Technical perfection we have in plenty today, but of depth we have but little. Struthers Burt points this out by saying, in the Introduction to the O. Henry Memorial Award Prize Stories of 1945, "The most dangerous temptress in American life has always been the streamlined goddess of technique; a lady without lights, liver, and other viscera," and he adds that the final determination of any work of art is "the mesh of the sieve of its maker." The best mesh is the mesh of deep insight which reveals characters fully and satisfyingly in such a way as to stand analysis.

One must learn to understand the depths of his subject matter. Good material often presents several possible approaches. The richer the material is inherently, the more numerous the approaches. The good writer today knows that he must "go beneath." He asks himself: Just what basic conflicts do my characters have in this situation? What reactions and conflicts do they produce in the other characters? Who is up against what obstacle? What does it do to him? What does he do to it? Always, always, must the writer know *why* his characters act the way they do. The "knowing why" is what we call insight. If we understand the factors that underlie dramatic conduct, we shall certainly know how to select "threads worth pulling," and we shall know how to pull them to the best advantage. One cannot help wondering what Henry James, so intent upon deep vision, would have made of analytic psychology, what "threads" he would have pulled had he been more aware of the force of the unconscious.

Thomas Mann, in his essay "Freud and the Future" has

indeed pointed the way for the writer of today and of the future:

The analytic revelation is a revolutionary force. With it blithe scepticism has come into the world, a mistrust which unmasks all the schemes and subterfuges of our own souls. Once roused and on the alert, it cannot be put to sleep again. It infiltrates life, undermines its raw naïveté, takes from it the strain of its own ignorance, de-emotionalizes it, as it were, inculcates the taste for understatement, as the English call it—for the deflated rather than for the inflated word, for the cult which exerts its influence by moderation, by modesty.[1]

Mann closes his magnificent essay with a paragraph in which he envisages a man who can meet the Faustian ideal of a free folk. "The free folk are the people of a future freed from fear and hate, and ripe for peace."

Mann has in this pregnant sentence put his finger upon two of the most important factors in all conflict: fear and hate. They come from infantilism, regression to childhood and, says Mann, "what a role this genuinely psychoanalytic element plays in all our lives! What a large share it has in shaping the life of a human being; operating, indeed, in just the way I have described. . . ."

"Shaping the life of a human being . . . !" What a marvelous phrase! The writer's task is, first and foremost, to show the shaping of a life. And is not the shaping of a man a matter of his ability to handle relationships with other people, with environmental factors, and above all with himself?

It is only by showing cause and effect that we can give our fiction reader the greater understanding that he craves. Life can easily show him the effect, the man in action, but life less often shows the causes for the action, the relationships between things. The average man sees Mrs. So-and-So behaving strangely, but he does not see why. He can't read beneath the surface. The psychological writer tries to show

[1] *Op. cit.*

what goes on beneath the mask; he tries to uncover the real woman. He often does not understand the full intricacy of human motivations (Who does?), but he does show step by step in vivid scenes both the nature of the conflict and its results. Sometimes his picture is merely revealing and ironic, sometimes emotionally moving and tragic.

Conflict betrays itself by its production of opposing desires and alternating emotions. One line of reason says to the hero, "You ought to do this," but another line says, "No, you ought to do that." Such a conflict may be merely an intellectual duality, but what complications appear when strong emotional drives enter to confound reasoning and say it nay! What inner and outer confusion when the emotional urge defies the intellect!

De Maupassant shows in "Moonlight" a memorable struggle born of the Abbé Marignan's fixed belief that he knew God and was able to penetrate his designs and of his love for his niece whom he had destined to be a nun. The Abbé hears of clandestine meetings going on between his niece and a young man. Having cut himself three times while shaving, "swollen with rage and resentment," he finally starts out, cudgel in hand, to break up the evening tryst. Then an involuntary emotional reaction to the beauty of the moonlight night, to "such a splendor of moonlight as you seldom see," stops him.

> He began to breathe deep, drinking the air as drunkards drink their wine, and he walked slowly, being ravished, astounded, and almost oblivious of his niece.

> The distant nightingales "mingled their scattered music, which makes one dream without making one think—their music gay and vibrant, made for kisses, for the seduction of moonlight."

> The priest resumed his march, his heart failing him, without his knowing why. He felt himself enfeebled and as it were, suddenly

exhausted; he wished to sit down, to remain there, to contemplate, to admire God in His work.

Down there, following the undulations of the little river, a long line of poplars could be traced in serpentine perspective. A fine mist, a white vapor which the moonrays traversed, silvered and made luminous, hung suspended above and around the trees, enveloping all the tortuous course of the stream with a sort of light and transparent haze.

The Abbé Marignan stopped again, penetrated to the depths of his soul by an irresistible emotion. And a doubt, a vague disquietude invaded him, while there arose in his mind one of those interrogations which he sometimes proposed to himself.

Why had God made this? Since the night is intended for sleep, for unconsciousness, for repose, for forgetfulness of all, why did he render it more charming than the day, sweeter than the dawns and the evenings? And this slow and seducing star, more poetical than the sun and which seems destined, so discreet is it, to illumine things too delicate and mysterious for the garish light of day—why does it come to make the shadows so transparent?

Thinking about all the glories of nature with this "half veil over the world," stirred by the sensuous beauty of the night, the Abbé Marignan finally sees the couple embracing.

They suddenly animated this motionless landscape, which enveloped them like a divine frame made for them alone. They seemed, these two, like a single being, the being for whom this calm and silent night was destined; and they came towards the priest like a living response—the response which his Master made to his interrogation.

Finally, deeply stirred by the sensuous beauty of the scene, the Abbé believes that he has seen here "some Bible story, like the loves of Ruth and Boaz, the accomplishment of the will of the Lord in one of those great scenes talked of in the holy books." And he says to himself, "God perhaps has made such nights as this to clothe with the ideal the loves of men." And he flees from the scene bewildered, "almost ashamed, as if he had penetrated into a temple where he had not the right to go."

Thus the Abbé has, in this scene, gone through the steps

of recognizing a situation, starting to act to prevent the assignation, reacting to the atmospheric stimulus of the moonlight, and reversing himself. The moonlight has softened his stern belief in chastity and the dedicated life of the nun. The Abbé's conflict was one that could be solved by intellectualization. It had no realistic irreconcilables. Maupassant chose a relatively easy problem here.

But quite different and not to be solved at all is the conflict of the mother in Katherine Anne Porter's story "He." The mother here can find no way out because the idiot child is one duty and the husband and other children are another and conflicting duty. The idiot child poses an impossible problem. The mother struggles valiantly against any partiality to the other children, but in spite of herself she gives Him the difficult and even dangerous tasks. Then her inexorable conscience flays her and throws her into an agony of self-blame. Finally we see her taking Him to the hospital: "she had loved Him as much as she possibly could, there were Adna and Emly who had to be thought of too, there was nothing she could do to make up to Him for His life. Oh, what a mortal pity He was ever born!" The mother here has followed the familiar pattern of facing her problem, recognizing it, trying to solve it, and finally acting. But her action is at best only a compromise that must confront her all the rest of her life. She has been caught in a moral trap, and, whatever decision she makes, her conscience will crucify her. There is in all reality no possible escape for her. There is only the agony of guilt.

5

Building the Structure

THE best situation from which to develop a plot is that which offers no easy solution. The expected, the patterned, the cliché, is thoroughly bad. The writer must, as we have seen, strive for a new configuration. He need not invoke unrealities, however. The reader may be able to guess the outcome of the conflict, in which case suspense must arise from excitement as to the ways in which the outcome is brought about. Often the suspense depends upon how the character will react—upon, as Henry James said, "the interesting face presented by him to *any* damnable trick." The way the characters react to their situation is often the main story.

Life supplies not so much a ready-made plot as it does the germ. Henry James reports in his Preface to *The Spoils of Poynton:*

most of the stories straining to shape under my hand have sprung from a single small seed, a seed as minute and wind-blown as that casual hint for "The Spoils of Poynton" dropped unwittingly by my neighbour, a mere floating particle in the stream of talk. What above all comes back to me with this reminiscence is the sense of the inveterate minuteness, on such happy occasions, of the precious particle—reduced, that is, to its mere fruitful essence. Such is the interesting truth about the stray suggestion, the wandering word, the vague echo, at touch of which the novelist's imagination winces as at the prick of some sharp point: its virtue is all in its needle-like quality, the power to penetrate as finely as possible. This fineness it is that communicates the virus of suggestion, anything more than the minimum of which spoils the operation. If one is given a hint at all designedly one is sure to be given too much; . . . . Life being all inclusion and confusion, and art being all discrimination and selection, the latter, in search of the hard latent *value* with which alone it is concerned, sniffs round the mass as instinctively and unerringly as a dog suspicious of some buried bone.[1]

The buried bone for James in this case was the chance remark at a dinner party that "a good lady in the north, always well looked on, was at daggers drawn with her only son, ever hitherto exemplary, over the ownership of the valuable furniture of a fine old house just accruing to the young man by his father's death." James goes to great pains to point out, however, that he did not work his story out in "the regular way." He saw it "all for himself." James always did see things for himself, in a very special way, with a great sensitivity to fine issues, for shades of moral judgment, "latent value."

Latent value, arrived at after a thorough consideration of all the possibilities, should be the concern which determines the form of a story, the line of an action. "Tragedy is an imitation," said Aristotle, "not of men, but of an action and of life, and life consists in action, and its end is a mode of action, not a quality." Aristotle thought that the incidents and the plot were an end in tragedy and that character was "subsidiary." Most modern critics and writers would disagree with him. But, it must be remembered, fiction is never static and characters are not static. Therefore Aristotle's concept holds when all is said and done, at least it holds so far as serious dramatic writing is concerned.

Fiction, as we have noted, involves both character and action integrated into an organic whole. Structure, development of character, event, and outcome, then, all rest entirely upon the author's concept of the whole value. The five stories of Jewish persecution examined in the preceding

[1] *Op. cit.*, pages 119–120.

chapter can be broken down analytically into five different thematic and emotional values, each with its special tone and revelation. The form is determined in each case by the latent value which is the author's special vision. The events of one story could hardly be transferred to another without destroying its special meaning. It is important that the selection of events, their order, and their tone shall be worked out so as to bend the story in the direction of the author's intention and integrate it. Each scene, each plateau must be determined in relation to the desired artistic effect. Anyone teaching beginners is surprised to discover how few really know what their end product is to be—a state of mind that comes from a superficial view of the materials, a too immediate concern with action in itself, and a resulting failure in theme and philosophy. The result of such ineffective planning is that the reader puts the story down with a feeling of "So what?" In other words, the story has not *come off*. It lacks the final intensity and impact of a truth convincingly demonstrated.

The answer to all this is, of course, careful planning. Some people call this "plotting," but the word conveys so much of the idea of artificial and bad organization that the "plotter" has come to be disliked and distrusted. Much of what has passed for plot since the time of O. Henry has been so bad that many critics have fully accepted Sherwood Anderson's idea that plot is "poison." But such rejection of a good, old-fashioned word because it has been misunderstood and abused is really not justified. We need a word that conveys the meaning that was originally contained in Aristotle's analysis.

Assuming that we have fully determined our desired effect, how do we go about getting it? How do we construct our edifice? Just like any builder, with bricks and mortar. The bricks are the scenes, the mortar is the necessary material for binding all together; and they are put together in accordance with a clearly determined plan. As James pointed out, one may, and often does, change his architectural scheme as he comes to see the possibilities of his materials more clearly; but always there is a plan.

A plan involves an awareness of the many possibilities of the scene and the plateau. It involves a reckoning of the number of scenes required and the amount of binding material. The scenes are the peaks. They are important moments, moments of minor or major crisis that the author wants to reveal in detail. The scene brings the character or characters before us, acting as they would act upon a stage, talking, moving, *breaking out* in revealing ways. The plateau also has many uses and many possible abuses. It is used to convey facts like any exposition. The facts may be antecedent to the action about to take place and the form of the plateau may be that of the flashback (author explanation), or retrospection (character explanation in terms of either thought or speech). It is used to *describe* the characters and their setting. It is also used for transition: to go from one time to another, one place to another, or one person to another.

Plateaus are not always necessary, however, and we shall soon see that a very interesting and moving story can be told almost entirely without scene. What folly, then, it would be to try to lay down set rules about even these fundamental aspects of fiction writing! We can show, however, what a scene is and what a plateau is, and the writer who understands these matters should then be able to construct a story if—and what a big "if"—he really has a story to tell.

Irwin Shaw's famous story, "The Girls in Their Summer Dresses," [2] is a perfect example of scene and the one-scene story, which is so frequently found in *The New Yorker*.

[2] Copyright, 1942, by Irwin Shaw. Reprinted by permission of Random House, Inc.

Shaw's characters are there before us, revealing themselves, their conflict, and the comic irony of the situation.

"Look out," Frances said as they crossed Eighth Street. "You'll
break your neck." Michael laughed and Frances laughed with him.
"She's not so pretty," Frances said. "Anyway, not pretty enough
to take a chance of breaking your neck."

These words give us the clue to the line of action and the
cause of conflict—Michael's propensity for looking at women
and noticing things about their appearance.

We hear Michael and Frances discussing their program.
They will not accept the Stevensons' invitation. They will
have "a planned Sunday in New York," ending with a
good dinner and a French picture at the Filmarte. Frances
talks on.

"Sure," he said. He took his eyes off the hatless girl with the dark
hair, cut dancer-style like a helmet, who was walking past him.

Again, the conflict is indicated. The very words that Shaw
selects are pregnant with meaning. "Took his eyes off" implies that Michael's gaze has been long and concentrated.
We can quite readily recognize that this is an important moment when Frances comes in:

"You always look at other women," Frances said. "Everywhere.
Every damned place we go."

Now the conflict is becoming clearer. The irritation expressed by the word "damned" is significant.

Michael now admits that he likes to "look at women and
men and subway excavations and moving pictures and the
little flowers of the field. I casually inspect the universe."

"You ought to see the look in your eye," Frances said,
"as you casually inspect the universe on Fifth Avenue."
Michael assures her that he has not touched another woman.
"Not once. In all five years." But Frances goes on talking

about it and he confesses just how much he likes to look at women, all women, in all places, at all times including "the girls in their summer dresses." His wife asks if he loves her then and he assures her that he does and that she is beautiful.

Then Frances opens Pandora's box. "You'd like to be free to—". . . . "Sometimes I feel I would like to be free," he replies, and she says, "Well, any time you say." He tells her not to be foolish, but she goes on. "Someday," she says, crying, "you're going to make a move." Goaded, he finally says, "Maybe. . . . How the hell do I know?" More discussion and then Frances begs Michael to do her one favor:

"Stop talking about how pretty this woman is or that one. Nice eyes, nice breasts, a pretty figure, good voice." She mimicked his voice. "Keep it to yourself. I'm not interested."

She finally gets up, leaves the table, and says, "Do you want me to call the Stevensons?" and he replies, "Sure. Call them."

Our brief conversation has run its course and the couple's "program for a planned Sunday in New York," starting so lyrically, ends in their effort to escape being alone together. The scorned invitation of the Stevensons will be accepted, and the acceptance is symbolic of a complete change of mood. Michael's idiosyncracy, fully explored, and Frances' jealous reaction, also fully explored, have brought about the illumination of a common situation.

But Mr. Shaw is not content to let it rest at that. He has a final illuminating note to add. He tells us that Frances walked to the telephone and Michael watched her, thinking, "what a pretty girl, what nice legs."

The basis of this conflict is the husband's exaggerated interest in women, all women, and his wife's resentment of it. Jealousy is one of the most ancient and commonplace themes in the world. Any high school child could write a story about jealousy. But Mr. Shaw's story is about a very particular cause for jealousy, an exaggeration, almost a distortion of the normal. The story, therefore, for all its trivial subject matter, has a special interest. It pulls old elements together in a new configuration, offering a new interpretation of everyday facts at once ironic and revealing.

The house of fiction has "not one window, but a million," said Henry James. People watching the same show see things differently. The window through which one looks is especially important.

The entire action of the Shaw story takes place in a matter of ten or fifteen minutes; yet it is a satisfying structure with a beginning, a middle, and an end, and, granting the character traits as they are, a good deal of inevitability. We note that it contains a small amount of explanatory material, indicated in the first extract, but for the most part it is told in direct conversation. The reader gets the story by hearing the actors talk, exactly as if they were on a stage before him.

The number of scenes in narrative is, of course, dependent upon the scope of the action and the period of time covered. One cannot always be sure in advance of how many scenes will be needed. A short story may become, in the working out, a long one, even a novelette, like *Ethan Frome;* or it may grow into a novel of several hundred pages. Henry James noted this when he wrote of his "false measurements":

The little ideas one wouldn't have treated save for the design of keeping them small, the developed situations that one would never with malice prepense have undertaken, the long stories that had thoroughly meant to be short, the short stories that had under-handedly plotted to be long, the hypocrisy of modest beginnings, the audacity of misplaced middles, the triumph of intentions never entertained—with these patches, as I look about, I see my experience paved: . . . [3]

It is important for the writer to view all of the possibilities of his subject matter. Then he must limit himself to that which has a unity, otherwise he will try to tell in short story

[3] *Op. cit.,* page 100.

form of events and character developments that require novel length and can only be summarized in a short story.

And the summary is one of the most common mistakes of beginners. The summary is merely a fairly complete outline briefly and directly presented. One sees the distinction between summary and artfully narrated story when he looks at the outline of previous action that is usually presented at the beginning of each installment of a "continued" story. To look at the synopsis and then at the dramatization that follows is to understand how much elaboration and expansion the art of fiction involves. The length of a story is nearly always determined, not by author's whim, but by the number of words required to convey the dramatic action and theme in view of the author's very specific intention.

The number of scenes or, to put it differently, the number of crises, has a good deal to do with the length of the narrative. A scene may not appear to be critical, but it should have its justification as a moment in the story worth noting. It is the author's way of saying to the reader, "Now stop and look at this." We shall discuss scene more analytically in the next chapter. We bring it in here because the idea of scene is basic in planning the structure of a story.

Unless the story has only one scene, there is usually plateau material which is necessary for complete understanding of what is going on. It may give us the antecedent events, it may supply descriptive detail, or it may provide transition. Plateau is the thread which holds together the scenes upon which attention is focused. It can provide an atmospheric or explanatory frame for them. It is not, as a rule, exciting in itself, but it leads to things that are exciting. All cannot be crisis in fiction any more than in life, and plateau provides that lessening of tension, that relief, that calm, which brings out the contrasting excitement of the important moments. Plateau may also, on the other hand, serve to build up expectancy and suspense. It can be extremely effective, as we shall see later in discussing Joseph Conrad's *Lord Jim*.

The author's plan for his story will tell what the scenes are to be, what each is to accomplish, how each will advance the action, and what plateau material is needed. But, as our quotation from James implies, his plan may change as he writes, until the narrative has lost much or even most of its original plan. It is not important that one should know in advance how *long* his story is to be, but he should have, in the short narrative, at least, an idea of the number of scenes necessary to dramatize it.

Scenes may be used to imply the lapse of time necessary for an action or a growth of character development to take place. A novelist often uses scenes that way, the short story writer less often, because the short narrative by its very form and nature deals with a more immediate and limited range of experience. Edith Wharton has spoken of the typical short story as "the foreshortening of a dramatic climax connecting two or more lives." The typical novel, she adds, "usually deals with the gradual unfolding of a succession of events divided by intervals of time, and in which many people, in addition to the principal characters, play more or less subordinate parts." [4]

Sometimes, especially in the novel, it is very important to establish this sense of time. It takes real skill to do it in the short story, as we shall see in our discussion of "Something Jolly," which illustrates the handling of both time and scene. There are many ways of implying time, the more obvious being the use of transitional phrases or clauses—"Meantime the day had grown cold and dark." More subtle delineations reveal time through concrete detail describing characters as changed in appearance or situation.

Time elements are now often conveyed through what is

[4] *The Writing of Fiction*, copyright by Charles Scribner's Sons, 1925.

called the "flashback." This is done either by direct author explanation, telling about what has gone before, or by some character who either talks or thinks. The terms "flashback" and "retrospection" are often used interchangeably, but the word "retrospect" should be kept for the character's thought.

Tchekov, after introducing his hero in "Old Age" as an architect returning to his native town to restore the church, immediately informs us that "He was born in the town, he had grown up and been married there, and yet when he got out of the train he hardly recognized it. Everything had changed." This is direct author summary, or flashback of the simplest kind.

But Walter Van Tilburg Clark, introducing an old man in "The Wind and the Snow of Winter," [5] reveals facts much less directly, much more slowly, conveying a feeling of the passage of time by means of the character's thoughts and finally by the changes that he finds when he reaches his destination. Clark has used a surprisingly long introductory plateau, giving many details of the mountain trail, as well as description of the old man and his burro. In fact, two thirds of the story really consist of memories; and, if the author had not been extremely skillful, if he had not been a master of description and atmosphere, the quiet narrative would repel the reader who has been conditioned by most modern writers to the immediate and scenic.

In this story, Mike Braneen is a miner coming down the mountain to spend the winter in a settlement. When he gets there he finds everything is changed, his old friends have died, and the settlement itself is dying. The significance of the story is much greater, however, than these words imply, for the old man himself must be near the end. "It was a place that grew old with a man, that was going to die sometime too."

[5] *The Yale Review*, Winter 1945, copyright Yale University Press.

How does Clark make such material interesting? By revelation through long descriptive passages conveyed through Mike's mind: first, his awareness of the casually drifting snowflakes, the mountain scenery, and the newly paved highway, not good for his burro Annie. Mike's thoughts mingle facts viewed through a failing memory with their previous emotional impact to show a life that has been so long that Mike is not sure how long it is. The only other character during these passages is the burro, who has shared his life. Clark skillfully indicates Mike's confusion of past and present by changing the burro's name from Annie to Maria, an earlier burro, and back again to Annie at the end of the story. We meet no scene of present importance until we come to page eleven of a total of fourteen. Here is a daring technique. All the factors are perfectly integrated to produce the mood and the feeling of life running down as inevitably as the season changes to the wind and snow of winter. Especially significant are the intimations of a dimming mind, that crowning indignity imposed upon those who live too long. The only present scene is that in which Mike meets a young stranger, asks questions about his friends and the places that he and Annie used to stay, and learns the truth. He accepts it with moving simplicity when, after hearing of Mrs. Wright's death, he says after a long pause the one little word "Oh."

We shall study this beautiful story in more detail later when considering the angle of narration. It is significant for many reasons, not the least of which are the unusual techniques for conveying a sense of time and the inevitability of change and death. All is so skillfully devised as to make one feel the illusory quality of experience. Interestingly enough, retrospection is the perfect device for the theme. How unexciting this quiet narrative sounds, and how thrilling it really is! Thrilling because it is a work of art illuminating the universal and philosophically significant. Only an accomplished writer could so perfectly integrate subject matter and form.

Allan Seeger's introduction in "The Conqueror," in the O. Henry Memorial Award Collection for 1945, is also slow moving, with a great deal of emphasis upon the tavern's interior appearance and, for a reason not very clear, the teeth of the bar tender. The leisurely detail includes description of a picture portraying "a struggle between a mounted Arab and a man on foot. The horse was white, rearing and frightened, and his eyes bugged out like billiard balls. (Foreign horses have big eyes perhaps.) The Arab was dressed in flowing bed-sheets and he was swinging a curved sword." Still further details follow about the Arab scene, which reminds the soldier of a town called Marrakech in North Africa. More description is given, during which the soldier has a beer; then he calls in "a loud confident voice," saying, "Hey, gimme another beer!" This hints at his adolescent quality, which is the main character element. He is compensating for his lack of confidence. His absorption in the romantic and unreal chromo is also part of the effect of unsophistication, and we see, at the end, that it is a symbolic forecast of the outcome, which is simply *recognition*. The reader, of course, does not know this when he first meets the picture, and hence there is danger that he may decide that the writer is unselective and boring. But the danger is cleverly lessened by the use of amusing detail, perhaps even by the description of the teeth, which seems irrelevant otherwise.

"Parts that prepare,"—plateau, retrospect, description, exposition—can be handled, it is clear, so that they are just as interesting as scene. They are in many ways more difficult, taking greater artistry. They constitute a test of technical skill. One way to acquire such skill is to study the best writers intensively. The writer is faced with the necessity for coming close to technical perfection. Otherwise, no matter how interesting his material, he can hardly succeed.

Beginnings may be either plateau or scene. As a rule the amateur will, as we have noted, have to guard against a tendency to write a long introduction. Introductions are difficult and critical in that they usually determine whether or not a reader will stay with the story or throw it down. Long plateaus of any kind give a sense of delayed action. They inhibit suspense, that feeling of rising excitement which is one of the chief elements of drama. Only the stylist dare risk delaying the immediacy of scene and action. Thus it is that a great majority of today's stories begin near the climax or point of excitement and tension. Many begin very close to the end and then go back by means of plateau or retrospect to tell what has led up to the impending crisis. In general, the reader wants to have an idea, early in the story, of the problem or the struggle to come. And it is often far easier to handle the scenic and immediate.

But we do not need to knock our reader down with our first sentence. Above all, we do not need to make our first words a direct quotation hanging in the air without any setting or introduction of characters whatever. More often than not contemporary writers begin with a few words which explain the situation—in other words, an introduction. The introduction usually sets the *time* of the action.

For instance, the fear that is the basis of Frances Gray Patton's story, "A Piece of Bread,"[6] is revealed by the author's telling us in the first paragraph:

Lida was afraid to cross the street where the chain gang was working, but she knew she had to. She had promised Mother to come home and bathe at five, and besides it was wrong to be afraid, and besides what could possibly hurt her? The Negro prisoners were all coupled together by heavy chains at their ankles, and a white man with a gun was watching them. She would go quietly across in a grown-up way, and nobody would even notice her. Of course she could walk down and cross at the corner and then walk back up to

[6] *The Kenyon Review*, Autumn 1944.

her own house on the other side. But that would be going out of her way for no real reason; Mother might see her and ask her why she was coming from the wrong direction. And she would have to say she had been afraid.

This introduction is directness itself. It tells us the main facts about the situation confronting the little heroine, it defines the line of conflict—the fear of acknowledging fear. We see, as we go on, an overly conscientious child, sensitive to the feelings of others, worried about imagined "lies." Then the Negro asks for a piece of bread and Lida is terrified. Later she is at home and we are in her mind, realizing that her mother doesn't want her to be afraid of anything and has in the past forced her to do things she feared. (This is conveyed through retrospect.) "That was how grown people were. If they saw you were afraid to go somewhere they made you go." And now Lida is also worrying about keeping her fears from Mother who "might die." (This indicates an alarming development of guilt sense.) Then there is a scene with Mother and the maid, who is factual and frightening. Capitola said "everybody had a right to be afraid of something." After this we are in a plateau for some time, thinking Lida's thoughts as she gets ready for dinner and tries not to be afraid to make up her mind to take the Negro the piece of bread. Finally comes the scene at the dinner table, a very charming picture of carefully reasoned family life and child guidance. Lida tells about the Negro's asking for bread, and is praised for not going back to him. But she withdraws "into a dreamlike loneliness, gazing through the window at the street. . . ."

And out of the gathering darkness one shadow, darker than the rest, lengthened, and invaded the innermost recesses of her mind. It brooded there, black and shapeless, tingeing all her thoughts with the somber hue of its trouble.

The devices of scene, explanation, and retrospect are extremely well handled in this story; so cleverly are they woven together that it is difficult even to identify them. There are many hints that reveal what the family does to prevent the child's fearing things and at the same time show that their method is not working. They are defeating their own ends by suppressing the child's natural and legitimate fears. The maid, Capitola, seems wiser. Capitola says, "She ought to call me when the road's full of wild men." Father and mother are overly careful, casual, about the Negro. Grandmother is less wise and amusingly beside the point. Father and mother talk of other things, revealing their technique of handling the child. This is how Lida has *been* handled and—we finally see—unfavorably conditioned. Lida thinks how Father "might hold your hand and go with you. But he made you go." (Present thought.) That refers to a time when she had been afraid of a dog. (Retrospective thought for several sentences.) Capitola thinks people have a right to be afraid of something; but the child thinks, "It was natural for colored people to be afraid, because their ancestors came from the African jungles, where lions and tigers and other dangerous animals were always prowling around." The kind of training that Lida has been given is in many ways correct, but the effort to forestall fears has been overdone and Capitola, realistically afraid, has played her role as an undermining influence. The reader can see, from time to time, what the child's fear-history has been. Retrospect is used lavishly but the *effect* is presentness. The concluding paragraph is, of course, portentous. Little Lida has been conditioned, by the most careful parents, in the wrong way.

Still another story in this collection, "Understand What I Mean?" [7] by Bill Gerry, handles plateau material skillfully.

[7] *The Yale Review*, Autumn 1944, copyright by the Yale University Press.

It begins with a device for arousing suspense: "To tell this story is difficult, and I approach it with misgiving. For I do not like what I have seen, I do not like what I have heard, and I shall not like it when you laugh and say, 'Look what turns up in a barbershop.' " This, of course, tells us that the narrator is concerned about something which he thinks others may treat casually. We note that he has been told to take medicine for his heart. First he shows us the barbershop and the people in it; all is very detailed and slow for two pages. We look through the window at things outdoors, military things that serve the purpose of building up reader awareness of war and soldier sacrifice. We have no clue to the main action until we reach the top of page two and someone, we do not know who it is, says, "More damn niggers!" From this hint at the theme, talk goes on very casually between the barber and the sergeant from Arkansas who wants "niggers" kept in their places, while the narrator thinks back (retrospect) over his friendship with Brownie at the induction center a year and a half earlier. He is now out of uniform, and he remembers that this barbershop used to be on Brownie's mail route. There is more casual barbershop talk and general goings-on, with some description of the sergeant and more of his hatred of Negroes, which stirs the narrator very deeply: "stiff and excited like an animal, and the old pain was cutting off my breath." When Brownie enters, again carrying mail, there are bitter words between the sergeant, Brownie, and the narrator. Finally the sergeant leaves and the story ends with the narrator so upset that he seems close to a heart attack. As Brownie goes out, he says, "There goes a man—and a friend." But in the last paragraph the barber, who has heretofore not revealed his attitude, goes leisurely about his work and finally answers, "with indulgence," "Yeah—pretty good nigger, that one."

The story is masterly in its combination of the realistic,

the casual, and the significant. Vivid characterization comes out; for instance, the barber and his old wife with "birdlike eyes" which pierced the hero "venomously and then fluttered to one side." And the action is socially illuminating, especially in the words spoken by an apparently mild barber which reveal so much of the common attitude. The words "pretty good nigger, that one" tell a whole story.

The descriptive detail here has been generous and the movement is really slow; but the realism is strong and interesting and the very small amount of action is entirely convincing. We see how harmless, mild, average people can take on racial antagonism and superiority.

The principle of *expectancy* is used. There must be a reason for all this barbershop detail. One "smells a mouse" even when nothing much is going on. And this is important; the careful building of background, of setting, while it is plateau, nevertheless implies that something important is going to take place. It is like the spot "marked with a cross." It retards action but it nevertheless brings suspense. Plateau and retardation of action permit a slight dropping of suspense through a loss of immediacy; but they can convey a sense of waiting which is important in itself. All is in abeyance before the impending action.

The novel makes more use of plateau than do most short stories. Obviously it *can*; it has more time and consequently needs less speed. Intense rapidity is not expected of it. The short story is, by its very nature, more rapid, more a flash in a pan, more immediate. But the novel can take time to develop the necessary details, time elements, changes in character, growth, and development.

Joseph Conrad has used long plateau passages with the greatest possible effect in his description of scene on the night that was to prove so disastrous to Lord Jim. The reader should note how the passage below conveys a mood of calm and beauty that contrasts with the tragedy about to take place.[8]

> A marvelous stillness pervaded the world, and the stars, together with the serenity of their rays, seemed to shed upon the earth an assurance of everlasting security. . . .
> Jim on the bridge was penetrated by the great certitude of unbounded safety and peace that could be read on the silent aspect of nature like the certitude of fostering love upon the placid tenderness of a mother's face. . . .

On the deck the pilgrims slept all unaware, disturbed only by "a faint and patient sigh at times," "the exhalation of a troubled dream."

> The thin gold shaving of the moon floating slowly downwards had lost itself on the darkened surface of the waters, and the eternity beyond the sky seemed to come down nearer to the earth, with the augmented glitter of the stars, with the more profound somberness in the lustre of the half-transparent dome covering the flat disc of an opaque sea. The ship moved so smoothly that her onward motion was imperceptible to the sense of men, as though she had been a crowded planet speeding through the dark spaces of ether behind the swarms of suns, in the appalling and calm solitudes awaiting the breath of future creations.

In addition to peaceful mood, Jim's feeling of safety, the pilgrims' defenselessness—all highly important in contrast with what is about to happen—the reader (and Jim by implication) is made to feel the smallness of man before the planetary universe with its "profound somberness." All this conveys the implication of something important ahead, perhaps an ironic stroke by Fate, ironic because so much in contrast with the peace and "unbounded safety."

And then it happens. Note the great restraint with which disaster is revealed, so delicately that only the very careful and aware reader will realize what is happening.

---

[8] From: *Lord Jim* by Joseph Conrad, copyright 1899, 1900, 1928 by Joseph Conrad, reprinted by permission of Doubleday & Company, Inc.

Something made the men on board stagger, they knew not what. They could not understand; and suddenly the calm sea, the sea without a cloud, appeared formidably insecure in their immobility, as if poised on the brow of yawning destruction. . . . A faint noise as of thunder, of thunder infinitely remote, less than a sound, hardly more than a vibration, passed slowly, and the ship quivered in response, as if the thunder had growled deep in the water. The eyes of the two Malays at the wheel glittered towards the white men, but their dark hands remained closed on the spokes.

That is how Conrad deals with the sensational material of a wreck at sea. He turns the descriptive plateau into a pregnant scene with faint thunder and glittering Malay eyes! But a man's life is about to be wrecked and, for all the reader knows, a boatload of sleeping passengers is going down. This is a tremendous scene—pictured, oh so quietly.

In concluding our discussion of plateau, we should, however, warn the beginner against the very long and slow introduction. It can be effective in the hands of an accomplished writer, but it is dangerous for the inexperienced. Only the well trained reader has patience for long descriptive passages. Therefore, especially if the author is writing for "the market" —whatever that implies—he had best speed up. The sooner he hints a predicament, the more likely he is to hold reader attention. Indeed, one of the outstanding characteristics of the fiction of the last twenty-five years or so has been its immediacy, its skillful use of early implication to catch the reader firmly in his fears for the characters and his sympathy for them.

The techniques of the past were far less skillful and far more obvious to any adult mind. One needs only to think of Poe to see how methods have changed in the last century. Poe's mechanics seem cumbersome and obvious. But, since they are so visible, they are worth a moment's attention, despite their obviousness.

First, the titles often imply exciting developments: for

instance, "The Tell-Tale Heart," "The Masque of the Red Death," "The Pit and the Pendulum," "A Descent into the Maelstrom," "The Premature Burial," "The Murders in the Rue Morgue," "The Fall of the House of Usher."

Second, Poe's opening paragraphs strike the reader with considerable impact and shock him into attention. In "The Tell-Tale Heart," for instance, our hero reveals his dangerous madness in the first sentence.

True!—nervous—very, very dreadfully nervous I had been and am; but why *will* you say that I am mad? The disease had sharpened my senses—not destroyed—not dulled them. Above all was the sense of hearing acute. I heard all things in the heaven and in the earth. I heard many things in hell. Now, then, am I mad? Hearken! and observe how healthily—how calmly I can tell you the whole story.

The narrator's protestations of sanity actually inform the reader that he is, in truth, insane. They also tell us that the illusions have to do with hearing. In the paragraph following, the still protesting narrator has murdered an old man because he did not like his eyes. Eventually, we are in the never-to-be forgotten story of the tell-tale heart heard only by the insane murderer, who is driven by his guilty conscience to shriek out, "I admit the deed!—tear up the planks! here, here!—it is the beating of his hideous heart!"

Again in "*Ligeia*," Poe's second statement reveals that the narrator's memory is "feeble through much suffering," while the quotation beneath his title sets the theme that "man doth not yield himself to the angels, nor unto death utterly, save only through the weakness of his feeble will." We easily guess that the story is going to reveal a struggle to overcome death itself. The first paragraph of "The Cask of Amontillado" explains that a man has been done an injury and has vowed revenge of a sort that will enable him to "punish with impunity" at the same time that the avenger is known to the man who has done him wrong. The narrator in the second paragraph smiles "at the thought of his immolation," thus revealing his sadism.

"William Wilson" can hardly be rivalled for direct thrilling statement.

Let me call myself, for the present, William Wilson. The fair page now lying before me need not be sullied with my real appellation. This has been already too much an object for the scorn—for the horror—for the detestation of my race. To the uttermost regions of the globe have not the indignant winds bruited its unparalleled infamy. Oh, outcast of all outcasts most abandoned!—to the earth art thou not forever dead?

This introduction implies exaggerated guilt sense or that the hero is an insane man, a man victimized by his own imagination. The machinery creaks loudly.

Yes, Poe resorted to the most extreme means to gain attention and frequently gave clear indication of the general kind of action to come. Few writers today, outside of the pulps which appeal to an audience of crude and adolescent tastes, would dare use such obvious devices.

An illustration of equally direct intimation, given in the modern idiom with more subtlety, is found in Josephine Johnson's "Safe," [9] where the heroine opens the story she is to narrate:

I don't know why things come this way. If I'd known before—but we never know, we always find things out too late. Each day she asked about the mail, pretending at first that she expected bulbs, was anxious that they should come before the winter. Then the bulbs came, and the seed catalogue, and there was nothing else she could seem to be waiting for except his letters.

In this retrospective monologue we meet the narrator who is going to tell us about a serious mistake found out too late. It has to do with a woman's expectation of a letter, an ex-

---

[9] Reprinted from *Winter Orchard and Other Stories* by permission of Simon and Schuster, Inc. Copyright, 1935, by Josephine Johnson.

pectation which she is at pains to *conceal*. That is all. It sug-gests the ancient plot of the intercepted letter, and that is indeed, what the story is about—the terrible results of the narrator's cruel and determined opposition to her sister's love affair.

Here we find, not the chronological, natural order, but a more calculated and effective order of art. Instead of begin-ning with *A* and running through to *Z*, the action begins at *Z*, which is the final catastrophe of insanity. The tragedy has already happened as the narrator suggests when she says, "We always find things out too late." Then she goes back and tells about the sister's love affair, about her own resent-ment of it (this unwittingly), about the interception of the lover's letters and the resulting effect upon the sister's hap-piness and mood—always in terms of action shown retrospec-tively. The very title serves to point up the irony inherent in the smug sureness of infallibility, of always doing right. The word "Safe" ironically prophesies the opposite condition, which is, in this case, the ultimate human catastrophe.

We have been talking about beginnings. We have said little about order: where to begin, how near the chronological beginning, *A*, how near the middle, *M*, or how near the end, *Z*. The answer is that suspense values, thematic emphasis, and incidental technical problems must determine the be-ginning. Many stories begin with *A* and run straight through chronologically to *Z*. The one-scene story does this, as we saw in discussing "The Girls in Their Summer Dresses." But stories can begin anywhere. Often they begin close to the end, or even *after* the end, in which case, of course, the author very often goes back to *A* and follows through chron-ologically. That is what Sherwood Anderson does in "I Want to Know Why." Beginning fairly close to the end has the advantage of conveying to the reader a sense of crisis, as we have seen. But it involves long retrospect or flashback, which can be difficult and full of pitfalls for the beginner. In the Poe stories just discussed, the order is usually from Z back to *A* and then chronological. In Seeger's story, however, the order is entirely present and chronological, going on before our eyes. But where we need to understand what has gone before the crisis, we often start fairly near it. Hemingway starts with a scene immediately following what has been a crisis in "The Short Happy Life of Francis Macomber," which we shall discuss in the next chapter.

First, however, let us look at Edwin Granberry's wonderful story "A Trip to Czardis," [10] which arouses the most immediate kind of suspense in the opening sentences and then goes on to the chronological account of a memorable day.

We begin with two little boys waking up cold and sleepy. "Hit's the day, Dan'l. This day that's right here now, we are goen. You'll recollect it all in a minute."

"I recollect. We are goen in the wagon to see papa—" Uncle Holly comes in and says, "You're goen to take them after all?" implying that there has been doubt about taking the children, perhaps with good reason. And the mother replies, with moving simplicity, "He asked to see them. Nobody but God-Almighty ought to tell a soul hit can or can't have." These words imply that papa may be going to die and at the same time characterize the mother. The economy is good and conveys its own impact and emotional response. The idea of papa's dying is built up further when the boys decide to take a pomegranate to papa and the mother says, "I guess we won't take any, Jim . . . But I'm proud it come to you to take your papa somethen." Later the mother says, "When we get to the place we are goen, you won't know your papa after so long. He will be pale and he won't be as bright as you

---

[10] From *Selected Short Stories*, edited by Dorothy Scarborough, Rinehart & Company, Inc., New York.

recollect. But don't labor him with questions but speak when
it behooves you and let him see you are upright." The paleness
"after so long" is, of course, another signpost. After this,
the hints come thick and fast, and gradually—and this is the
point of this moving story—the little boys come to realize
that something terrible is happening. The farewell scene with
the father at the prison is shown with the greatest restraint.
The father and mother speak "a few low words" and touch
one another. And the father finally gives one boy his watch
and the other his chain and says, "And I want you to always
do what mamma tells you." Then they start home in the
wagon.

"Is papa coming home with Uncle Holly?" Jim asked in a still
voice.

His mother nodded her head.

Reaching the woods once more and the silence he knew, Daniel
whispered to his brother:

"We got a watch and chain instead, Jim."

But Jim neither answered nor turned his eyes.

The use of the word "instead" is masterly. It tells the story:
Daniel *knows*. And Jim's wordless response also tells that
he knows. The story is simplicity itself, a chronological account of a tragic day in the life of this little family, so poor,
so quiet, so restrained in their terrible hour. The reader never
knows why the father is being killed by the state, or whether
he is innocent or guilty. This is the story of the mother and
the two boys, how they acted in their crisis, and how realization came to the children. The suspense arises not from complication, but from beautifully wrought, closely knit scenes
of rising dramatic interest.

6

Scene and Conversation

WE have noted that scene can be very effective dramatically. This is because action is more convincing than words;
words tell *about* events; the scene shows events; and also because the scene can accomplish so much with a minimum of
words. This *economy* is one of the main characteristics of
scenic writing. Never before has economy been carried to
such a degree of perfection. Ernest Hemingway, Irwin Shaw,
John O'Hara, Dorothy Parker, and Dorothy McCleary, for
instance, can give a vivid realization of the pattern of a whole
life within the compass of a few hundred words. They have
many imitators; but, unfortunately, the young person who
imitates them is often unaware of the high degree of sensitivity and selectivity that has made their writing what it is;
and so the imitation is often mechanical, barren of emotional
impact, and lacking in significance. What looked easy was, in
reality, the result of great labor and great skill and talent.

The student may come to see the art in this economical way
of writing if he will apply himself to the discipline of a careful word-by-word, scene-by-scene analysis of any one of
these writers. Such an analysis involves an alert mind and an
awareness of innuendo and psychological import, together
with an eye for mechanics of transition and for symbol. One
must become language-conscious if he is to see how an
author brings about his effects.

Great virtuosity in writing is revealed in such an analysis

of Dorothy McCleary's moving story, "Something Jolly," [1] which illustrates the art of building tension through a series of closely related and economically wrought scenes in which every word counts. Here we see growing realization reaching a climax of recognition, explosive in its intensity. Two middle-aged women are bent on a good time together after a good many years. A few sentences tell us about the meeting, time, and place. Then a vivid scene shows their first embarrassment and their childish excitement, with Miss Bertie Quade, the hostess, struggling to take charge of the luggage. Then Jessie Downs mentions Papa. It would please him if Bertie would visit in Melville. They move on to "a little sandwich shop" where they look at each other and there is a moment of letdown after all the anticipation. "Each was secretly shocked." "Would they ever be able to talk to each other again freely and naturally, in the old familiar way?"

Jessie talks about her old father, who, we gradually see, has her completely helpless before his invalidism. " 'I felt like a sinner, I can tell you!' " And there is nothing to be done about it. To put him in the hospital, "at the mercy of strangers? . . . . 'That *would* be the death of me.' " Jessie must return tomorrow, too, after waiting twelve years for this good time. " 'But when Papa takes it into his head to say no—.' "

Again the scene changes. They are riding in a taxicab, seeing The Great White Way. But Jessie keeps seeing her father, and finally she murmurs, " 'Bertie, life is such a terribly complicated proposition, don't you find?' "

Next, they are in the theater, about to see Ibsen's *Ghosts*. Papa has read Ibsen, Jessie says. They are reminded now of their high school plays and the boys they have known. Nazimova's acting absorbs them and Jessie wonders about a

[1] Copyright 1939 by Story Magazine, Inc.

"kind of universal motherhood" portrayed. Had she "any such deeps inside of her"? Yes, "she would have been quite capable of it, was still quite capable of it."

Her growing realization seems to rise "to a crescendo of feeling within her. Poor me! There are things in this world that I know nothing of. . . . I have been cheated of something." Jessie weeps as the play proceeds. Bertie asks, " 'Does this make you want to get married?' " with a "wry laugh" and adds, " 'Not me. No, thank you.' "

During the interval between scenes, they talk, and finally Jessie says, " 'I'd like to live the way she does, where you're boss of the whole ranch, where your word goes—Do you know, Bertie, I'd be a different person if I lived down there.' "

At the end of the play, Jessie, deeply moved, says " 'She oughtn't to have let herself kill him.' "

They move out onto Broadway and go into Childs for "a nice little nightcap." Again Jessie thinks, "This is the place to live, all right. Lucky you." After excited argument they decide to have "just a very weensy little bit of sherry" and Bertie even lights a cigarette. (Jessie does this at home only when Papa's asleep.) They are very lively and Jessie's tongue is loosened in such a way that the reader realizes her frustration about men. Why does Jessie not talk the "way Nazimova does, where every word *means* something"? And from this they come to their old conversations when they "didn't know much" about "it." Jessie adds, " 'Well how much do we know now?' " and they have to agree that it is nothing. But they can "*surmise* a great deal—." Miss Quade even implies that " 'once, just once—,' " and Jessie finally says, " 'And if you'd ever gone off and—well, had the experience, if I must say it—there'd be just me left, do you see, out in the cold.' " Then they talk about the times when Jessie "went" with Arthur, for whom she still has some feeling, though he is married and has three children. Again discussion of girlhood dreams of marriage and children. At last they are back where they used to be.

Jessie feels she ought to put in a long-distance call to see how Papa is. Bertie says no.

Then they are on their way home in the subway, giggling, "choosing their favorite men" among the passengers, having a wonderful time, "the most fun in twelve years."

When they reach Bertie's room, the author pauses for a plateau skillfully used to describe the characters through the kind of ridiculous adornments and keepsakes displayed. Bertie and Jessie get into bed in the dark and Jessie whispers excitedly, " 'Now we can talk. Now we can *really* talk.' " Whereupon, the whole pitiful story comes out, bit by bit, until Miss Quade finally says, " 'Your father scares off any man that sticks his nose inside the house—that's why.' " And finally she adds, " 'When Nazimova gave her son that poison, in the play, the thought came to me and hit me right in the face: I wish Jess could get rid of her father as easy as that.' "

Jessie registers shock, but finally she admits that she, too, has had the terrible thought. " 'A fine daughter I am!' " And again it all comes out: " 'Because if I was absolutely free,' Jessie added, 'then any time any—well, romance—came walking around loose I could make a grab for it, just like anybody else. And, boy, would I grab!' " She attempted to giggle "but sobbed instead." The story ends with the following passage: " 'Oh I don't suit me!' said Jessie, kicking her feet out angrily against the soft covers at the foot of the bed. 'I don't suit me a little bit!' "

This story is wrought almost entirely through the use of scenes, through direct dramatization, and it reveals characters clearly in a commonplace but tragic situation fully realized. It has a beginning, a middle, and an end—a perfect structure, economical, tight-woven, and brilliantly focused. It has character awareness and final *denouement* of recognition. Even

Jess's words that she does not suit herself have psychological import, the hatred that the self-punishing, guilt-ridden person feels for himself. All is accomplished by the slow, increasingly moving revelation of seven well planned scenes. There is almost no dependence upon author explanation or character thought-processes.

Such a story, if carefully studied, makes the writer aware of dramatic techniques and the business of "plotting," which beginners find mysterious and baffling. Looking at each scene, analyzing its achievements in terms of character development and action advance, one comes to an understanding of mechanics and of how writers work to bring out values, "all that is within the hour."

Usually in fiction the end of a scene comes with a *change of place*, someone leaves and goes someplace else. Perhaps there is a change in time which requires its own special technique. The beginner is often awkward in handling transitions, to the very great detriment of his plausibility.

One can get a clear idea of how to handle transition by going through the story we have just discussed in its original complete form and underlining the transitions. He will need one colored pencil for the transitions by means of *author exposition* or direct description, and another for transitions conveyed by speech. For instance: after the meeting at the station, Miss Quade says, " '*In here, then*,' " and the author writes, "*They took seats in a little sandwich shop*." In one place the idea of change is conveyed when the author tells us that Miss Quade *helps Jessie into her coat*.

These transitions are good in that they are so easily, so smoothly managed that they are quite unnoticed by the reader, who moves along held by the emotional impact of the story itself. But they are there and they give a feeling of movement in space and time during this significant evening beginning just before "dinner" and ending in bed.

The handling of *time* is an extremely difficult matter. It is absolutely necessary to master the handling of time in writing fiction, which requires both an initial placement in time and a sense of the intervals and *passage* of time. Neither character nor action can develop in a timeless void. One of the real technical feats of "Something Jolly" is that by means of the retrospective conversation so intricately wrought, so well scattered through the different scenes, one gets a feeling of *erosion* through the years. This feeling occurs over and over again and is the means by which a full awareness of suffering is conveyed. Perhaps six or seven hours have elapsed during this "jolly time"; but during those hours the whole negative, destructive pattern of their lives has been made clear to the characters. Dorothy McCleary has avoided all the pitfalls of the amateur. She has broken up her opening exposition with conversation, and she has broken her conversation with just enough direct narration or stream of consciousness. But there is never any sense of interrupted action, never any reader awareness of the mechanics. The integration of subject matter and technique has that perfection which makes a work of art. The characters speak for themselves and the author offers a minimum of comment or interference in attempted explanation. The length of each scene, too, is just right for its purposes.

This matter of the length of a scene is interesting. We have pointed out the necessity for slowing down at the important moments and rendering them in their full intensity and reality. One might here suggest the practical expedient of acting the scene before a mirror. The result of such procedure should be adequate dramatization, by which we mean a scene not too long, not padded, but economical and right, a scene with just enough detail, just enough words to convey its full impact.

Scenes vary greatly in the number of words which they

require. In the Shaw story, "The Girls in Their Summer Dresses," all is told by means of one general scene running approximately twenty-five hundred words. Yet the conversation which it represents could perhaps have taken place in ten minutes. In Miss Porter's "Downward Path to Wisdom," on the other hand, the opening scene runs two pages and is just a beginning. In "All the Years of Her Life," by Morley Callaghan, the opening scene takes about eight hundred words, including the explanatory material, and the boy's thoughts are about thirty-five words of this. The scene between mother and son on the way home, if we include the author explanatory material and the boy's thoughts, takes about two hundred words. When Alfred finally watches his mother with her tea in the kitchen, however, Mr. Callaghan takes one hundred and forty-three words for one moment of revelation. Then he uses another one hundred and twenty-five or so to sum up Alfred's feelings, a very eloquent summary indeed. This summary gives universality to the mother's gesture and the son's sudden recognition of her sacrifices. The reader becomes aware of its symbolism for him. Most of us have had such moments of revelation as those that come to Alfred.

To attain such effects, every scene should be constructed with minute care. One puts into a scene all the materials necessary to convey its full meaning and effect. Then one uses some kind of remark, thought, or movement which takes the characters out of that scene and into another. This device naturally means an assertion at the *end* of the paragraph or at the beginning of a new paragraph, or sometimes both.

Too often young writers do not understand how to handle the speeches and the expository material in relation to each other. They put the actual words in quotation marks and then, in a new paragraph, tell how the characters are acting, moving, or thinking. They should recognize, however, that these materials usually belong *together* in one paragraph. They should also recognize that it is good technique to *begin* a speech with the use of gesture or thought. Gesture often, in reality, comes before speech.

"The Girls in Their Summer Dresses" reveals the possibilities of skillful handling of both talk and supplementary material. After the two characters have become involved in their discussion, we get a sense of the rising tension when we see that "Frances' tone was a good imitation of the tone she had used at breakfast and at the beginning of their walk." The word, "imitation," of course, tells the story of strain, self-consciousness, effort to conceal something.

Shaw has cleverly put immediately before or after the remarks descriptive material which both reveals the character and the gesture and at the same time advances the action. For instance, after Michael has admitted his liking for looking at the girls:

> Frances finished her drink and swallowed two or three times extra. "You say you love me?"

and later:

> "I'm good for you," Frances said, pleading. "I've made a damned good wife, a good housekeeper, a good friend. I'd do any damn thing for you."
> "I know," Michael said. He put his hand out and grasped hers.

The explanatory material here tells as much as the spoken words. The technique is very economical and very effective. It is revealing because it conveys the *whole* of the action. Yet the average reader may be scarcely aware of it. The machinery is so perfect that it is invisible.

In order to make developments clear and plausible it is often important that each scene shall contribute to the revelation of character attitude. One should ask himself, "What is this character thinking and feeling about the situation?" not only at the outset and the end, but in each scene, making clear how the attitude changes, how the tension, resentment, worry, or fear increases to the final breaking point. One of the main purposes of the scene is to show emotional development as the action progresses from beginning through the middle to the end, thus revealing the character's full experience at each stage. Thus in a way each scene is a little story in itself and at the same time an integral part of a movement toward an end—the end being the *summation* of the whole experience, which has been given form and significance.

Sometimes the order of scenes is anything but chronological and direct, effectiveness being bound up with other scenes that have gone before or with considerations of time.

Hemingway's fascinating, technically perfect story, "The Short Happy Life of Francis Macomber," [2] employs scene and plateau in ways that are complicated and extremely effective in bringing out shades of character, as well as maintaining suspense. We first meet the three main characters, the husband, the wife, and the guide, as they sit in a dining tent "pretending that nothing had happened." Flashback through cleverly devised conversation gives emotional impact very early. Macomber, it is clear, has "very publicly" played the coward in a lion hunt. His wife is upset, and, when he tries to lighten the situation with reference to his "red face," his wife replies, "No. It's mine that's red today." This remark implies, as soon becomes clear, the egocentricity of the wife. Why should she take her husband's unhappy failure as damaging to her self-esteem? The reason appears right away. She enjoys torturing Macomber. For a moment we are in the guide's mind, seeing Mrs. Macomber as an attractive woman. But she speaks cruelly, in innuendo. She will go with the next

[2] From *The Fifth Column and Forty-nine Stories*, copyright, 1938, by Ernest Hemingway, New York: Charles Scribner's Sons.

party. "I wouldn't miss something like today for anything."
Now the guide sees her cruelty and so, obviously, does her
husband.

That night Macomber lies awake in his tent thinking of his
shame, filled with a "cold, hollow fear." Next morning he admits his nervousness at having heard a lion roar during the
night. Again there is a lionhunting scene, again Macomber
fails in the crisis, and the guide has to kill the lion. Then we
are in Macomber's mind, feeling his shame. His wife openly
repulses him and then kisses the guide. The story's forward
movement stops momentarily while Macomber thinks of the
sordid facts of his wife's attitude toward him, of events of the
past, and decides that now she is "through with him." Later,
in the middle of the night, Macomber's wife comes *back* into
his tent, clearly returning from a visit to the guide. Again she
is cruel. Macomber is resentful. We can see that her infidelity
is an old story. Finally comes another day of hunting, and
now we see Macomber proving his courage at last. But at the
climax, Mrs. Macomber shoots from the car, killing her husband. The guide, addressing her, reveals his suspicions of the
"accident." He is angry. "I'm through now," he says. "I was
a little angry. I'd begun to like your husband." The woman
begs him to stop and finally he agrees after she says,
"Please."

Events here cover considerable time and a good deal of
history. The scenes are delicately wrought with the facts
clearly brought out despite the telescoping of time elements,
producing an effect of great economy and presentness. Yet
nowhere is dramatization skimped. Scenes are highlighted
with a maximum of characterization and portent, always
moving toward the end which is so right. Talk leads casually
from one thing to another, naturally, smoothly, revealingly,
without disgression or irrelevant detail. There are none of
those extraneous remarks which amateurs think necessary to

produce the illusion of casualness and reality. Thus, both the conversation and the accompanying action are drawn into a focus, a focus of which the scene is the aim. We see the woman getting more and more ugly and sadistic, more and more abandoned in her relations with the guide; we see Macomber growing more and more humiliated both by his own "cowardice" and by his wife's infidelity, wantonness, and open contempt; we see the guide's opinion of Mrs. Macomber changing until he finally sees her as her husband's murderer. There are also skillful intimations that the "cowardice" in the hunt is symbolic of psychological sexual impotence, and by this means all becomes richer and more intense, with more at stake in proving bravery. At the climax, when Macomber finally overcomes his cowardice and truly lives for the few seconds before he is shot, we are hit by the tremendous irony of Hemingway's title. We realize, too, that the author has subtly taken the victory away from Mrs. Macomber and given it to her husband.

Thus Hemingway has brought together highly dramatic motivations and kinds of struggle into scenes of strong emotional impact. He has indeed worked his material "for all it is worth"; and it is no wonder that his mastery of technique in this story has attracted a very great deal of attention.

Complicated orders are the special forte of William Faulkner, who is also a master of the vivid scene. Unspeakably sinister is the moment in the rat-infested barn in *Sanctuary*, for instance, when the young girl, Temple, cringes before the approaching Popeye; and its portent is enhanced by the fact that we are uncertain as to what happens. We are not even sure who it is that she is calling to but finally decide it is the old man sitting outside the barn on the porch of the house. This happens at the end of Chapter 13, and we leave Temple there frozen in her terror. We next glimpse her passing the house "with eyes that did not wake"; and then we do not see her until Chapter 18, when she drives along the country road with Popeye, her face "like a sleep walker's," and Faulkner refers to "her blood seeping inside her loin's." Still we do not know exactly what happened in the barn. She hangs back when they reach town, speaking of what people might see. Popeye handles her threateningly. "You want some more of it, don't you?" After that she is in Minnie's sinister house and the doctor has come. Temple's thoughts after he leaves are feverish, going back to her companions in college. Then Popeye comes in and we see the unforgettably depraved scene, with Popeye making "a high whinnying sound like a horse."

In Chapter 23 more horrible details come out as Temple tells Horace about the night following the barn affair. Her talk keeps shuttling between the house that night and the corncrib of the day before, telling how she prayed to be changed into a boy, how she imagined that she was a boy, and how she finally "went to sleep." She had, of course, fainted. Horace thinks that it were better if she were dead and then ponders on "the logical pattern to evil," which phrase seems to sum up Faulkner's philosophy of life. We finally, in Chapter 28, close to the end, discover through the courtroom scene exactly what Popeye did in the corncrib. We have had to put together for ourselves the evidence given through the various chapters of the novel and that very fact is an important means of suspense, implication, and climax. It would be difficult to conceive of more powerful writing. The delays are maddening, yet the material interpolated between the big scenes in which Temple figures has its own function as a sort of backdrop of horrible realities and dreamlike comings and goings in sordid, evil surroundings. The whole novel has a nightmarish craziness that arises from both the action and the elusiveness with which it is shown. And finally—this is the crowning tribute to Mr. Faulkner's power to do as he wishes with the reader's sympathies—in the last chapter, when we learn the real facts about Popeye and his ghastly childhood, we actually feel pity for him, sadist from early childhood that he was. Indeed, he might "well have been dead" after the fire.

Just how much the effects in this novel arise from the order and the way in which the story is told, is a matter of conjecture. The subject matter is, in itself, horrible enough to leave an unforgettable impression. But it seems that the slow revelation which makes the reader piece together a good deal is an effective device. The student should note, when he reads the novel, the skillful way in which Faulkner implies sexual degeneracy, never going over into the actual chronological depiction of the scene itself. "Plotting" by Faulkner is extremely complicated, intricate, always stimulating to the reader's imagination however annoying it becomes in its various digressions. It would be dangerous for an inexperienced writer to attempt such complicated writing; but it is well for him to recognize that there are many ways of using scenes—one of which is to break up the main scene, interrupting it, and then to return to it, again and again. Needless to say, not every dramatic scene could stand such treatment; only a scene powerful in itself would hold up very long under such handling. If the final truth were not sufficiently terrible, the reader would feel let down upon reaching it.

Most people recognize the importance of making conversation realistic, but they are not always aware of the many uses to which it can be put. Ideally, it should do more than just make characters come alive. It should do several things at once: indicate character nuances, advance the action, and indicate thematic trends. Never should conversation be thrown in for padding or filler. Filler is bad anywhere and in conversation it is worst of all because conversation focuses attention upon a given moment. One should not focus on filler! It is true that conversation is often used retrospectively to show what has already gone on before the story begins, but this past action may deserve conversational emphasis, as it does in "The Short Happy Life of Francis Macomber," where we are slowly made aware in the first scene of the unhappy events of the day just past.

In Faulkner's famous story, "That Evening Sun," the child reveals in retrospective monologue the trouble that the Negress Nancy has been in, describing vividly the jail scene in which Nancy has tried to kill herself. This is done, not in a present scene, but in a kind of aside to the reader; and finally the child reports what seems to be a present scene (though the past tense is used) in the kitchen where the angry Jesus threatens the white man.

This conversation is memorable for two reasons: first, the terror conveyed, and, second, the semi-comic relief afforded by the continual interruptions of the delightfully inquisitive Caddy. The Negroes are in deadly earnest and the children reveal a sensitivity to innuendo and sexual talk that induces a reader-feeling of universality and reality. Their persistence is as laughable here as it is maddening in family life. The technique of this writing is subtle and it gives that fourth-dimensional feeling so characteristic of today's best writing. It also creates a growing suspense and horror. At the close of the story, Faulkner leaves the reader to fill in for himself the ghastly details of the murder from the ditch that he is sure awaits the helpless Nancy. The device of having her reveal her terror through her pitiful attempts to keep the children near—bribing them to stay in her cabin, offering popcorn and stories, being entertaining when she shakes with fear—is powerful. At the end, however, we revert to the alleviating and amusing note as the quarreling children argue about who is brave and who is cowardly. This argument serves the double

rtistic purpose of conveying the over-all theme of white
people's indifference to the fate of Negro servants, and of
offering that comic element which is so often close to the
tragic. Comic relief is used in close juxtaposition with pity
and fear.

Another extremely effective use of conversation is to be
found in Katherine Anne Porter's story "Rope," [3] where the
comedy is that of husband and wife bickering over trivialities,
the kind of bickering that reveals underlying tensions, larger
issues. It is interesting to study this unusual technique. Paragraph one introduces the scene with the husband returning
from the grocery store. Paragraph two asks:

Had he brought the coffee? She had been waiting all day long for
coffee. They had forgot it when they ordered at the store the
first day.

Paragraph three contains the germ of the conflict:

Gosh, no, he hadn't. Lord, now he'd have to go back. Yes, he
would if it killed him. He thought, though, he had everything else.
She reminded him it was only because he didn't drink coffee himself. If he did he would remember it quick enough. Suppose they ran
out of cigarettes? Then she saw the rope. What was that for? Well,
he thought it might do to hang clothes on, or something. Naturally
she asked him if he thought they were going to run a laundry? They
already had a fifty foot line hanging right before his eyes? Why,
hadn't he noticed it, really? It was a blot on the landscape to her.

This paragraph is woven with the intricacy and craftsmanship which one expects from Miss Porter. First it sets a *tone*
of mild irony and amusement at the sight of the young couple
quarreling about nothing at all. This situation itself is so common that the reader also experiences the feeling of having
seen it many times. (Dorothy Parker used it in "Here We
Are," with much the same effect, but nowhere near the same

[3] From *Flowering Judas and Other Stories*. New York: Harcourt, Brace and
Company, Inc., 1935.

degree of artistry.) This sense of truth to life is brought out
primarily though the exact reproduction of bickering conversation, tones, rhythms, and oratorical questions in particular. These questions are ironic and sarcastic and they also
show that the young couple are "on" to each other's ra-
tionalizations and psychological processes. (This fact is conveyed through their pointing out to each other the interest
in coffee or cigarettes, which are the special concern of one
or the other—very human, indeed is this.)

Most revealing is the way in which the author has shown
a mountain growing out of a mole-hill: all this excitement
and tension about a rope! The quarrel advances steadily from
its trivial inception to its happy ending, which makes one
wonder if this isn't a case of quarreling in order to make up.
The tension mounts with each question and answer; slowly
but consistently the wife's irritation is revealed, largely
through her sarcastic questions and her observation of the
man's ability to remember his own cigarettes. One can easily
supply the implied italics of her emphasized words: "What
was *that* for?" "run a *laundry*," "*already*," "right before his
eyes," "*really*," "*blot*."

It would hardly be possible to pack more revelation of
scene, conflict, character, more human nature into a few
words. The economy is clear and the tonal integration is
memorable, however slight the narrative itself. And this
brings us to our last point in regard to this story. It is very
important.

One can make a big lather out of a little soap—if one is an
artist! This is very simple, everyday material available to all
of us. But how many of us could do with it what has been
done here? The achievement is, as we have noted, similar to
the kind of thing accomplished by Dorothy Parker. The effect in this kind of writing arises largely from skillful reporting on human foibles. But to the student of techniques—and

every writer had better be a student of techniques—there are the added values of craftsmanship.

The mechanical details to be noticed here, the devices used, are *original*, or at least uncommon. The Porter story in no way depends upon techniques used earlier by Dorothy Parker. It does, indeed, go her one better as a reporter of conversation. The student will observe that there are neither quotation marks nor "saids." But—and this is not always the case when either is omitted—the action is entirely clear. We always know who says what and we know it at once, without any annoying looking back and checking over. (One of the commonest faults of amateurs in attempting to dispense with quotes and saids is a maddening obscurity. Every teacher of narration will certify to this!) Dispensing with the customary devices and forms, Katherine Anne Porter has accomplished results simply by her knowledge of speech rhythms and accents used by bickering people, and by an exact reproduction of these sound elements. She has attuned her ears to recognize the revelations of everyday talk in moments of emotion. And she knows that emotions out of proportion to the situation are in themselves revealing of underlying frictions. One sees this clearly as one goes along with the story to the end. "It's all," we are prone to say, "in the way a thing is said." By that we mean tone and emphasis as well as phraseology.

To catch and depict the idiosyncracies of a person, one needs to observe what kind of words he uses, as well as grammar, sentence structure, and general "style" of speaking. Such characteristics enable one to place the speaker with a good deal of accuracy. They tell us so very much about the social and educational background that has formed the person. They tell us a great deal about how much economic opportunity he has had, what part of the city he lives in, what part of the nation he comes from. The hill-billy will not talk like a city man; the New Englander like a Mid-westerner, a Southerner, or a Westerner; a Negro like a white.

And so one resorts to localisms, narrowly colloquial expressions, dialect, and pronunciations. But never to stock ideas about how people talk! Always from knowledge. Dialect is tricky, indeed. And it is, above all, usually repellant to the reader who anticipates, when he sees it, that he will be involved in obscurities. One uses it only when he must use it or when he happens to know it well enough to do it skillfully, and then in moderation. A little goes a long way. If it is good it adds flavor, but one seldom needs an overwhelming dose. Chunks of dialect are, visually speaking, a handicap in getting attention.

For high skill in dialect treatment one turns, as one often turns for stylistic matters, to Hemingway. In *For Whom the Bell Tolls*[4] Hemingway has turned idiom into a stylistic device of great charm. He has accomplished the difficult task of conveying Spanish gypsy idiom, rhythm, and tone in terms of the actual language of the country; and yet there is no obscurity for the reader ignorant of Spanish. Spanish phrases abound in this book; and so cleverly are they used, together with English words hinting at their meaning, or with gesture, or author exposition, that the reader experiences no difficulty. These strange and different people become very real to us, so real that we are able to tell by the words themselves who spoke them. Characterization of a fairly sizeable group acting together during the three-day period is distinct and individual. Even the obscenity, and it is very obscene, serves to enhance the charm and humor, as well as to reveal the extreme tension felt by the actors in the drama. It is Pilar's nerves that ask "What passes with the obscenity of an *Inglés?*"

And this brings us to the frequent student question: Shall I use obscenity? There seems to be a general idea that to do

[4] See page 391.

so indicates "bad taste" or worse, and that editors "will not stand for it."

The answer to the first objection is that whether or not it is "good taste" depends upon the extent to which the obscenity serves any real artistic purpose. (Yes, "artistic"!) If it does, as in *For Whom the Bell Tolls*, it should be used. If it does not, it is better left out. The artistic purposes should be clear by now: they are characterization that is necessary in terms of the action and the organic whole, comic relief which is a value in itself as well as a sound dramatic device, and revelation of the character's emotion. All of these purposes are legitimate and any devices that further them are legitimate—unless, indeed, one has religious or puritanical reasons for objecting. But art is never concerned with the onlooker's personal bias; and the real artist is very likely to refuse to yield to even a public bias. He continues to write to please himself and the people that "speak his language." And if Boston objects—well, the resulting publicity is not without its own ironic and satisfying results from a material standpoint.

Practical considerations there are, it is true, if one has his eye—and who does not to some extent?—upon the box-office. There are many readers who will not have published obscenity in their houses; there are many editors who cater to such readers in a very big way, who respect the real or falsely imagined objections of the group that constitutes the family from grandma to grade school. This fact is, of course, largely responsible for the overwhelmingly low level of mine-run fiction, to say nothing of Hollywood with its many entirely inconsistent evasions. The worst of this evasion comes most often in the field of sex, where the movie gives little of any truth or revelation and a very great deal of false romanticism, sentimentalism, and downright pernicious sex stimulation by means of the strip-tease, the bedroom scene, and the just-around-the-corner seduction which we never really see or even come to. Plenty of sex emphasis, oh yes! But no truth, no honesty, no sincerity, no revelation of the infinitely varied elements in any sexual situation. Mae West but not the sleeping bag of Maria! It is this kind of thing which the literary rebels of our century protested about so violently during the renaissance that produced Dreiser, Anderson, and Sinclair Lewis, and which newer writers are still protesting about. Literature has "come of age" in America, however low the level of the magazines of the vast "home circle" scope. Even the women's magazines have begun to move a bit in the direction of greater attention to psychological depths and greater fidelity to reality. Perhaps they have been stimulated by the growing popularity of such magazines as *The New Yorker*, *Mademoiselle*, and *Harper's Bazaar*. But they do not yet accept obscenity.

But to return from considerable, if related, digression. One need not run wild with obscenity. There *are* boundaries and criterions of good taste. Obscenity *per se* really is just so much bad taste. It is seldom even interesting. It is far more likely to be *boring*. And there is, from a practical standpoint, no use in risking offence unless real ends are to be gained. The writer must, too, be especially warned against the use of the "four letter words." Editors are afraid of them; they have constituted a legal basis for many censorships. It seems that certain words are just unbearable in the eyes of the law or at least of the city authorities.

What constitutes good taste is, of course, any man's guess or judgment. *De gustibus non est disputandum*. What is good taste in the mid-west may be bad taste on Park Avenue. What is bad taste in Middletown may be good taste on Fifth Avenue. But we might note, in conclusion, that modern aesthetic theory admits frank realism and admits it to the "highest" circles. The Art Institute is no longer afraid to show a picture of the good old "outhouse"; nor is the Public Library *always* afraid of James Joyce. Newer times bring newer *mores*. It is a good idea, perhaps, to be sure that one's "likes" are not too far behind the times in which he lives, and also that they are in accordance with that honest fearless approach to facts which is supposed to distinguish the adult from the child.

What kind of conversation our fictional characters use is therefore a matter of sincere and honest approach, as well as of taste, charm, or even eloquence. Good talk is always at a premium in literature, as it is in life.

7

The Angle of Narration

MODERN writers are intent, as we have seen, upon showing the whole of a given experience. They have striven for a "fourth dimension," a greater reality of both inner and outer life. This business of reality is intimately bound up with the angle of narration, the vantage point from which the story is told. Especially interesting is the development of "stream of consciousness" writing (which we shall discuss in some detail in the following chapter) because of the light it sheds both upon characterization and upon the nature of experience. Always we must keep in mind that writers are now attempting far more than has been attempted before. To phrase it in the language of the existentialist Jean-Paul Sartre, who speaks, in *The Atlantic Monthly* for August 1946,[1] of the enthusiasm of French writers for the work of certain contemporary American writers:

What has aroused our enthusiasm among the recent novelists whom I have mentioned is a veritable revolution in the art of telling a story. The intellectual analysis which, for more than a century, had been the accepted method of developing character in fiction was no longer anything but an old mechanism badly adapted to the needs of the time. It was opposed to a psychology of synthesis which taught us that a psychological fact is an indivisible whole. It could not be used to depict a group of facts which present themselves as the ephemeral or permanent unity of a great number of perceptions.

We shall see more clearly, when we finally arrive at a discussion of Steinbeck, Dos Passos, and Hemingway, what this

[1] "American Novelists in French Eyes," *The Atlantic Monthly*, August 1946.

somewhat complicated statement means. Now let us turn to matters involved in an understanding of the angle of narration.

Little does the novice realize the importance of selecting the best angle from which to tell his story. Often, indeed, he is unaware that there *is* an angle; he "just tells" his story in blithe, naïve simplicity. And, it must be admitted, if he is artist enough he may instinctively select the best angle and handle it correctly, thereby achieving that unity, reality, and dramatic intensity which his brother craftsman attains only through conscious struggle.

The natural angle from which to tell a story is that of the narrator who begins, "Once upon a time—" This method may work famously with children's minds, but it is not so good for the mature mind, which is prone to ask questions having to do with plausibility. It is not good at all for the sophisticated literary mind or for the intelligent reader's mind, which nowadays has come to demand great illusions of reality.

The "once upon a time" angle is, of course, an *objective*, all-seeing, omniscient angle; it is the angle of a god looking down upon human beings, recording what they did, how the scene looked, how the characters looked, and even what not only one but several characters thought. Using this angle, writers of the past thought nothing of intruding themselves, labeling characters and taking sides openly for or against them, and pointing the already obvious moral. This widest angle—viewing action from the outside—is, nevertheless, a good one to start with; it makes later shifts into various individual minds easier.

Petronius, in "The Matron of Ephesus," for instance, goes about his tale in the most baldly omniscient way, interrupting his narrative to pin ironic labels and to comment on human nature. (Italics are used to indicate the author intrusions.)

A matron of Ephesus was of such notable chastity that women came from miles around to gaze on her. So, *naturally*, when her husband was buried she was not satisfied by the popular fashion of following a corpse with streaming hair, and beating the naked breast in front of the crowd: she went with the dead man into his very tomb, an underground sepulchre in the Greek style, and settled down to watch and weep day and night. Her parents and other relations could not divert her from tormenting herself, or from leaving herself to die of hunger; the government officials finally went away discouraged, and she dragged through her fifth day without food, mourned by everyone as the unique example of womankind. A faithful maid sat beside the miserable lady, wept *just the proper number of tears* with her, and kept the light in the tomb burning. Only this one tale went the rounds in the city, and people of every class agreed that it was an unrivalled example of chastity and love.

Meantime, Petronius continues, a soldier is set to watch the crosses upon which some thieves have been crucified nearby; eventually he offers food and wine and attempts to seduce the devoted wife. Petronius comments: "People usually listen when they are asked to eat or live; the lady, hungry and thirsty from five days of starvation, let her resolution be broken down, and ate as greedily as the maid who had yielded before her." Then the author comments. "Well, you know what generally tempts a well-fed human being?" And a little later he says, "Why delay the story?" And further along, at the end, he tells us that, after the soldier has put her husband's corpse on the cross to replace the stolen corpse of one of the crucified men, "The soldier profited by the sagacious lady's ingenuity." Here the word "sagacious" is clearly a comment, just as were the words, "Why delay the story?" reminding the reader that he is being told a story and thereby taking him out of his make-believe world for a moment, destroying to that extent his illusion of reality.

Author comment was quite the thing as late as Hawthorne's day. In the first chapter of *The Scarlet Letter*, Hawthorne comments (italics indicate author comments):

The founders of a new colony, *whatever Utopia of human virtue and happiness they might originally project*, have invariably recognized it among their earliest practical necessities to allot a portion of the virgin soil as a cemetery, and another portion as the site of a prison. In accordance with this rule, it may safely be assumed that the forefathers of Boston. . . .

Later in the paragraph he uses the words, "Certain it is that," and further along he comments, "Like all that pertains to crime, it seemed never to have known a youthful era," and at the end of the brief chapter he goes all out in his role of commentator.

He speaks of an historic rosebush (italics indicate the intrusions by the author):

This rose-bush, by a strange chance, has been kept alive in history; but whether it had merely survived out of the stern old wilderness, so long after the fall of the gigantic pines and oaks that originally overshadowed it, or whether, as there is fair authority for believing, it had sprung up under the footsteps of the sainted Ann Hutchinson as she entered the prison-door, *we shall not take upon us to determine. Finding it so directly on the threshold of our narrative*, which is now about to issue from that inauspicious portal, *we could hardly do otherwise than pluck one of its flowers, and present it to the reader. It may serve, let us hope, to symbolize some sweet moral blossom* that may be found along the track, or relieve the darkening close of a tale of human frailty and sorrow.

One would search far in any modern collection of stories, or even a modern novel, for examples of such bold-faced author intrusion. In most modern writing the author remains *out of the picture*. As Professor Joseph Warren Beach says, the author

does not wish to be caught standing apart from the character and saying clever things about him. He wishes instead to read himself right into the consciousness of the character, to identify himself with him in impression, feeling, outlook, to reproduce with absolute fidelity of tone the character's reaction to everything in his experience. He wishes to give as consistently as possible, an inside rather than an outside view of things.[2]

[2] *Op. cit.*

The modern technique, no matter what angle it uses, whether inside or outside, is a technique of *dramatization*. Dramatization, let us repeat, means *representing*.

We have pointed out that Petronius used the omniscient angle, the outside view, with occasional comment. This angle was also much used by French writers, who refined it. For example, let us consider a quotation from the opening of Daudet's story "The Little Pâtés."

That Sunday morning, the pastry-cook Sureau, of the Rue Turenne called his apprentice and said to him,——

"Here are Monsieur Bonnicar's little pâtés. Carry them to him, and return at once, for they say the army from Versailles has entered Paris."

The boy, who understood nothing of politics, put the pâtés, still warm, into his tart-dish, the tart-dish in a white napkin, and balancing pâtés, dish, and all upon his cap, set out on a run for Île Saint-Louis, where Monsieur Bonnicar resided. The morning was glorious, sunshine everywhere,—that warm May sunshine that fills the fruit shops with bunches of lilacs and clusters of cherries.

Now this is telling us what happens. The author gives us time and place, a snatch of spoken order from the cook, description of what the boy did, and comment about the quality of May sunshine. Here is omniscience, the widest possible angle. At times, the author comments directly as the story progresses. The omniscient angle is maintained rather consistently. This angle requires the least writing skill, the least art. It is, as we have said earlier, the natural angle of a story-teller. Maupassant used it a great deal. In "The Necklace," he states the facts about his heroine very simply, with some notes of comment.

She was one of those pretty and charming girls who are sometimes, as if by a mistake of destiny, born in a family of clerks. She had no dowery, no expectations, no means of being known, understood, loved, wedded, by any rich and distinguished man; and she let herself be married to a little clerk at the Ministry of Public Instruction.

Maupassant is here describing and explaining his heroine and he continues to do so until he tells us, "She thought of the silent antechambers," . . . whereupon we are in the narrower angle of her mind. Then the method becomes that of alternating between telling us about Madame Loisel and giving her thoughts: "She thought of the long *salons* fitted up with ancient silk." Here the author has assumed the privilege of jumping in and out of a character's mind. This is a very common technique.

Usually in the short story, the writer goes only into *one* mind and that is the case here, except for one sentence in which Maupassant says that the *husband* "reflected that he must be at the ministry by ten o'clock." The total impression of the story, however, is clearly that of objectivity. There is little author comment, editorializing, or injection of self or author's point of view toward the subject matter. Maupassant *tells us about* what is happening or lets us hear the characters speak.

This *telling. about* is usually avoided by the best contemporary writers, except in the novel of broad scope, as we shall see in Chapter 11. The tendency is all toward a more complete dramatization, dramatization either of action—as we have seen in our study of "The Girls in Their Summer Dresses" and other stories discussed under "Scene and Conversation"—or of the *character's thoughts*. The suitability of this latter method becomes clear the moment one stops to think that what is interesting to human beings is the inner view of other human beings: what seems important to them, what gives them pain or pleasure, what motives they have, what struggles, what concepts of ethics and morals, what values and what ideas about the society in which they live. What the characters see and feel is quite as dramatic as what they do.

One may select the mind of *any character* in the story for

the purpose of reflecting and interpreting what happens. Which one is selected depends entirely upon the artistic purpose. One may use the hero's mind or that of a less important person, either a subordinate character who plays a role, entering into the action, contributing to the complication, or one who plays no real role except to relate and to interpret—to see, in other words.

A word of warning is necessary here against confusing the form of first or third person with the concept of who tells the story: you can tell a story from the angle of the hero, for instance, and use either the pronoun "I" or the pronoun "he." Either will do, but usually one is better than the other for a given purpose. The "I" angle is important if one wishes to report sensory impressions and atmospheric impressions, and if one wishes to lend plausibility to the weird or fantastic or unbelievable. Marcel Proust employed it to report childhood impressions in great detail, using his magnificent gift to make us *feel* the beauty of provincial France, the whistling of trains, the note of a bird, the shimmer of light upon a church, the cosy warmth of his bed, the moonlight through the shutters.

The "I" angle is important if one has a tale to tell as Poe did, about an ever descending pendulum threatening to kill a man caught in a pit, or about the horrors of a descent into a maelstrom. It is important if one wants to report such adventure as Conrad takes us through in "Youth," where we need to share the atmospheric effects of ocean, storm, fire at sea, and a wonderful wakening from nightmare of danger in a peaceful Eastern port. It is important here also in that it gives the author a voice for his philosophy that youth is the best time, youth symbolized in the sea voyage with all its perils. The narrator concludes:[8]

---

[8] From "Youth" by Joseph Conrad, copyright, 1903, by Doubleday & Company, Inc.

"By all that's wonderful it is the sea, I believe, the sea itself—or is it youth alone? Who can tell? . . . wasn't that the best time, that time when we were young at sea; young and had nothing, on the sea that gives nothing, except hard knocks—and sometimes a chance to feel your strength—and that only—what you all regret?"

Sometimes the "I" angle is used to report on a character in the story. Conrad used Marlow in *Lord Jim* (in the "frame" device) to tell us about Jim, to explain at times what he hears about him, and to interpret Jim for us. The "I" angle is the perfect device for the story *Safe*, where, as we have seen, the villainess is the main character. This woman's self-revelation is the core of the story. Miss Johnson could have told this story using the third person pronoun, "she"; and if she had handled it with her usual skill, she might have brought it off; she would, however, in order to achieve her effect, have had to go into the character's mind. That would have involved problems that are more easily solved by using "I."

Editors are always saying that they do not like the first person; there is a tradition that they do not. But "I" has its important uses, as we have seen, and we find it appearing frequently. That it has its limitations goes without saying: one can record only what the "I" is able to see, hear, and feel, and, if the character is to be admirable, considerations of proper modesty may inhibit him from telling his story with due emphasis. In other words, "I" offers a restricted scope.

The first person is, of course, the usual angle in a mystery or detective story, where it helps to reinforce the plausibility of events that have happened to the teller and where it gives the teller a chance to employ all kinds of theories and clues that serve to increase the complication, the suspense, and the mystery. Poe used it in "The Murders in the Rue Morgue" and in the ever popular "Gold Bug," models of the good detective story.

The reader will have noted, earlier in this chapter, that

the determination of angles in a given piece of writing is not always easy. Often it seems to involve hair-splitting. Why is all this necessary, you say. What do we gain by it? What we gain is understanding and, eventually, *mastery*. Make no mistake about it: the *angle of narration is vital* to both plausibility and style. Its proper handling is the mark of the writer who knows his craft, its clumsy handling is the mark of the amateur.

The fact that the more sensitive and subtle writing is, the more difficult it is to analyze, is significant of the intricacy of the art of narrative. It is significant, for instance, that two of the finest stylists in America today, Katherine Anne Porter and Eudora Welty, are difficult, even baffling at times, to the student of the angle of narration.

In "Livvie Is Back," [4] for instance, beginning in the all inclusive third person, apparently with the author's telling us about Livvie's marriage, Eudora Welty eventually *seems to be* Livvie herself. She has, before her story ends, completely projected herself into the character of Livvie. The narrative begins:

Solomon carried Livvie twenty-one miles away from her home when he married her. He carried her away up on the Old Natchez Trace into the deep country to live in his house. She was sixteen then. People said he thought nobody would ever come along there. It had been a long time, and a day she did not know about, he told her himself, since that road was a travelled road with *people* coming and going. He was good to her, but he kept her in the house. She had no thought that she could not get back. Where she came from, people said an old man did not want anybody in the world to find his wife, for fear they would steal her back from him. Solomon had asked her before he took her, "Would she be happy?"—very dignified, for he was a colored man that owned his land and had it written down in the courthouse; and she said, "Yes sir," since he was an old man then and she was young, and just listened and answered.

[4] From *The Wide Net and Other Stories*. New York: Harcourt, Brace and Company, Inc., 1943.

Here Miss Welty seems to be telling us about this couple as if she knew all about them and had heard them talk. Then in the next paragraph she writes:

It was a nice house, inside and outside both. In the first place, it had three rooms. The front room was papered in holly paper, with green palmettos from the swamp spaced at careful intervals over the walls. There was fresh newspaper cut with fancy borders on the mantelshelf, on which were propped straight-up photographs of old or very young men printed in faint yellow—Solomon's people. Solomon had a houseful of furniture. . . .

What has happened here? We have entered, unobtrusively, into Livvie's mind. Who but Livvie would think such a house was "nice"? Certainly not Miss Welty! Over and over again throughout the story we feel that we are *in* Livvie's mind, even though Miss Welty maintains her third-person angle. Sometimes, it is true, she frankly enters Livvie's mind, saying, "she felt her heart beating in her left side. . . . It seemed as if her heart beat and her whole face flamed from the pulsing color of her lips." At other times the penetration of Livvie's mind is less obvious, but the reader *feels himself* there. Note this clever device:

Livvie knew she made a nice girl to wait on anybody. She fixed things to eat on a tray like a surprise. She could keep from singing when she ironed; and to sit by a bed and fan away the flies, she could be so still she could not hear herself breathe.

The effect produced by this story is, as Esther Forbes pointed out in the Introduction to *The O. Henry Memorial Award Prize Stories for 1943*, that of seeing life as it seems to the people who are living it. "Old Solomon's three-room house, with its neat mouse-traps inside and its bottle trees outside seems as marvelous to us as it did to Livvie, and old Solomon as kind, and Cash as beautiful." Hershel Brickell, the editor of the collection, adds that Miss Forbes "has hit upon one of Miss Welty's most notable abilities, her complete

identification with her characters, the sure mark of genuine
talent in fiction, short or long."

One device that brings a sense of identification is the use
of child-like Negro metaphor. For instance, when Miss Baby
Marie, the cosmetic agent—who is, by the way, in a class by
herself—asks Livvie a question, Miss Welty writes:

"No'm," Livvie tried to say, but the cat had her tongue.

Livvie's story *could* have been told in the first person—
'Solomon carried me twenty-one miles," and so on. But it
would have had a completely different effect upon the reader.
Or it could have been told from the angle of a neighbor,
who looked on and observed the events. But the angle chosen
was that of the author who was in Livvie's consciousness.
The reader can see how far away this angle is from Maupassant's angle, yet both he and Miss Welty use the third person.
Maupassant has *told us about Madame Loisel*, Eudora Welty
has *shown us life through Livvie's eyes*.

Katherine Anne Porter has achieved inner reality in many
ways. In "Theft" [5] she uses an introductory explanation, part
author, part consciousness:

She had the purse in her hand when she came in. Standing in the
middle of the floor, holding her bathrobe around her and trailing a
lamp towel in one hand, she surveyed the immediate past and remembered everything clearly.

Direct consciousness is used in the next sentence, which
is the last one in the paragraph:

Yes, she had opened the flap and spread it out on the bench after
he had dried the purse with her handkerchief.
She had intended to take the Elevated, and naturally she looked
in her purse to make certain she had the fare, and was pleased to find
forty cents in the coin envelope. She was going to pay her own fare,
too, even if Camilo did have the habit of seeing her up the steps and

[5] From *Flowering Judas and Other Stories*. New York: Harcourt, Brace and
Company, Inc., 1930.

dropping a nickel in the machine before he gave the turnstile a littl
push and sent her through it with a bow. Camilo by a series of com
promises had managed to make effective a fairly complete set o
smaller courtesies, ignoring the larger and more troublesome ones

This is our old friend "retrospect," going on for seven page
of *past and pluperfect* tense and through the retrospectiv
scenes with three different men. Then we are brought bacl
to the present moment. The italics are mine.

There, she *now remembered distinctly*, she had taken the letter ou
of her purse before she spread the purse out to dry.
She had sat down and read the letter over again: but there wer
phrases that insisted on being read many times, they had a life o
their own separate from the others, and when she tried to read pas
and around them, they moved with the movement of her eyes, and
she could not escape them . . . "thinking about you more than
meant to . . . yes, I even talk about you. . . ."

Then the author uses simple past tense for the character'
record of what has happened and her feeling of "a deep almost murderous anger at the janitress." This anger is important because its violence indicates pent up, accumulated
anger or frustration—it is more violent than the loss of the
purse warrants. Accusing the janitress of the theft, the character makes a little scene. This scene is again recorded in
past tense. One gets the impression that the scene is being gone
over retrospectively in the heroine's mind, though it could be
a dramatized, past-tense record of action of the more usual fictional type. A transitional phrase beginning "She remembered" indicates, however, that we have been in our heroine's
mind all this time. Now she goes on remembering certain
facts about her life, in a technically brilliant passage of
philosophical retrospect using the pluperfect tense, summariz-
ing other "losses" not material, and finally concludes: "all
that she had had, and all that she had missed, were lost together, and were twice lost in this landslide of remembered
losses."

In the next paragraph Miss Porter uses the past imperfect, "was following," to describe a second scene with the janitress but soon returns to the simple past tense, "the janitress thrust the purse towards her." The story is continued for the next few paragraphs describing this scene, in the simple past tense until the final sentence most brilliantly concludes:

She laid the purse on the table and sat down with the cup of chilled coffee, and thought: I was right not to be afraid of any thief but myself, who will end by leaving me nothing.

Any analysis of Miss Porter's brilliant handling of angle here can hardly give the sum total impression of wholeness, presentness, and complete integration of subject-matter and method. The student should study the story for himself. In it he will find a good deal of technical interest, especially the expert treatment of *tense*. Now tense is the bugaboo of any amateur. It is difficult and no rules can be laid down. Yet, in the best use of tense lies much of the secret of artistic skill.

Ernest Hemingway has achieved this same identification in his third person story about Nick in "Indian Camp," and again in "The End of Something," both stories from the collection *In Our Time*. If the reader will turn back to the quotation on page 27, from "Indian Camp," he will see how masterly is the craftsmanship by which the author-narrator has become a part of the boy, Nick, with, of course, a result-ing reader identification. In "The End of Something" We *are there* with Nick, as he lies on the shore. The technique after the opening paragraphs seems to be that of pure, objective dramatization: we see people move and hear them talk. But all the time, we are somehow in Nick's mind; yet not by direct implication except when the author says that Nick "could hear Marjorie rowing on the water" and again when he tells us that "he felt Bill coming up to the fire." But just the same there has taken place that magic identification: *author is character*.

It is all rather casual, as is the case in much of Hemingway' most moving writing. The very casualness has its own specia effectiveness, that quality which the British call "under statement" and which, indeed, is a result of the highest re straint. This is the method of synthesis, of perfect reproduc tion of life itself, with its forms of inner and outer aware ness.

The dramatic objective method contributes speed as wel as illusion. The story moves through action itself, rather thar through the medium of the author's description or exposition Many of Dorothy Parker's stories, it is clear, move along scenically; that is to say, in direct conversation. The author'; only intrusion is that she puts up an occasional sign post to tell us who said what, or a bit of stage direction placing the characters in the scene. In "Here We Are," she tells us that a young couple are in their Pullman compartment, briefly describes their nervous concentration upon settling them selves, and tells us what the girl looks like. After a page or so of this, the young honeymooners begin to talk and the author disappears completely, except to indicate who makes the remarks. The story could well be a one-act dialogue.

Another dramatic objective device is that which Dorothy Parker used in "Lady with a Lamp," in which the entire story is revealed through the steady, uninterrupted mono logue of the catty bedside visitor. Nowhere is there one single word of author intrusion, one word of stage-direction We only listen to one woman talking. The same thing hap pens, of course, in Browning's poem, "My Last Duchess," where the husband of the dead woman tells his story of obses sive jealousy, giving at one and the same time a picture of the wife and of himself. The economy and directness of such a method is clear indeed. Scenic detail, if any, comes in only as a part of the monologue: "There she stands as if alive," and "since none puts by the curtain I have drawn for you, but I."

Economy and speed in writing may often, however, come at the expense of other values, prohibiting a full, rounded development through a leisurely building up of characters and scenes. Slowness often has its own importance. For instance, in the beautiful Clark story referred to earlier, "The Wind and the Snow of Winter," the author's leisurely description of the coming of winter combines with the character's wandering thoughts to give us a strong sense of old age which is slow and of that passage of time which is so important to the main theme of the story. And this is definitely a story of theme and symbolism. The story opens with the words, "It was near sunset when Mike Braneen came onto the last pitch of the old wagon road which had led into Gold Rock from the east since the Comstock days." More description and then suddenly we are almost in Mike's mind. "Mike didn't like cars anyway, and on the old road he could forget about them and feel more like himself." The *effect* here depends upon leisurely techniques. The technique of this story is the very common one of author omniscience, combined with character angle. There are countless variations in modern writing, and the contemporary author often does little more than set the scene or indicate gesture or movement from one place to another, or tell us who says what. But more often than not, we spend a great deal of our reading time in the mind of one character, usually the main character.

It is interesting to analyze how a skilled writer brings about these shifts of which the average reader is probably entirely unconscious. Clark writes, after describing the signs of winter on the mountain: "Yet Mike Braneen was not deceived. This was not just a flurrying day; it was the beginning of winter. If not tonight, then tomorrow, or the next day, the snow would begin which shut off the mountains, . . ." Clark uses the words, "he had thought drowsily." Later he takes us into his hero's mind by saying

that he could or could not remember certain things. This
device also promotes the all-important sense of *time*. Then
we are directly in his mind remembering with him: "It had
been in Hamilton. He had felt unhappy, because he could
remember. . . ." After a while, however, at the end of the
story, there is another man present; the two men exchange
some pregnant questions and answers, and the story ends
with the author's statement about the men's moving off. The
general impression here is that of being in the old man's
consciousness.

Finally, the very beautiful and symbolic last paragraph
is pure author narration:

> They came up onto the crossing under the light, and the snow-
> laden wind whirled around them again. They passed under the light
> and their three lengthening shadows before them were obscured by
> the innumerable tiny shadows of the flakes.

The words "passed," "lengthening shadows," "obscured,"
all serve to indicate the idea of annihilation and death, just as
the words "innumerable tiny shadows of the flakes" suggest
man's infinitesimal and fugitive role in a vast universe. And
this metaphysical view is combined with universality. Such
effects are the result of a mastery of technique, a perfect
command over the subject-matter.

This command is shown in another story from this same
collection,[6] "Flesh and Blood" by Laurence Critchell. How
is it achieved? The first sentence seems to be author statement. "It was still raining outside. It was so wet that even
the crows had ceased their arguments from tree to tree. The
only sounds in the whole local English world were the
dripping of water on the tent walls and a lonesome fragment
of music now and then from the direction of the area where
the enlisted men lived." Then we are in Lieutenant Stack's
thoughts, missing his wife, wondering what to do. He is feel-

[6] *O. Henry Memorial Award Prize Stories of 1945.*

ng sorry for himself and he finally goes forth to his infidelity. The author has, after all, scarcely come into the
story at all; the necessary information, with the exception
of a few passages of dramatic scene, is conveyed through
the hero's thoughts. The story ends most philosophically and
quite satisfyingly in his summing up of his feelings, and the
final paragraph shows the symbolic clearing of the rain.

To study almost any of the stories in the annual collections
is to become aware of the innumerable gradations of angle
possible and of the skill with which good contemporary
writers handle them. The novice must realize that the angle
of narration can make or break his work.

A consistent angle is an invaluable aid to both unity and
intensity. There are, indeed, several well known teachers
who maintain that the angle of narration should never be
changed in a short story. But how far from the truth, as we
have just seen! Even the stories that give the greatest impression of unity contain shifts. The idea of a single angle is vital
for the beginner and the dogmatic prohibition against shift
is important as a teaching device and a warning against
dangerous practices. But the truth is that the best of writers
do shift. They shift not only from omniscience to character
mind, but they even at times shift to the mind of more than
one character—a highly dangerous proceeding for the un-
wary. The best writers shift and, by so doing, gain highly
important ends.

Let us consider Hemingway's treatment of angle in "The
Short Happy Life of Francis Macomber," analyzed earlier
in Chapter 6. Here we find the master of dramatic narrative
and the objective method blending it constantly with the
angle of a character in the story; not only with the angle of
one character either. Yet careful study will indicate at once
how perfectly justified is each shift and how much it contributes to the story and its effectiveness.

First the author describes a scene in which the character are "pretending that nothing had happened." Then we are suddenly in Mrs. Macomber's mind, thinking about Wilson the hunter. More conversation reveals that something embarrassing has happened. Then we are momentarily in Wilson's mind: "Wilson had seen it coming for a long time, and he dreaded it"; then, in the next sentence we are almost in Macomber's mind: "Macomber was past dreading it." There is more conversation and gesture and then, after only a few sentences, we are again in Wilson's mind. We come and go in Wilson's mind. Sometimes Hemingway writes "he thought" and sometimes he just *is* in the mind, as when he writes, without any quotation marks to indicate that this is Wilson's thought, "This was no better." This method, provided it is clear, as it is here, is superior to that which he uses in the next sentence. " 'Good God,' he thought, 'I am a diplomat, aren't I?' " A little further along Hemingway writes, without quotation marks, *So he's a bloody four-letter man as well as a bloody coward, he thought*. Here we have the thought directly, but it is accompanied by the *author* statement as to whose thought it is. (Italics are mine.)

No wonder the student of technique becomes confused as to mechanics! To use quotation marks or not to use them? The truth is that one may do as he pleases, provided he makes himself clear; and it really is surprising how clear one can be without the conventional punctuation. Contemporary usage grows more and more varied. Each writer is something of a law unto himself, using devices that seem to him best suited to his subject-matter and the style of his writing.

But to return to our story analyses: There are several pages of excursions into Wilson's mind combined with some direct author statement. Then we come to Macomber's thoughts by means of a transitional time and place phrase "But that night after dinner. . . . as Francis Macomber lay on his cot . . .

it was not all over." By that clever statement we have made the transition to still another angle, Macomber's. Now in his retrospection we get his feeling about his cowardice with the lion.

Then comes the dramatic hunt episode of the following day when we are even momentarily in the *lion's* mind. And after this hunt scene we are again in Macomber's mind thinking of his relations with his wife and why it is that despite her treatment of him, she does not worry about his leaving her for another woman. He knows full well what material considerations keep her from divorcing him. Following this day-time, after hunt, disgression explaining Macomber's past life with his wife, we reach the transitional statement "It was now three o'clock in the morning. . . ." Now Macomber after a frightening dream about a lion again lies awake. He is aware that his wife has been out of the tent for a long time. "At the end of that time his wife came into the tent. . . ." And now we are watching a scene between the two. After other more general scenes we again come back to Wilson's mind, and his final conclusions about Macomber's death. The story ends with his significant words to Mrs. Macomber. Wilson is an active, but not a main character, definitely a witness of Mrs. Macomber's sadism and clearly an interpreter of her personality.

Our analysis shows that this short story can effectively use several angles—as many as four, not including the lion's: those of omniscience and dramatic objective (considered as one), of subordinate character, and of two main characters.

It is interesting to dwell further upon Wilson's role. He is active as the man who stages the hunt for a price, as the man who saves Macomber's life in the hunt, and finally as a reflecting and interpreting agent. He sees a great deal, and by his reactions he indicates his changing emotions toward both Macomber and his wife. He is a most useful agent but still

subordinate to the main story, which is Macomber's story
and especially the story of his relationship with his wife
Wilson is a man of some intelligence. He seems to fulfil
James' requirement of the central intelligence in dramatizing a story. He cannot perhaps be called a "*fine* central intelligence," his very occupation makes him somewhat brutal,
extrovert, and unintellectual. But he does highlight and in-
tensify as well as record the story.

The writer who studies James' Prefaces in *The Art of the
Novel* will gain a great deal of understanding and apprecia-
tion of the values to be brought out and especially of the enhancement in unity and intensity coming through a skillful
use of an angle correctly chosen. The discussion of *The Ambassadors* is especially revealing. Over and over again, James
makes the point that he has literally squeezed out the values
of his material through Strether who "wore this glow" of
goodness and beauty, this man so imaginative, so discriminating of ethical and moral values. "Strether's sense of these
things, and Strether's only, should avail me for showing
them; I should know them but through his more or less
groping knowledge of them." James speaks also of the "large
unity" of his angle—that of the hero—and of its "grace of
intensity."

It is true that James is discussing a two-volume novel here,
which, by reason of its leisureliness and length offers every
opportunity for fine-spun psychological study and development. It is the great fault of the short story, as we have seen,
that it affords so little opportunity for a thoroughly satisfying treatment of character. The short story is often mainly
a character sketch, and it can be only a sketch as a rule. It
is usually very limited in the length of time covered; and
character development involves the passage of time. Development also involves fine shades of meaning, implication, and
nuance; fine sensitivities, awarenesses, and analysis of moral

problems. Obviously, the story built around one scene, one moment in a character's life, cannot be as convincing as a series of scenes.

James' method, of course, was exercised upon much *longer* works than the average short story. Thus he had opportunity, as any novelist has, to give inherently psychological and analytical treatment in the round and to satisfy more thoroughly the reader's desire for full information about characters. It is to be remembered always that the educated reader is reading for illumination and for values that life itself does not offer. Such values may consist either of character and personality understanding or of social or philosophical theory. And James' novels, especially *The Ambassadors* and *The Golden Bowl*, with which this writer is more familiar, offer this gratification. The people who move through their pages become old friends, well known and familiar.

James' characters seem, as Professor Beach points out, "unitary beings responsible for their choices"; but in contemporary fiction, people are not unitary and they are far from responsible for their thoughts. James was an advance guard of the new psychological fiction. He came at the end of one century and the beginning of another, when two very great minds were coming into play. Proust, the novelist, was to illuminate consciousness and subconsciousness through his novel *Remembrance of Things Past;* and Freud, the psychologist, was to emphasize the power of the unconscious and to open new vistas for the understanding and therapy of mental problems. Both men were primarily concerned with the involuntary stream of consciousness and the buried experience of the past. A fourth man, James Joyce, was to develop the technique by which the associative processes were dramatized far more effectively than they had ever been before.

8

Stream of Consciousness

THAT angle which goes directly into the mind of a character and represents without benefit of author is the most realistic for the depiction of thought processes. If it is rigidly adhered to, as it is in parts of *Ulysses*, it almost becomes phonographic. But the writer will, in such a process, sacrifice direction and pattern and perhaps drama. The technique affords, however, a far greater degree of realism than does ordinary writing about thought. The inner view is deeper.

In its extreme form the technique reveals disordered, uncontrolled mental processes that are spontaneous and that represent the inner man just as truly as do his conscious, directed thoughts, the things that he *lets* himself think. This revelation can be very important for fiction, especially where deep characterization is desired. It is also valuable in compulsive or obsessive states, and delirious states, as we shall see. But its inconsequence, its very lack of apparent direction, may detract from the dramatic power of the narrative. Drama is, after all, traditionally concerned with the "free" activities of a man with enough will-power to determine, to some extent at least, his own destiny.

But we are not concerned here with such problems. We are only interested in discovering what values such a technique has and how they can be turned to account, perhaps in more traditional writing which tells a real story. Let us look, for a moment, at *Ulysses*, which uses both traditional and new consciousness techniques. This novel affords a view of the lives of several people living a day in Dublin and presents a slice of life revealed chiefly through the consciousness of these characters. It is an absorbing slice, indeed.

Here we shall attempt to show by illustrative quotation *how* Joyce wrote; then later in the chapter we shall try to show adaptations of this method or similar methods employed by contemporary writers.

The opening paragraphs of *Ulysses*[1] use the familiar dramatic objective method, with the author outside the characters, and show the scene at its best. They are vivid and direct, with a minimum of author intrusion.

Buck Mulligan came from the stair head, bearing a bowl of lather on which a mirror and a razor lay crossed. A yellow dressinggown, ungirdled, was sustained gently behind him by the mild morning air. He held the bowl aloft and intoned:
—*Introibo ad altare Dei.*
Halted, he peered down the dark winding stairs and called up coarsely:
—Come up, Kinch. Come up, you fearful jesuit.
Solemnly he came forward and mounted the round gunrest. He faced about and blessed gravely thrice the tower, the surrounding country and the awaking mountains. Then, catching sight of Stephen Dedalus, he bent towards him and made rapid crosses in the air, gurgling in his throat and shaking his head.

Here the author has told us how Mulligan appears and what he does. He has used no quotation marks whatever in recording the conversation. He has merely substituted an introductory dash; he has not used any mark to indicate the end of a speech.

After two and a half pages of this kind of treatment Joyce suddenly is in Stephen Dedalus' mind. (My italics indicate when he is completely in.)

Stephen, an elbow rested on the jagged granite, leaned his palm against his brow and gazed at the fraying edge of his shiny black coatsleeve. Pain, that was not yet the pain of love, fretted his heart. *Silently, in a dream she had come to him after her death, her wasted body within its loose brown graveclothes giving off an odour of wax and rosewood, her breath, that had bent upon him, mute, reproachful, a faint odour of wetted ashes.* Across the threadbare cuffedge he saw the sea hailed as a great sweet mother by the wellfed voice beside him. The ring of bay and skyline held a dull green mass of liquid. (Are we in his mind here? It seems so. But Joyce has used the words "he saw," to that extent acting as the recording writer. The next sentence leaves no doubt.) *A bowl of white china had stood beside her deathbed holding the green sluggish bile which she had torn up from her rotting liver by fits of loud groaning vomiting.*

The technique used in this last sentence is not new to any student of today's writing. It is the use of direct character retrospective, flash-back consciousness. No quotation marks are used and none are necessary. The succeeding passages, however, return to the method used in the opening paragraphs. It is easy to find examples of a similar technique used by other writers.

Now let us go a step further with Joyce's technique and consider the pure stream standing alone, without introduction or explanation. We find it in the famous chapter beginning:

Ineluctable modality of the visible: At least that if no more, thought through my eyes. Signatures of all things I am here to read, seaspawn and seawrack, the nearing tide, that rusty boat. Snotgreen, bluesilver, rust: coloured signs. Limits of the diaphane. But he adds: in bodies. Then he was aware of them bodies before of them coloured. How? By knocking his sconce against them, sure. Go easy. Bald he was and a millionaire, *maestro di color che sanno*. Limit of the diaphane in. Why in? Diaphane, adiaphane. If you can put your five fingers through it, it is a gate, if not a door. Shut your eyes and see.

In the next paragraph Joyce says, "Stephen closed his eyes to hear his boots crush crackling wrack and shells." Then again we are immediately in Stephen's mind:

You are walking through it howsomever. I am, a stride at a time. A very short space of time thru very short times of space. Five, six: the *nacheinander*. Exactly: and that is the ineluctable modality of

the audible. Open your eyes. No. Jesus! If I fell over a cliff that
beetles o'er his base, fell through the *nebeneinander* ineluctably.

This writing is very obscure, as much of Joyce is obscure. To understand him requires knowledge of several
languages, of the classics, and whatnot. But the student can
see that it represents natural but chaotic associative processes,
the free associations of a highly educated poet. This is not
meat for the average palate; but it is meat with a very special
flavor for those with taste to enjoy it.

Now for a more easily understood and equally famous
passage we turn to Marion Bloom's coarse, lusty mind as she
lies day-dreaming in bed—a passage forty-four pages long,
without any punctuation or paragraphing and without capital-
ization to mark the beginning of a sentence. This chapter also
represents direct, freely associative thought. Joyce has given
it no introduction whatever, no explanation of who is thinking or under what circumstances. These facts eventually become clear through the thought itself.

Yes because he never did a thing like that before as ask to get his
breakfast in bed with a couple of eggs since the *City Arms* hotel
when he used to be pretending to be laid up with a sick voice doing
his highness to made himself interesting to that old faggot Mrs
Riordan that he thought he had a great leg of and she never left us
a farthing all for masses for herself and her soul greatest miser ever
was actually afraid to lay out 4d for her methylated spirit telling me
all her ailments she had too much old chat in her about politics and
earthquakes and the end of the world let us have a bit of fun first
God help the world if all the women were her sort down on bathingsuits and lownecks of course nobody wanted her to wear I suppose she was pious because no man would look at her twice I hope
I'll never be like her a wonder she didn't want us to cover our faces
but she was a welleducated woman certainly and her gabby talk
about Mr Riordan here and Mr Riordan there

This is the pure stream of consciousness of a very impure
mind, as one discovers later. It reveals the woman, fully and
amazingly, including her attitudes toward her husband, with

whom we have also become intimately acquainted through the use of the same technique. What brilliant revelation of the associative processes! And it has possibilities for telling a good deal more of a dramatic story, although there is really plenty of story, unorganized story, in this chapter. Its reality and the directness of its impact are tremendous. It makes all other methods of portraying thought seem relatively clumsy and indirect because they always offer some element of author interference.

Even Marcel Proust, whose *Remembrance of Things Past* is unquestionably one of the most revealing novels ever written about consciousness in its thousand variations, is always *present*, whether he is identifying himself as the "I" of the narrator, as "Marcel," or is in Swann's mind. He is portraying thought that is guided by a kind of unifying thread. This is, as Clive Bell wrote, the work of "a psychologist writing out of himself, digging deeper, ever deeper, lowering his bucket to the very bottom of his own subconsciousness." But Proust the writer is there watching his own consciousness, studying his own sensory impressions, and even his own memory processes. A passage describing his reactions to a telephone call to his beloved grandmother will indicate the difference between Proust's technique and Joyce's.

Suddenly I heard that voice which I supposed myself, mistakenly, to know so well; for always until then, every time that my grandmother had talked to me, I had been accustomed to follow what she was saying on the open score of her face, in which the eyes figured so largely; but her voice itself I was hearing this afternoon for the first time. And because that voice appeared to me to have altered in its proportions from the moment that it was a whole, and reached me in this way alone and without the accompaniment of her face and features, I discovered for the first time how sweet that voice was; perhaps, too, it had never been so sweet, for my grandmother, knowing me to be alone and unhappy, felt that she might let herself go in the outpouring of an affection which, on her principle of education, she usually restrained and kept hidden. It was sweet, but also how sad it was, first of all on account of its very sweetness, a sweetness drained almost—more than any but a few human voices can ever have been—of every element of resistance to others, of all selfishness; fragile by reason of its delicacy it seemed at every moment ready to break, to expire in a pure flow of tears; then, too, having it alone beside me, seen, without the mask of her face, I noticed for the first time the sorrows that had scarred it in the course of a lifetime.

Was it, however, solely the voice that, because it was alone, gave me this new impression which tore my heart? Not at all; it was rather that this isolation of the voice was like a symbol, a presentation, a direct consequence of another isolation, that of my grandmother, separated, for the first time in my life, from myself.

Then, finally, Proust describes his sensations upon the breaking of the telephone conversation:

I was shaken by the same anguish which, in the distant past, I had felt once before, one day when, a little child, in a crowd, I had lost her, an anguish due less to my not finding her than to the thought that she must be searching for me, must be saying to herself that I was searching for her; an anguish comparable to that which I was to feel on the day when we speak to those who can no longer reply and whom we would so love to have hear all the things that we have not told them, and our assurance that we are not unhappy.[2]

The reader will see at once that this is an entirely different kind of revelation from Joyce's; that it is an evocation of thought processes that are intellectualized, for all of their emotional tinge and content. There is really nothing haphazard or "freakish" here at all. The man that we are looking at is a highly sensitive intellectual who combines in his attitude toward his materials a remarkable degree of both subjectivity and objectivity. We have here what someone has called "an exquisite synthesis of his sensibility." And just as we hear with him and feel with him and think with him, we can in hundreds of other passages of his novel share

[2] Copyright, 1936, by Random House, Inc. Reprinted by permission of Random House, Inc.

equally revealing experiences of his world of sight, taste, and smell—all made symbolic and universal by his art, an art which reveals both "normal" and "abnormal" people so clearly that we know them better than we know living people. The technique itself is not new and startling like Joyce's. It is more on the traditional side, in so far as its *mechanics* are concerned. Its novelty and its achievement lie in the completeness of its revelation of experience. That completeness arises from Proust's *style*, his inexhaustible patience in the use of detail, his careful elaboration, and his command of many symbols, metaphors and similes of the utmost freshness and poetic impact.

Proust belongs in a way to the stream of consciousness school, yet he is by no means closely related to Joyce as a technician. He is closer to Henry James, who followed the more traditional methods but also, as R. P. Blackmur says, "rendered shades and refinements of meaning and feeling not usually rendered at all." It is rewarding to study Proust on many levels; but most of all, for the writer, to observe his use of intensification and to realize how much depth it gives to his revelation of the inner life. Indeed, to study other great writers of the last fifty years is to recognize that they also are not afraid of going into sufficient detail to convey the exact measure and content of experience. We have dwelt a great deal upon the contemporary stylists who are distinguished by economy of treatment. But James, Proust, Joyce, and Mann, all experts in revealing consciousness, are distinguished for their disregard of economy and their emphasis upon depth and fullness. And, as we have pointed out in our discussion of "The Wind and the Snow of Winter," today's writers are again tending toward the more leisurely exploration of subject-matter.

To turn now to contemporary techniques for describing

consciousness, let us first consider James Thurber's well-known story, "The Secret Life of Walter Mitty." [3] It comes to mind because it borrows some of Joyce's techniques. In paragraph one we find Joyce's device of throwing us directly into the mind of the hero. Thurber departs from it only in that he puts quotation marks around the things that Mitty imagines are being said by himself, as Commander, and by his men.

"We're going through!" The Commander's voice was like thin ice breaking. He wore his full-dress uniform, with the heavily braided white cap pulled down rakishly over one cold gray eye. "We can't make it, sir. It's spoiling for a hurricane, if you ask me." "I'm not asking you, Lieutenant Berg," said the Commander. "Throw on the power light! Rev her up to 8,500! We're going through!" The pounding of the cylinders increased: ta-pocketa-pocketa-pocketa-pock*eta-pocketa*. The Commander stared at the ice forming on the pilot window. He walked over and twisted a row of complicated dials. "Switch on No. 8 auxiliary!" he shouted. "Switch on No. 8 auxiliary!" repeated Lieutenant Berg. "Full strength in No. 3 turret!" shouted the Commander. "Full strength in No. 3 turret!" The crew, bending to their various tasks in the huge, hurtling eight-engined Navy hydroplane, looked at each other and grinned. "The Old Man'll get us through," they said to one another. "The Old Man ain't afraid of Hell!" . . .

Now Thurber uses conventional dramatic technique:

"Not so fast! You're driving too fast!" said Mrs. Mitty. "What are you driving so fast for?"

"Hmm?" said Walter Mitty. He looked at his wife, in the seat beside him, with shocked astonishment. She seemed grossly unfamiliar, like a strange woman who had yelled at him in a crowd. "You were up to fifty-five," she said. "You know I don't like to go more than forty. You were up to fifty-five." [We italicize here the fragment using the newer "stream" technique.] Walter Mitty drove on toward Waterbury in silence, *the roaring of the SN 202 through the worst storm in twenty years of Navy flying* fading in the remote, intimate airways of his mind. "You've tensed up again," said Mrs. Mitty. "It's one of your days. I wish you'd let Dr. Renshaw look you over."

Paragraph two, of course, serves to interrupt Mitty's day-dream through Mrs. Mitty's back-seat driving. It brings the reader up sharply since it is his first intimation that something strange is going on, something at first confusing. The next paragraphs indicate two things: Mitty has been going a bit too fast, perhaps absent-mindedly; and Mrs. Mitty is a bossy woman. They also throw us again into Mitty's day-dream ("the roaring of the SN 202" etc.); and they further reveal that Mr. Mitty is "tense" and that it is not the first time.

The implications of that word "tense" are great, but just how great the reader will see only as the story progresses through several compensatory day-dreams in each of which Walter Mitty is playing an important and heroic role. The device which Mr. Thurber uses of having each fantasy *suggested* by some external reality is both original and clever, lending psychological validity. And finally we come to the last fantasy in which Mitty faces an imaginary firing squad: "erect and motionless, proud and disdainful, Walter Mitty the Undefeated, inscrutable to the last."

This story is extremely well knit, perfectly integrated, and very real. The device of contrast is handled with great effectiveness. Mr. Mitty's silly name, his subservience to his dominant wife, and the trivial errands she makes him do are all in contrast to his dreams of grandeur and power. Some people are only moved to laughter by this story, but the contrast here is in reality pitiful and moving. Mr. Mitty is the symbol of the tragic disparity between our dreams and our realities. His compensatory dreams also have their tragic significance, for his implied fate is perhaps life's greatest tragedy—insanity.

Mr. Thurber has used the method of *Ulysses*, in that he has thrown us repeatedly into Mitty's mind, without introductory statement. Joyce would probably, however, not have used any quotation marks to indicate the imagined conversation; and it is conceivable that his technique would have had still more realistic impact, for that very reason.

Studies of this kind, dealing with psychopathic states, appear far oftener in today's fiction than most people would think. Indeed, we seem to be having a sort of epidemic of borderline or actually insane fictional characters. Three stories in *The O. Henry Memorial Award Prize Stories for 1946* deal, as the preface admits, with "madness." The two war stories also deal with consciousness, perhaps of "normal" men under the impact of battle and wounding.

Since the prize-winning story, "Bird Song,"[4] by John Goss, deals with actual madness, let us consider it first. It uses no startling techniques, but it does illustrate the possibilities for handling mental material with extreme reality and at the same time dramatic effectiveness.

Beresford is first awaiting his wife's visit to the insane asylum. Then he gets word that she cannot come and is sending a taxi for him. He is permitted to go to see her for a short time. He is thinking about his talk with the doctor and how he has proved his rationality. The mechanics used are as follows:

When you sat beside the doctor before his wretched "class" and, when your turn came, finally answered his questions, quickly and naturally as anyone should:

"What day is it?"

"Wednesday, the thirteenth of November, 1940, Doctor."

"How old are you? When is your birthday?"

"Three weeks ago I was forty-six, Doctor."

(I'm living, Doctor. I am of my own generation. I am not a child nor an old man, not unborn or dead, just miraculously George Beresford, groped back out of oblivion to consciousness, to sanity.)

"Good! Very good indeed, Beresford. Nicely oriented. I am proud of you. One of my best patients."

It is clear that we have here the usual technique of reporting a scene dramatically, combined with the use of a parenthesis without any quotation marks, to show what the

[4] *The Atlantic Monthly*, February 1946.

character remembers having thought. Since this memory shows his rationality, it contributes to our understanding of the present situation in which he is to have his trial flight into the world of reality with his wife. We see that he has at least a fair degree of sanity. The story is wonderfully constructed. Beresford leaves with the taxi-driver who, he notes, is a bit afraid of him. Then the driver reveals that they are heading for "Bertha's place." "Ain'cha never been there? Say, is that little Frenchy your wife?" This, of course, startles Beresford. "What was the fool saying?" Then they reach their destination.

"Oh, my Lord, it can't be a—*bordel*." Say it fast Beresford. Say it in French and you won't be sick.

One will note the interesting way in which this ghastly information is conveyed to the reader at the same time that Beresford's words to himself show his natural but very intense reaction of horror. The technique used is smooth, natural, and perfectly clear, for all the difficulty of the narrative problems.

From here the story moves rapidly, as certainty grows for Beresford and for the reader that the French wife is living in a brothel again (the implication is that he took her from one in France) and under particularly sordid conditions. She herself has degenerated into drunkenness. We see Beresford fighting his sick reactions, forcing himself to think of their former happy life at the farm.

Back to the farm? Back to the old furniture, the silver, the pictures on the walls? Go fishing in the creek again with Denise, work in the garden with her, play with the dogs? What about that letter from the bank? There was no money. What was it that he had to do about that? He must see about everything, so many things. Not now— some day. He couldn't think about them now.

This paragraph has high economy: it shows the old life with its happy normalities; then the financial situation which evidently helped bring the breakdown; and the fact that

Beresford now cannot think about the money problem. If he cannot, he is obviously not well-adjusted to reality. He is slipping back. He also shows (in the "now") time confusion.

We cannot here go into the many artistically woven details of this finely integrated story in which, moment by moment, Beresford is confronted by increasing realistic horror until he finally breaks completely and fancies himself, as he looks upon some canaries in cages, the victim of a hospital plot against him.

"It was a beastly scheme they were trying out on him. They were showing him he could not get away even for a day. They knew what he was doing all the time—they would always know."

Finally we see him returning to the insane asylum with—and this is tremendously ironic and even philosophically significant—"a feeling of freedom. He felt superior and privileged, as if he were a senior in college again, and he trod with a firmer step."

In the last scene he is sitting with Graber who says:

"Anyway, a guy sits here and forgets how screwy things were in the world. God, look at this sheet." Graber extended the magazine he had been reading to arm's length and slapped it violently to the floor. "Things aren't perfect out there, Beresford, by a hell of a sight —whatever you've been hoping. What was the matter? Wasn't your cute little wife glad to see you? Or was she living on the wrong side of the tracks?"

Grabers comments further: "I've seen plenty of guys get knocked off balance again the first time they stuck their heads out"; and we last see the two men sitting together smoking in the sunlighted room. Beresford is smiling—"two businessmen they might have been, two men of affairs anywhere, idling an hour in their club lounge in the hush of a Sunday afternoon."

The reader will see for himself what a really wonderful conclusion this is, how true to the temperament which cannot bear the impact of disillusionment or adversity; and at the same time how philosophical its startling implication that for such a sensitive person a life of retreat into the ivory tower of the asylum is not necessarily unhappier than is life in "the world."

To turn to less morbid subject-matter, we can consider two war stories in the same O. Henry collection which depict consciousness in situations of terror, physical suffering, and expected death: "Waves of Darkness" and "Breathe Upon These Slain." "Waves of Darkness," [5] by Cord Meyer, Jr., won the special prize for a first published short story. It offers no new techniques; but it is an interesting treatment of the impacts of battle fears and horrors, carrying at the same time symbolic and philosophical overtones that are significant.

The lieutenant lies in a trench at night with his friend, thinking of the day just passed, when he led his men through the attack; thinking of how they suffered and died. Staring into the blackness of a clouded sky (important to the plot), he tries to rationalize his fear of the death that he feels is surely approaching. Extremely vivid details take us into his present crucial situation; facing Jap night attack, he is very much aware of the darkness "a curtain behind which some fantastic tragedy waited." He thinks indignantly of the makers of war as he and his friends are "bracketed" by the ever closer Jap fire. Then his friend is killed by a grenade and he himself is seriously wounded, evidently, he thinks, in the face. All is blackness. "Truth was never more terrible" than at that moment when, fearfully, he raised his hand and found that his left eye had been shot out. Then for some time he contemplated the horrible thought of total blindness, facing its imagined realities, not daring to explore his other eye with his hand, and still facing a black sky.

[5] *The Atlantic Monthly*, January 1946.

In all its poverty his life as it would be appeared before him. All other things, he felt—the mutilation of his face, the loss of his limbs, —would have been endurable, but not this: the dark dragging hours, the mocking blackness of his nights, the loneliness of a world where people are only voices which if beautiful are more bitter to hear, the unassuageable regret provoked every memory of the lighted past, the cheerful self-sacrifice of kind relations to goad the sense of his own parasitic uselessness, and always the mind growing more deformed in its crippling attempts to escape the dark of prison.

The memory returned of how as a boy he had almost drowned. It seemed that again he struggled upward through the black water. An illusory hope filled him that he could break the confines of the dark that pressed down on him as the ocean had so long before, but the excitement passed quickly. Above this ocean no sunlight flashed on white waves. It was infinite, and extended in blank perspective from that moment to the day of his death, when, he thought, one form of eternal night would be exchanged for another devoid of anguish and regret. Behind the sightless eyes, his mind would burn down like a fire in a room the guests have left until, mercifully, darkness was all.

He reaches for his gun to end it all, but cannot find it and so he resigns himself to his "dark fate." "With a new severity, he contemplated the few short years of his life to discover some strand of meaning running through the trivial sequence of days and nights stretching back to the earliest memory." And he comes to reconciliation for the death that he has convinced himself is close at hand. The universe is alien and men wander in it like strangers. He thinks of the stars in their wandering courses and waits for death.

Then suddenly, he feels a tear and a smarting "where his right eye should be." He starts to explore with his hand, but what use? He has now rationalized himself into accepting death; why "disturb that profound indifference?" But he does nevertheless explore the eye. It is there! He searches the "blackness above for a sign. Gone was all indifference. Light was life." And he waits for "a frail miracle."

Then down the long corridor of the night it swam into his vision. Out of focus, it trembled for a moment hazily, and then burned steady and unwinking. Fearing that he might have created it out of the intensity of his wish, he let his lid close and then forced it open again. The star still lay in the now soft and friendly dark. It flooded his being like the summer sun. He saw it as the window to Hope. Another appeared, and another, until the whole tropic sky seemed ablaze with an unbearable glory. Joyful tears rose in his heart. Gently, he permitted the torn lid to shut. Warm on his cheek and salty in his mouth were the tears of his salvation.

Life has affirmed itself for him in terms of light and the vast solar universe. As one of the O. Henry Memorial Award judges said, the hero "might be a symbol for all sensitive soldiers wounded by life as well as weapons." And thus the narrative takes on those overtones and larger implications which are to be found in philosophic writing.

Equally important overtones are to be found in another stream of consciousness story printed in this collection: "Breathe Upon These Slain" [6] by Meridel Le Sueur, who wanted, she writes in a letter, "to show that the primal jungle life of our civilization is 'unconscious,' and leaves us darkly unconscious in our conscious life—often automatic, if not as this boy utterly inarticulate without myth or symbol to use as coin of exchange between himself and others—in fact his only contact was the deathly one night-marishly destructive."

In this technically interesting story, we meet the hero as he crawls through the jungle, crying to Slim, who is dead. Finally he reaches a tree into which he can hoist himself to escape the pursuing Japs. He keeps whispering to keep from "the horrors of sleep that now resembled death too much." And all through the story his whispers, growing into long monologues, are indicated by the use of italics. If the Japs do not get him at daylight, his own ships will. "*My own ships. What ships are mine, Slim?*" He, too, reviews his life as he faces death, reviews it bitterly: he "couldn't fool himself now. *Don't kid yourself, baby. It's bad. And it's always*

[6] *The Kenyon Review*, Summer 1945.

been bad for you. It's stacked against you. You never won a game." He thought how his whole life had "been something like it was now, as he was strapped to a tree in a thick fog with enemies on all sides of him, and a promise of ultimate disaster in what might happen within the hour."

He sees his own city, Chicago, but it does not seem to really be "his" city. He tries to remember what other fellows have told him about history and about the ideals they were fighting for, but they had "families to die for." He even sees his death as a hero reported in the Chicago papers.

In that moment he saw himself become dear to them in Chicago. He saw them stop and think of him.

There would be a little convulsion along the streets of Chicago for love of him.

Again he cries out in whispers to his comrades and dreams in his delirium:

He was holding back the sun with his bare hands. He was hunting on the beach for Slim. . . .

Then he apostrophizes the sun and finally calls to Slim

When the sun comes roaring up there, shining up from America right over Chi . . . right over us . . . let's all go together in the face of the sun sky high, baby, sky high. . . .

Now he felt a kind of joy.

He had a community now; five dead men and those who would mourn him in Chicago, and those now lying on the beach head dead.

Thus we leave him hanging in his strap in a tree. The last sentence is: "The sun, hours before, had moved from the black shadows of Chicago and the Illinois prairie."

The impression here is of man's isolation, concretely described in the action and emotion of the story, and implied as symbolic of many men's isolation. The story lacks the lift at the end of "Waves of Darkness." Here all is dream-like agony, a nightmare, and illusion, except for the hero's faith in his buddies, who have given him the only love and companionship he has ever known. This affirmation, however, is very significant and very beautiful. It is usually and especially notable in the writings of ex-servicemen who have been in actual battle.

9

Characterization

THE fiction writer's task is to make the reader feel with or about his characters. By means of his insight he will show us, as James said, "the interesting face presented by" the character "to *any* damnable trick." What happens to our hero is interesting, but still more interesting is his way of meeting it. We have to see what traits he brings to bear upon his situation or his problem, how these traits develop, how his relationships change, how he feels toward others and toward himself, and what comes of it all. If the story is short, the amount of character revelation must be limited and flat; if it is long, the revelation may be much more round and complete. In any case, we are dealing with a "lighted figure" which is the center of the action.

The "short-short" story has been popular in this country during the last twenty years or so; and the result of its influence has been a good deal of poverty of characterization, even in longer stories. Compact, invented for the hasty reader intent upon a single incident and a single trait, the device was to be expected in an age of tabloids, digests, and radio condensations. Its meagerness, however, becomes tiresome and unsatisfying to the more serious reader who wants something to get his teeth into. Hence, perhaps, the popularity of some very long novels in more recent years; hence, perhaps, the current excitement about Henry James, who was for some time formerly looked upon as "tiresome and hair-splitting." Even the expert and revealing short stories of *The New Yorker*, good as they are, and imitated far and wide, eventually come to seem of rather transitory interest. One craves a more intimate relationship with fictional people than is possible within the compass of one or two thousand words. Life itself can give us this much if we look for it; we expect fiction to reveal more, to give more intimacy with people and their inner life. We expect it to break down the walls between us and others.

Very often the short-short story deals almost entirely with incident. If the incident is striking and significant, well and good; if it isn't, or if it has been written about too many times and has been too thoroughly explored before, then its poverty is most obvious.

Characters simply cannot be developed thoroughly in a few words. The clear exposition of what people are like, of the nature of their crisis, and of how they meet it, is all implied in the phrase "adequate characterization." Whether the writer starts from situation or character, he must come quickly to an analysis of traits. Too often the analysis is, as we have already suggested, woefully superficial and general. Jealousy, we have noted, is a common theme, but jealousy has many faces. So have ambition, vanity, revenge, self-sacrifice, and many other "themes," as they are wrongly called by those who think only in terms of the general. Generality here, as elsewhere, gets one nowhere unless it is coupled with the specific. Every narrative needs the specific quality, the exact shading of the general emotion dealt with. We have pointed out the illustration of this principle in our discussion of the two stories about fathers and sons by Stegner and Hemingway.

The writer of a short story is definitely limited in canvas. He can show only one trait or group of closely related traits.

If he can give us the sure test of character, the certain highly significant and symbolic act, we shall remember his hero. Such is Shaw's fortunate portrayal in "The Girls in their Summer Dresses."

Highly consistent characterization, characterization which makes the reader feel that he knows the hero and can depend upon him to act in a given way, is of the very essence of fiction writing. It is brought about by the use of details which, gradually yet very surely, as the story moves forward, point the way. Coming then to the end of the tale, we say, "Yes, that is just the way he would finally act." Thus it is that in Katherine Mansfield's story "A Cup of Tea" we are fully prepared for the final act, the closing revelation. We have seen Rosemary first by direct author statement. Paragraph one tells us, thru her cleverly implied view of herself, that she wants to be "pretty," that she is smart, exquisitely dressed, and that "her parties were the most delicious mixture of the really important people and . . . artists—quaint creatures, discoveries of hers, some of them too terrifying for words, but others quite presentable and amusing." This last sentence characterizes by depicting thought.

Then we see her shopping, first buying flowers lavishly and posing affectedly for the benefit of the salesman. Then we see her impressing the antique dealer, whose flattery she absorbs as she toys, again self-consciously, with the idea of an expensive little box. Then we see her mentally dramatizing her role as the patron and rescuer of a starving waif; we see her posturing, promising much. And finally we see her dropping the shivering and pitiful girl like a hot-cake, sending her again into the cold, wet night, merely because her husband has remarked upon the girl's prettiness. As the story ends she is lying to her husband about the girl's forced departure. She has obviously dressed to enthrall him, and she is sitting on his knee asking him if *she* is pretty.

A group of similar traits is used by Mansfield in "Mr. Reginald Peacock's Day." Here the *tone* is quite different, however; the portrait is different and equally memorable. In the first paragraphs we observe that the hero is resentful of the way in which his wife awakens him in the morning. "She did it on purpose, of course." We see him thinking of himself as a "sensitive person" and imagining all sorts of ugly motives in his wife's simplest act; seeing her as "trying to drag him down to her level"; sentimentally visualizing himself as being awakened by his "latest, most charming pupil putting her bare, scented arms around his neck and covering him with her long perfumed hair." Then he is acting operatically in his bath, then doing his exercises so as to stay thin, admiring himself in the mirror, using a little French phrase because someone has asked him the night before if he was English. Then he is posturing before his small son, exacting silly obeisances from him; later he is accepting adulation from his women pupils and from a distinguished host. And finally he has come home to his wife, who, we know, has been very busy all day around the house. He is thinking, "I could have anyone I liked by lifting a finger"; and he sees his wife as an "enemy, even in her sleep." He throws off his boots and wakes his sleeping wife whom he is, however, "for some fiendish reason" only able to address in the words of a matinee idol. "Dear lady, I should be so charmed—so charmed!"

The general traits that these two Mansfield characters have in common are clearly egocentricity, selfishness, vanity, self-dramatization, exhibitionism, and cruelty to others. But how very different the two portraits! How clear and individual! Because the means used are specific and perfect, the artist can be said to have realized her ideal in each case.

Katherine Mansfield has avoided abstract statement, all author explanation, all labels, all commonplaceness. The *types*

are well known to any halfway observant person; but the
characters are *individual* and specific. There is no tall hand-
some hero, with brown eyes, regular features, and a pleasant
smile; there is rather, a man whose every little act and thought
serves to draw his picture. We see him as the typical musi-
cian sought after by his women pupils; but, oh, how unique
he is! Nor is Rosemary at all like the heroine one meets so
very often in the women's magazines, "deliciously lovely,"
"smoothly groomed," "taut," "sleek," "patrician," "sophisticated."

The point to be noted here is that human beings do fall into
types; but they are also a good deal *more* than types, they are
individuals. The degree to which the type becomes individual
and the degree of charm and interest with which the writer in-
vests him are the important considerations. Coldly analyzed,
for instance, many of William Saroyan's characters are
"stock" and often they are highly sentimentalized. But often,
too, and this is undoubtedly the reason why Saroyan is
granted a place among competent writers, they are delightful
to know. Telegraph operator Grogan, the good-natured,
kindly alcoholic in *The Human Comedy*,[1] is highly typical,
but he is given individuality by Saroyan's technique of
putting a certain tone of polite formality into his conversation
with the boy, whom he treats as an equal in age and experience. Delicately explaining his weakness to the young messenger, Homer:

"I shall on occasion," Mr. Grogan said, "ask you to run an errand
for me, to join me in song, or to sit and talk to me. In the event of
drunkenness, I shall expect of you a depth of understanding one may
not expect from men past twelve. How old are you?"

Then Grogan tries to prepare Homer for his duties in case
of drunkenness:

[1] New York: Harcourt, Brace and Company, Inc., 1943.

"A splash of cold water in the face if I do not respond when shaken —this is to be followed by a cup of hot black coffee from Corbett's."

"Yes, sir," Homer said.

"On the street, however," Mr. Grogan continued, "the procedure is quite another thing. If you behold me wrapped in the embrace of alcohol, greet me as you pass, but make no reference to my happiness. I am a sensitive man and prefer not to be the object of public solicitude."

"Cold water and coffee in the office," Homer said. "Greeting in the street. Yes, sir."

And here the reader has a forecast of the action and a clear indication of the traits of two characters.

Saroyan's boy in "Corduroy Pants" [2] is definitely typical of the sensitive, intellectual, imaginative, under-privileged child who feels himself alien and different. He reads Schopenhauer, Nietzsche, and Spinoza at fourteen. Badly dressed in his uncle's old pair of pants, "very patched," and "not the style," he took to despising other boys who had good pants. But he imagined them offering him their old pants and his reply, "I don't want your old pants, and I don't want your new pants. I want my own God damn pants, and nobody else's. I'm in the world, and I want my own pants." Have the boys with the corduroy pants "read Schopenhauer? No. Do they know there is no God? No. Do they so much as suspect that love is the most boring experience in the world? No. They are ignorant. They are wearing the fine corduroy pants, but they are blind with ignorance. They do not know that it is all a hollow mockery and that they are victims of a horrible jest."

Saroyan's "Laughing Sam" is another sensitive boy, afraid of everything in the world, trying to laugh at everything and as a result getting into all kinds of trouble. "He couldn't do anything without doing it at least partly wrong. . . . He even died wrong, and for all I know he was laughing at the time, or at least right until he realized he was being killed

[2] From *Little Children*. New York: Harcourt, Brace and Company, Inc., 1937.

by the elevator." This boy is tortured by other boys, and laughs; he falls down hurt, and laughs. He laughs when he shouts a newspaper headline about a lot of people being killed. But everyone knows that he laughs because his heart is breaking. He is symbolic. "Here is man; here is the poor agonized body of the ancient slave, undernourished, over-worked, ill, wounded, graceless, foolish; he is the body of our Lord outraged by the world." The boy is fantastic, but the more fantastic he is the more he will stand out in the reader's memory.

Methods of revealing character will become clear if the reader will go through a story marking the traits and the methods used to describe them. However boring such an enterprise may be, it serves to illustrate the processes by which authors make characters come alive. The reader will find a reiteration of the trait, not so much by direct words as by hints and oblique intimations. Dorothy Parker's work will bear close analysis of this sort, for she is a mistress of portrait painting, with a special ability for noting and revealing the little ways in which people show what they are.

Her Mr. Durant,[3] for instance, is sensual and sex-conscious to the point of obscenity, and quite unaware of it; so unaware that he sees no significance in his own reaction to the children's female dog. First he is enjoying a "renewed peace," smug and satisfied, feeling "twenty years younger" and taking "a healthy notice" of a young girl on the street car. He observed her figure and "pointed his tongue and moved it deliberately along his cool, smooth upper lip." He is especially observant of her legs. Then he sits in the street car thinking of his affair with Rose whom he has gotten into "trouble" at the office, Rose who asks nothing of him and whom he lets get herself out of trouble. He offers assistance

[3] "Mr. Durant" from *Laments for the Living*. New York: The Viking Press, 1930.

only to the extent of twenty-five dollars which he could have used "very nicely himself, just then, with Junior's teeth." The details are packed in every sentence, all pointing up the sensuality, the irresponsibility, the egocentric thoughts about his family and children, the would-be youth, and finally the obscenely "pure" attitude toward the presence of a dog that might have puppies. Even the description of Mr. Durant's den is significant, with its bad taste, its emphasis of a highly colored "September Morn" and an "unknown Indian maiden" on a leather pillow which "set off her distressingly dated figure." Even the books "were mostly accounts of favorites of the French court, with a few volumes on the private life of the ex-Kaiser, and the intrigues of the Russian throne room." Then comes the scene at the end.

Into his den Mr. Durant preceded his wife, and faced her, still frowning. His calm was not shattered, but it was punctured. Something annoying always had to go and come up. Wouldn't you know?

"Now you know perfectly well, Fan, we can't have that dog around," he told her. He used the low voice reserved for underwear and bedroom articles and kindred risqué topics. There was all the kindness in his tones that one has for a backward child, but a Gibraltar-like firmness was behind it. "You must be crazy to even think we could for a minute. Why, I wouldn't give a she-dog house-room, not for any amount of money. It's disgusting, that's what it is."

"Well, but Father—" began Mrs. Durant, her hands again going off into their convulsions.

"Disgusting," he repeated. "You have a female around, and you know what happens. All the males in the neighborhood will be running after her. First thing you know, she'd be having puppies—and the way they look after they've had them, and all! That would be nice for the children to see, wouldn't it? I should think you'd think of the children, Fan. No, sir, there'll be nothing like that around here, not while I know it. Disgusting!"

And thereupon Mr. Durant decides to kill the dog and to lie to the children about it. He pats his wife. "Again his mind wrapped itself in the knowledge that everything was all fixed, all ready for a nice, fresh start."

The perfectly clear and pointed comparisons here are perhaps too obvious to be extremely effective, but the irony is certainly bitter. Dorothy Parker, with each little stroke, builds Mr. Durant's portrait. He himself behaves like a male dog in the presence of females, but it is the female dog that is vile. He is quite unaware of his resemblance to the male dog and very smug in his righteous "purity."

Since fiction deals very largely with the portrayal of emotions and emotional happenings, the details chosen should obviously be such as can convey emotions. The exact emotion felt *by* the character and as much of it as possible, is our artistic goal. Mr. Durant is clear in the light of the things he *feels* and so are Rosemary and Mr. Peacock. Feeling interwoven with action, supporting action and supported by it, advancing with it, is the ideal.

"Big Blonde," [4] a deeper, more rounded, more sympathetic character than most of the people who wander through Dorothy Parker's collections, advances always in terms of both feeling and action. In her twenties, she was meeting lots of men and "laughing at their jokes and telling them she loved their neckties. . . . Popularity seemed to her to be worth all the work that had to be put into its achievement. Men liked you because you were fun, and when they liked you they took you out, and there you were. So, and successfully, she was fun. She was a good sport. Men like a good sport."

Thus, in directly expository narrative, Hazel Morse's basic motivation and trait are revealed in the first two pages of the story. Then comes an explanation of the resulting poverty of mind and resource for this woman whose one idea was to be a good sport. In her much desired marriage we see another phase of her character: she is essentially domestic, passionately in love with Herbie and marriage, tired from her earlier

[4] *Op. cit.*

efforts to attract and hold men, growing more and more blowzy, and relaxing more and more into a natural senti-mental weepiness. "She would cry long and softly over news-paper accounts of kidnaped babies, deserted wives, unem-ployed men, strayed cats, heroic dogs. . . ."

"Honestly," she would say to Herbie, "all the sadness there is in the world when you stop to think about it!"

But Herbie comes to resent this change from the girl who was a good sport and then "it seemed without transition, they were enemies." When Herb finally started to leave her, her "head was beginning to ache bumpingly and her voice had a dreary tiresome tone," but true to form, she gallantly offered a final drink and a "mud in your eye." Before he stepped out the door she said facetiously, "Pardon my wet glove."

Next in a succession of efforts to attract and then hold a series of supporting lovers, Hazel becomes more and more tired of the effort to be a good sport, takes to heavier drink-ing, and becomes still more deeply depressed.

More and more, her days lost their individuality. She never knew dates, nor was sure of the day of the week.

"My God, was that a year ago!" she would exclaim, when an event was recalled in conversation.

She was tired so much of the time. Tired and blue. Almost every-thing could give her the blues. Those old horses she saw on Sixth Avenue—struggling and slipping along the car-tracks, or standing at the curb, their heads dropped level with their worn knees. The tightly stored tears would squeeze from her eyes as she teetered past on her aching feet in the stubby, champagne-colored slippers.

Now here is a maximum of information conveyed about our heroine's emotional situation, the breakdown so near at hand: her confused sense of time, her tiredness arising, not from work but from depression; her sentimental concern for the horses with which she quite unconsciously identified herself. Parker's skill is at its height here in the use of the horses as symbols that set off Hazel's tears. The emotions are conveyed in a stream of consciousness, combined cleverly with author description of her teetering past in (of all things!) champagne-colored slippers. Here is our blowzy heroine again! It is easy to see why there is more and more necessity for effort if she is to get and hold her men.

Then finally Miss Parker gives it to us in direct statement: "The thought of death came and stayed with her and lent her a sort of drowsy cheer. It would be nice, nice and restful, to be dead." And now our heroine is reading about all the suicides in the papers. "There was an epidemic of self-killings—or maybe it was just that she searched for the stories of them so eagerly that she found many." And finally she comes to the veronal, repeating her old phrase to her image in the mirror as she uncorks the vial, "Well, here's mud in your eye." Her old humor comes to the fore, appealingly indeed, when, as she begins to feel sick she says to herself, "Guess I'll go to bed. . . . Gee, I'm nearly dead" and laughs. "That's a hot one!" But there is no such escape for her. She is brought back to life, praying as she faces a continued existence, that maybe "whisky would be her friend again. She prayed without addressing a God, without knowing a God" and again reverted to her old toast as she lifted her glass to the maid.

The *contrast* between Hazel's actions which the reader watches growing more and more *forced* and the things she *says* brings its own large measure of emotional intensity. There is often tragedy in the antics of the clown. The device of contrast is pointed out to every high school student by his Shakespeare teacher. It is very effective in implying suffering. It goes without saying, of course, that "Big Blonde," by virtue of its emotional quality, the degree of pity and sympathy which it conveys, is a much better story than is that of Mr. Durant, who is treated not as tragic but as depraved. Both characters, however, have symbolic values that give them places in any gallery of contemporary portraits. Mr. Durant is pretty much in one color, etched in bitter acid; Hazel is painted with the color and roundness of a Rubens. Both stories reveal the Parker acuteness, the Parker sense of economy, the Parker flair for focus. There is no loose impressionism here; no chance for the reader to miss the point. There is subtlety at times, but not the sort of obliqueness that makes Katherine Mansfield so challenging.

Focus is best secured, in the case of the writer none too sure of his way, by the use of a *list of traits*. He must, however, never give the reader his list; never bunch traits in direct description, telling about them. This above all he must avoid. But he may find it profitable to *use* a list made up in advance of writing. Such a list can serve to hold the character together into a consistent whole, especially if our writer knows what kinds of traits usually go together, knows even the consistencies between apparent inconsistencies. But if he writes from more direct inspiration and would be deterred by the intellectualizing described by Poe in building up "The Raven," then he may well profit by the making of a list after the story has been written, thereby perhaps eliminating any irrelevant material which might blur the picture. It may help him, if he prepares his list in advance, to write down the ways in which he will show traits; the gestures, conversational high-points and remarks, the acts. This sort of character *dossier* is used by a good many writers. It goes with a more intellectual working out of a story; it has not, perhaps, very much to do with inspiration. In any case the writer *must* be aware of shades of character, of nuances, of tones, as we have already said. And if you think that even the really inspired do not know these goals, are not aware of these tones, just read the notes, letters, and diaries of authors from Hawthorne to Mansfield.

Mansfield's notes about her work, in the collection *The*

Dove's Nest, are illuminating for one who wonders how she worked, how she developed her stories.

Today I begin to write, seriously, *The Weak Heart*—a story which fascinates me *deeply*. What I feel it needs so peculiarly is a very subtle variation of tense from the present to the past and back again —and softness, lightness, and the feeling that all is in bud, with a play of humour over the character of Roddie. And the feeling of the Thorndon Baths, the wet, moist, oozy . . . no, I know how it must be done.

Mansfield has another note under the title "A Weak Heart."

Roddie on his bike in the evening, with his hands in his pockets, *doing marvels* by that dark tree at the corner of May Street.

Some of her other notes are as follows:

Six Years After:
A wife and husband on board a steamer. They see someone who reminds them. The cold buttons.

Our Maude:
Husband and wife play duets: *And a one a two a three, a one a two three one!* His white waistcoats. Wifeling and Mahub! What a girl you are!

At Karori:
The little lamp. I seen it. And then they were silent.

This last example gives us almost the exact phraseology of the end of "The Doll's House" and thus affords another example of the way in which a writer starts with the particular act or speech which later comes to form his concluding revelation. These notes all deal, in reality, with the most delicate of characterization. They indicate how completely Mansfield knew what her tone was to be before she began writing. Hawthorne's notebooks also reveal this same specific and careful attention to the exact note. There is no better way to write than to have the end clearly in mind, even unto the hero's last words. Julia Peterkin once illustrated this point by telling how she came to write *Black April*. It began with her hearing the final words of a dying man, proud of his great size, whose legs had been cut off. "Bury me in a man's sized box," he said.

A clear picture of one's character needs, perhaps, more detail in the list or *dossier* than will ever appear in the written story. But somehow one's idea of the character to be written about must be very clear: how he looks, how he carries himself, moves, stands, walks; how he dresses; what he thinks about and how he thinks it; what drives, what conflicts, what motives he has; what they are going to get him into, and how he is going to feel about his fate. Above all the writer needs to know the character's attitude toward *himself*. Is he secure or insecure? Is he self-possessed or ingratiating? Is he servile or aggressive? And in what specific actions does he show his traits?

What kind of eyes does our hero have, shifting or steady? Staring or sparkling, kind or cold, gay or sad? What kind of mouth—narrow, set, thin, tight, tense, rigid, stiff, surrounded by lines of depression? Or is it upcurving, happy, confident, free? What are the hands like? Are they open and free or clenched and grasping? What is the voice like? Is it deep, mellow, jovial, assured, affirmative? Or is it thin, "castrated," uncertain, strained?

Above all, what few special traits will best reflect the inner man? What will best *symbolize* his nature and the character of his relationships with himself and others? All such matters are of immense concern to a writer. They are the very essence of characterization.

And yet we by no means always find details of characterization expressed directly in so many words. Indeed, we may form our own picture with a minimum of direct help from the author. Alfred in Morley Callaghan's "All the Years of Her Life," can be clear to each of us in his own way. The author tells us only that he wears a white apron in the store, that he has "alert, frightened blue eyes," and that he has a thin face with "tiny pimples over his cheek-bone." The pimples are, of course, symbolic of adolescence and a sort of weakness —of a state between childhood and maturity, and Alfred is just such an unformed personality. The fact that he is so un-formed gives his final vision of himself and his mother its affirmative quality; we feel that Alfred can use his new knowl-edge from now on. He has not come by it too late in life.

In "The Killers," by Hemingway, one begins to feel the ugliness before there is a word of direct description, merely through what the killers say. Then at the end of three or four hundred words of action we find that Al "wore a derby hat and a black overcoat buttoned across the chest. His face was small and white and he had tight lips. He wore a silk muffler and gloves." The other man was dressed in much the same way; and both men ate with their gloves on. This vivid characterization proceeds, except for these details, entirely by way of conversation. Later, the author says that the de-parting killers "in their tight overcoats and derby hats looked like a vaudeville team." This is the perfect delineation, im-plying an ironic contrast between the deadliness of their pur-pose and the ridiculousness of their resemblance to funny entertainers.

We are not told what Mrs. Whipple looks like in Kath-erine Anne Porter's story, "He," yet how clearly we see her! We see her through her thoughts and her speeches, and the little reference to her black shirtwaist put on because she "couldn't stand to go looking like charity." We come to know Mrs. Whipple very well and she is the main character in the story, rather than the idiot boy, powerfully as he is drawn. Miss Porter has been more generous with descriptive detail about the boy, but with him, too, the picture grows by the masterful use of various technical devices. Unforgettable is the picture of Him at last surprisingly aware of something happening, "scrubbing away big tears that rolled out of the corners of his eyes. He sniveled and made a gulping noise." And poor Mrs. Whipple kept saying, "Oh, honey, you don't feel so bad, do you?" for he seemed to be accusing her of something.

It is a mistake, we must emphasize, to oversimplify character to the extent of making it *only* the embodiment of a trait. One works, even in the shortest story, for the ideal combination of *main tone* and *overtones*. Overtones add richness. Thus Rosemary in "A Cup of Tea" is not only a self-dramatizing, posturing egocentric, she is also avid for admiration, materialistic, and greedy, and basically insecure in her feeling about her husband's love which is, to the reader, clearly whole. Rosemary has a dominant character tone, a composite of these related traits; and the result is a clear focus, a brilliant portrait. Great is the value of richness, of roundness, and of subtleties in characterization.

To see overtones is, of course, to see life not too simply. The impressionist hints at many things, conveying a sense of color and richness. Taking advantage of associative processes, he conveys the more interesting and exciting idea of a person who is more than one simplified trait. A feeling for relationships, resemblances, color, atmosphere, tonal effects, incongruous details, shapes, scents, and sounds, brings fresh revelation, greater awareness of shifting life and personality. The student of Conrad will know the artistry with which such impressions are created. Henry James also mastered it; and so did, above all, Marcel Proust, Thomas Wolfe, Virginia Woolf, and James Joyce. Such mastery usually comes through the command of oblique techniques and especially through use of the stream of consciousness, the adequate handling of indirect discourse, time elements, and effective symbolism and imagery. We have only, indeed, just begun to understand the intricacies of word association. The science of semantics is very new.

Earlier we emphasized the necessity of close unity, especially in characterization in the short story. Belatedly, in the foregoing remarks, we have tried to indicate other values arising from complexities. After all, the beauty of characterization in a work of art is, as James said, "the close, the curious, the deep." Speaking of Strether, the hero of *The Ambassadors*, James wrote: [5]

> I rejoiced in the promise of a hero so mature, who would give me thereby the more to bite into—since it's only into thickened motive and accumulated character, I think, that the painter of life bites more than a little.

Perhaps the formula for one's first efforts at characterization is to strive most of all for *focus*, beginning with the relatively simple, easily portrayed, and working toward a richer, rounder effect which will be more ideally satisfying to the discriminating reader. Complexity has its own values in fiction, as in life.

[5] *Op. cit.*, page 310.

.10.

Going Beneath the Surface

WRITERS from Petronius to Thomas Mann have dealt with the conflicts and inconsistencies of human beings; but it remained for the literature of our time to bring science to bear upon the analysis of character. With the rise of psychology and its rapid permeation of all concepts of human relations, it was inevitable that the fiction writer would be influenced by new considerations. We find, therefore, that he is attempting more and more, especially in the "literary" publications, and to some extent in the women's slicks, to portray characters that hold up under psychological analysis. Many are the stories, as we have pointed out, about children's being conditioned in the wrong direction. This is a relatively easy method of adapting psychological theory to writing. The other method—dealing with adults who have already developed given psychic tendencies—is more difficult. Carried to extremes it produces the case history, as obvious and as coldly intellectual as a laboratory report. The too-clear mother complex in the hands of a bungler is only boring. There is, moreover, no longer any point in just showing *general* mother fixation; here again we have come to the necessity for the special kind of fixation which takes our story out of the general and into the particular. The problem is to use material that is case history, to bury the psychological jargon and labels, and to give the characters that dramatic potentiality which arouses reader suspense and sympathy. In other words only literary art can make the case history an *emotional* experience for the reader. The whole analytic approach to writing is filled with perils; yet we cannot overlook it if our writing is to reflect the time in which we live.

The universals of analytical psychology, a few of which we pointed out in Chapter 4, are the particulars of the modern novelist. Analytical techniques and observations offer him tools and insights that are new to fiction. They do not, however, show him people who are different from the people of earlier times, because basic human nature does not change greatly. Human drives and urges remain much the same, modified in some of their manifestations, of course, by the cultures in which they exist. Hence it is that we must recognize that earlier writers produced characterizations that seem sound today and that they arrived at their conclusions about human nature simply by more direct and "inspirational" means; not inspired by the gods, as Plato believed, but by their own acute powers of observation. Earlier writers, let us say Chaucer, Laurence Sterne, Dickens, Balzac, Dostoyevsky, Proust—to say nothing of the greatest of them all, Shakespeare—gave us characters that could easily have been the product of contemporary analysis.

How modern is Hawthorne's Reverend Dimmesdale, supposed to be "a miracle of holiness" but guiltily conscious of being "a polution and a lie" and therefore overwhelmed both emotionally and physically by his sin! The extrovert Hester was not made ill, however, though she had to bear the scarlet letter publicly upon her bosom; she merely turned to good works and thus earned a place for herself in the same community which had ostracized her. Hawthorne's knowledge was extremely modern, more modern indeed, than that of some practising physicians who do not recognize the psychic basis of much physical illness. Hawthorne, deeply influenced as he was by the false assumptions of his Salem, nevertheless really belongs in our world.

In entering upon any discussion of the science of psychology and fiction, we are upon ground that is controversial, so far as creative writing is concerned. Yet to ignore the tremendous movement would be to present the subject of characterization inadequately. Let us at the outset say that the following discussion is offered tentatively; and that we shall fall back upon much more competent judgments, which are already numerous in the literary journals and in the books of the last twenty years.

Professor Herbert Muller, for instance, wrote in his *Modern Fiction*[1] that a great deal of modern literature would be "almost unintelligible" to one unfamiliar with the vocabulary of psychoanalysis. Dr. Muller makes the point that "the neat, rounded, transparent types still persist in conventional realism, still make pleasant companions, but many novelists now consider them too artificial, and the traditional explanations of behavior inadequate."

They have in the first place become interested in abnormal psychology, with its important implications for theoretically normal men. They have learned, moreover, that the dividing line between normality and abnormality is far from clear or fixed, and that much seemingly irregular behavior is lawful and natural. They are therefore apt, like Proust or Gide, to throw into sharp relief the irrational, incongruous elements of personality; they give us jagged characters impossible to fit into snug categories—characters not consistently and comfortably eccentric, like Mr. Micawber, because they are not exhibited as freaks and placed in side shows. Above all, novelists have discovered the immense well of the unconscious. Into this they may, like Lawrence, plunge directly and almost disappear from sight; or they may, like Sherwood Anderson, remain on the surface only to watch what comes up out of the depths and to picture the havoc wrought upon conventional designs for living. And the culmination of such interests has been an effort to expose the whole of human consciousness—the popular stream-of-consciousness is only the most

[1] New York: Funk and Wagnalls Company, 1937.

literal of the several methods employed. The final effect of all these innovations is at any rate the same: a breaking up of the familiar, more or less symmetrical patterns of personality, and an emphasis upon obscure, inconsistent, unpredictable, often inexplicable impulses and emotions.

Discussing the main schools of psychoanalysis, Professor Muller concludes,

But all these schools have united in emphasizing the concept of a divided or "split" personality struggling with itself, often unconscious of its own purposes, often seeking to fulfill these purposes by means that it refuses or is unable clearly to define.

Dr. Muller adds that artists have at any rate found Freud's system "stimulating, if only because it is more dynamic than the behavioristic psychology it in some ways resembles, and constantly stresses wilful action, purposeful striving—the element of conflict by which drama lives." He also pays tribute to the *Gestalt* theories in which the stress is upon "discrete *wholes* as the essence of experience." This school, he says, "buttresses the work of the impressionists" because it regards "immediate, naïve impressions as the primary means of apprehending reality, and introspection as artificial and secondary. Hence they confirm the value of the sensory impressions to which the artist of every age is especially sensitive. . . ."

Dr. Muller is only one of the many competent critics who have expressed themselves on the importance of the new knowledge about and point of view toward character. One must reiterate that the writer is now up against the necessity of a deeper insight into human nature. Whether he likes it or not, both editors and literary critics (to say nothing of the better educated readers) will bring the new theories to bear in their judgments of his work. Literary critics, Dr. Muller points out, have been "furnished with sharper tools." And he adds:

But the chief contribution of psychology is not the specific knowledge that critics have picked up. It is rather the new way of looking at things that has enabled them to see around the corner of habitual beliefs, helped them to escape the tyranny of habitual verbalizations. Psychologists have unveiled holy mysteries, stimulated direct thinking.

We have seen, more recently, the direct result of this tendency in the presentation by Hollywood of such movies as *Spellbound* and *The Lost Weekend*, as well as, earlier, *Of Human Bondage*, *Mädchen in Uniform*, and the Orson Welles version of *The Magnificent Ambersons*. The awards, the Oscars, indicate this tendency to recognize the superiority of dramatizations that have been worked out according to modern psychological theory.

Floyd Dell once wrote that the Freudian point of view has become "so wide-spread that the writer who has not learned to occupy it to some extent is out of tune with the age in which he is living." Mr. Dell thought that it was a necessary part of any writer's intellectual apparatus. And Professor John T. Frederick goes still further. He believes in the writer's understanding of the psychology not only of the characters in the story, but also of himself.

Any teacher who has met the fumbling efforts of writers who are attempting to put labels on human behavior on the basis of a little knowledge of psychology, who have a few catch words or a few stock explanations, will certainly agree that psychology can be a dangerous tool. Yet the more obvious facts do remain. "Exhaustive character study is an adult occupation, a philosophical occupation," wrote H. G. Wells in his *Experiment in Autobiography*, adding that he was taking more interest in it than ever before. He came to the conclusion that we are moving in the direction of freer discussion of living people and that as honest biography grows, the need even for fiction will decline. Be that as it may, there is freer discussion all down the line now. The writer should be prepared to make the most of it.

John Crowe Ransom, writing in *The Saturday Review of Literature*, as early as October 4, 1924, commented that our literary giants "hitherto have not been so conspicuously lacking in the depth of their psychology—that is in their power to psychoanalyze—as the new school might wish to believe." He then, however, points to Henry James, Joseph Conrad, and John Galsworthy and suggests that "with access to psychoanalysis proper they might have found truth and depth even readier to their hands and teeming with vaster multitudes of significant life forms."

Recognition of this mine of literary values was rapid in the 30's; and Frederick J. Hoffman, writing in 1945 his *Freudianism and the Literary Mind*,[2] was able to present impressive evidence of this continuing growth. His "selected bibliography" contains twelve pages of intriguing references, many of them from the statements of creative writers themselves. The most important literary man to go all-out for psychoanalysis was, of course, Thomas Mann, who not only used it extensively in his novels but also wrote essays about it. James Joyce made even more extensive use of it in his stream-of-consciousness writing, especially in his depiction of dreams and of "the several stages by which the individual recedes from consciousness, and of the aesthetic problem involved in each case," as Hoffman indicates. Joyce also "thought that much of character motivation could be more adequately developed by recourse to the psychoanalytic explanation of familial relationships, than by any other method." Hoffman says:

The twentieth-century artist wished to believe that he possessed more than an arbitrary device for enclosing a story within a framework. The dream was for him a way of pointing to the complexity of

[2] Baton Rouge: Louisiana State University Press, 1945

a character's motives and his diverse range of possibilities for action. For example, Conrad Aiken—who in 1915 had read Freud's *Interpretation of Dreams* in the English translation—considers the dream an essential means of explaining the sources of action.

Hoffman calls Sherwood Anderson, "psychoanalyst by default," and indicates that Anderson heard a great deal about Freud in his Chicago literary group, that he even submitted to "amateur psychoanalysis," and yet cannot be proved to have accepted it; indeed, he seems to have been sarcastic about it. Nevertheless Anderson, too, was much interested in the study of repressions, and he and Freud clearly worked "along parallel courses." Hoffman points also to Dostoyevsky who had this willingness to "explore and exploit all suggestions about the irrationality of man."

D. H. Lawrence knew Freud's work well, having read it in the original, and wrote essays attacking phases of it as too intellectualized and "scientific." But for all Lawrence's quarreling with Freud, Hoffman thinks, "he was ever aware of the fact that Freud was patrolling the same grounds," and Lawrence recognized "that his antagonist had made profound discoveries about that world in which the artist was most interested." Lawrence was especially interested in the Oedipus complex, the effects of which he portrayed in his writings.

Franz Kafka, who is the subject of widespread and intensive literary interest today, offers, Hoffman believes, the best case in twentieth-century letters for the Freudian, underscoring as he does "the significance for him of his lifelong struggle with his father whom he could neither renounce nor accept." Hoffman points out that Kafka's writings are "persistent demonstrations of an anxiety neurosis—a constant flight from anticipated affective danger." In a now famous letter to his father, Kafka referred to his lifelong belief in his "own incapability" which was instilled by his father and which prevented him from marrying. "There is no question about Kafka's knowledge of psychoanalysis, or its peculiar pertinence to his case." The knowledge clearly entered into Kafka's fictional subject-matter, which was concerned with father and son relationships and with man's relationship to God. But Kafka himself quarreled with some of Freud's views of religion and of the power of analytic therapy.

These are some of the most important fiction writers discussed in detail in Hoffman's book. Others also come in for illuminating and even more convincing discussion, since they have been frank about the influence of Freud upon their own writings. Among them are Waldo Frank, Conrad Aiken, Ludwig Lewisohn, Dylan Thomas, Henry Miller, Joseph Freeman, and Arthur Koestler.

Criticism has also been greatly influenced by Freudian theory, which entered on the one hand into critics' views of the fictional story told and on the other into their interpretation of the author's personality and life-view. Mr. Hoffman's conclusion here is as careful and objective as are his conclusions about Freudian "influence" upon creative writing.

Critical exploitation of psychoanalysis has been marked often by abuse and misunderstanding. Not only have critics often sinned against good critical sense by forcing the writers of the time into pigeonholes of theory; they have frequently mistreated Freud's original remarks about the psychological nature of the artist. Three at least of modern critics may, however, be said to have shown great intelligence in their appropriation of Freudian materials. These men— Herbert Read, Edmund Wilson, Kenneth Burke—have made important contributions to a sane estimate of Freud's meaning for modern aesthetics.

One approach to this field is such a book as Dr. Karen Horney's clear exposition for the layman, *The Neurotic Personality of Our Time*.[3] It affords an excellent introduction to analysis. Dr. Horney explains that the deviation from the "normal" which we call neurosis arises from the usually

[3] New York: W. W. Norton & Company, Inc., 1937.

unconscious conflicts arising within the individual as a result of his clashing infantile and natural desires. A neurosis, she tells us, has two easily seen characteristics: rigidity in reaction and a discrepancy between potentialities and accomplishments. The neurotic is unduly suspicious and spiteful without reason. Anxieties and defenses are common to all forms of neurosis, fears that are directed against imaginary evil, rather than real and justified dangers. The neurotic invariably suffers more than the normal person but often does not realize his own suffering. Dr. Horney defines a neurosis as "a psychic disturbance brought about by fears and defenses against these fears, and by attempts to find compromise solutions for conflicting tendencies." We all have basic problems of "competition, fears of failure, emotional isolation, distrust of others and of our own selves." We have attitudes of giving and getting affection; attitudes concerning evaluation of self, self-assertion, aggression, sexuality. In the neurotic the normal tendencies are exaggerated and even obsessive. Cultural factors of our time serve to increase the neurotic exaggeration of these normal traits which begin in childhood. Fear is justified if it is based on real dangers; anxiety is not so based and is out of proportion to any danger. "Hostility and anxiety are inextricably interwoven." The common childhood denominator of all is environment with lack of genuine warmth and affection; unjust reproaches; overindulgence suddenly changed to violent rejection; disturbance of the child's friendships, interferences with his interests and desires for achievement, parents "who loose their need for affection on the children."

All such psychological situations are of special interest to authors. Other trends that Dr. Horney points out are "dionysian impulses" toward religion and nature, ecstatic states, "going outside one's self." These tendencies become strong in the neurotic who needs to "break through the shell of individuality and be rid of its limitations and isolations"; yet this neurotic is often incapable of giving himself, sexually or otherwise. In a culture which overemphasizes love as the be-all and end of all troubles, many neurotic people are driven to over-emotional dependence, to over-estimation of values which they themselves are in reality incapable of giving. "The neurotic fears being caught in a web of real feeling," yet his demand for unconditional love is great and he often sets up tests that are impossible. He himself is "barren, selfish, domineering, demanding, possessive, incapable of give-and-take." "He wants to be helpless and taken care of" but at the same time "insists on being omnipotent." "Emotional isolation," says Dr. Horney, "is a calamity if it coincides with apprehensions and uncertainties about one's self."

This all too cursory summary will serve, perhaps, to indicate some of the many avenues of understanding, to say nothing of suggested conflicts and plots to be found in Dr. Horney's book. Her later book, *Self-Analysis*,[4] also offers valuable suggestions. She mentions, for instance, some of the things that can happen to a child who is forced to side with one parent against the other as the result of a mother's demand for "blind devotion." The child Clare's blind acceptance of her mother, coupled with her mother's obvious favoritism toward a brother, led to "a thousand little daily experiences" in which Clare was made to feel insecure: less concern when she was ill, less willingness to treat her as a confidante, less admiration for looks and accomplishments. Combined with this was Clare's feeling produced by the mother, that she had better be on the powerful side of the family, the side of the dominating, sophisticated, and attractive mother. The result was, according to Dr. Horney, that Clare never had a good chance to develop self-confidence. If she complained of unfair treatment she actually received, she was laughed at

[4] New York: W. W. Norton & Company, Inc., 1942.

as a child; in time she came to believe that she was really un-likable. We cannot go into all of Dr. Horney's analytic steps or her analysis of the resulting traits in Clare, but it is suffi-cient to point out here that there are *several* potential stories implied in this single case history. Take for instance, Dr. Horney's summary paragraph outlining the effects of this common family situation.

In consequence of all these factors three neurotic trends developed. One was a compulsive modesty as to her own wishes and demands. This entailed a compulsive tendency to put herself into second place, to think less of herself than of others, to think that others were right and she was wrong. But even in this restricted scope she could not feel safe unless there was someone on whom she could depend, some-one who would protect and defend her, advise her, stimulate her, approve of her, be responsible for her, give her everything she needed. She needed all this because she had lost the capacity to take her life into her own hands. Thus she developed the need for a "partner"—friend, lover, husband—on whom she could depend. She would subordinate herself to him as she had toward her mother. But at the same time, by his undivided devotion to her, he would restore her crushed dignity. A third neurotic trend—a compulsive need to excel others and to triumph over them—likewise aimed at restoration of self-regard, but in addition absorbed all the vindictiveness ac-cumulated through hurts and humiliations.

Dr. Horney's list of neurotic traits includes the ones named above and many others such as "indiscriminate need to please others," "neurotic need for power, domination over others, essential disrespect for others," "need to exploit others and by hook or crook get the better of them," dread of being "ex-ploited as stupid," neurotic "need for perfection, dread of criticism and reproach." All these attitudes, says Dr. Horney, are normal and of human value. What is wrong with them is that in the neurotic the traits lead to a failure to go out to others and to have the quality of "reciprocity." When these feelings lead to positive values and are accompanied by posi-tive feelings for others, they are not neurotic. "Neurotic per-suits are almost a caricature of the human values they resemble." They lack freedom, spontaneity, and meaning. "Not only are the neurotic trends devoid of the human values they mimic, but they do not even represent what the person wants." The person may be merely driven to want things that have no meaning for him when he gets them.

This last theme has appeared repeatedly in literature: one finds it in the works of Charles Norris, Theodore Dreiser, and Sherwood Anderson, to name but a few American writers. Above all, one finds it in Marcel Proust's *Remembrance of Things Past* where social success turned to ashes when the hero achieved it beyond his hopes; and success in love each time led to boredom and rejection of the mistress.

Most disastrous is the effect of the neurotic person upon the life of others. This theme has been used most successfully in countless novels and short stories. It scarcely needs amplification here; but one can offer, at first thought, the example of *Ethan Frome*, Mrs. Wharton's most successful and moving novelette. Here the bitter, complaining, neurotic invalid manages to destroy all joy for those about her. She only snaps out of her illness after she has driven her husband and the innocent girl he loves to an attempted suicide. The play about the Brownings, *The Barrets of Wimpole Street*, is a famous example of the blighting effect of the neurotic parent. Recent plays abound in this theme: for instance, "*Papa Is All*," and "*The Glass Menagerie*."

The portrait that Josephine Johnson's narrator paints of herself in "Safe," referred to earlier, is that of an unbalanced woman, unwittingly revealing her neurotic traits. The general plot is old; but it has been given a new turn by the emphasis upon psychologically consistent traits: envy, jealousy, hostility, insecurity, alienation from the rest of the world. Listen to her:

I began to hate Collin. Not for himself—at one time feeling even a sort of mild love and affection for him, although I was years older and not at ease with men—but hating him because he had come into our ife, and brought only pain in small places while he talked of lifting the whole earth's burden.

Later she says, defensively, "I was not jealous but full of fear. Whole afternoons I would stand thinking of them." The reader sees beneath the denial, of course, that the narrator *was* intensely jealous. Her words "not at ease with men" give us another clue and "pain in small places" indicates that other people's happiness only made her unhappy. The story begins when the harm has been done, at Z, with the older sister saying, "If I'd known before." Then we see that her sister did not confide in her, pretending to be looking for bulbs rather than Collin's letter. This lack of confidence is significant. The narrator speaks of the "water in the tubs grown cold, . . . my mind on them with a hardness of obsession"; of her intensity of feeling—she is "sick inside." Later she speaks of her sense of emptiness, futility, "Mary would be gone, myself alone, putting up jars of bean and apple to no purpose," to fill hours, empty years. Later we see her defensiveness, her guilt for her crime: "I felt sick and afraid enough to die, and yet strong with the sense of having done a hard but righteous thing." Then later comes, just as one would expect, the death wish: "I wished to God that I could die!" And finally we come to Mary's insanity and Abby returns to her opening self-defense: "How could I see this would happen to her? But she's safe now. She doesn't suffer. . . . Maybe it was the best thing after all. . . ." Nothing could be more revealing of Abby's complete failure to face the terrible result of her own actions; nothing more ironic than her use of the word "safe." The entire characterization is analytically consistent and it shows, too, how far gone Abby is in her failure to face the facts.

Now just how Abby *got* that way is not the point of this story. The point is the revealing portrait of the half-insane adult woman, so like other trouble-makers.

Another theme familiar to the psychologist is the mother-son complex. Dr. Karl Menninger shows, in his *Love Against Hate*,[5] how the buried resentments of a man too much dominated as a child by his mother, lead to an incapacity to love any woman properly. He mentions the woman who put a diaper on her seven-year old son; the mother who pushes her son's ears against his head and squeezes his nostrils together so that he will not look like a burly negro. Mothers often take out their resentments against their own inability to love their husbands properly by warping their children's attitudes toward love; they may also love the child too possessively. The woman who loathes her own life, built up with some idea of what is proper and ennobling for women, living an unhappy and unrewarding life with her husband, may make many wrong demands upon her children; may even try to keep them from marrying. Dr. Menninger reports that such a woman speaking of a woman who responds naturally to men, will often say, "Men may be attracted to such women, but they don't marry them."

Dr. Menninger also makes the statement that "plurality of direct sexual outlets," indicates the opposite of what it is popularly supposed to indicate. Such a man may assert his masculinity by having relations with two women, neither of which are satisfying because both loves are incomplete. His conduct may be prompted by fear of loss; he may feel safer with many women than with one. He may, however, like to keep his wife to fall back upon and hence shuns divorce. He keeps himself that way from feeling "completely in the power of one woman."

One main problem of the human being, according to analytic theory, is to achieve freedom from his fixation upon his mother as his first love object. The adjusted person has broken the bond; the maladjusted has not. A dominating mother may cause her son to hold his identification with her

[5] New York: Harcourt, Brace and Company, Inc., 1942.

all his life and thus ruin all his relations with other women. He may become effeminate, ever striving to be masculine and always failing and always aware of tensions within himself which he does not understand. Likewise a girl's too great need of her mother and hostility to her father may involve her in either unconscious or conscious attitudes which ruin her relationships with men. From such maladjustments come a horde of evils. The grown man who must consult "mamma" at all turns is an object of derision to others. Mr. Milktoast is a very real man. If he marries at all he is quite likely to marry a woman in the image of his mother and she, too, will rob him of his manhood.

Marcel Proust gave a marvelous picture of another type of mother fixation in *Remembrance of Things Past*. The little boy who longed so excessively for his mother's good night kisses kept on depending upon her emotionally. When she died and left him to stand on his own feet, he retreated more than ever from adult struggle with the outside world. Fortunately for the world, he turned his neurosis and his asthmatic invalidism into productive channels and, after years of comparative literary inactivity, produced the monumental novel which is one of the world's great masterpieces. The novel is faithful to the main facts of Proust's astonishing life.

D. H. Lawrence also wrote of the mother fixation, revealing the youth's identification with his mother and his efforts to break away and into a love relationship with another woman. In *Sons and Lovers* we leave him whimpering, "Mother." She was "the only thing that held him up." Lawrence was certainly aware of the awful sexual conflicts arising from such bondage, and there are many evidences of his knowledge in his writing which was so deeply concerned with sexual urges and frustrations, with, as Professor Beach said, "the welling up into conscious life of the great subterranean waters of unconscious vital force."

Now the concern of the fiction writer is very often, as we have already pointed out, chiefly the portrayal of character. But how seldom does he attempt to show the inner man or how he became what he is! Fiction has too often in the past been concerned largely with the hero's relations with other people only; or, at best, with his more or less conscious ideas about his own role and the conflicting desires which animate him.

Irwin Shaw reveals in "Main Currents of American Thought," the devastating effect of the selfish mother's demands upon her sensitive son, a script writer, who is torn between his sense of duty to her and his desire to do his work and make something of his life. "Don't give it [money] to me if you don't want to, Andrew," says his mother. And Andrew replies, completely broken in spirit, "I want to, Mom, I want to." But his thoughts are mixed up with plots and lines, and he wonders if he can keep it up through the years ahead. The sensitive youth tied body and soul to the demands of a neurotic parent is one of the most pitiful and tragic figures in the world. If he has been really tied in, really conditioned to helplessness before the parental demands, his conflicts are almost insuperable. They give him a feeling of true bewilderment. They are of the essence, then, for fiction.

"It seems probable that if we were never bewildered there would never be a story to tell about us," wrote Henry James; "we should partake of the superior nature of the all-knowing immortals whose annals are dreadfully dull so long as flurried humans are not, for the positive relief of the bored Olympians, mixed up with them." It is interesting in reflecting upon James' idea to remember that the Olympians were prone to get mixed up in their family relations, and that incest was common among them! The theme of unconscious wish to incest is far from uncommon in psychoanalysis.

Much of man's behavior only *seems* to be inconsistent. It

is the result of basic conflicting drives; sometimes they are unconscious, in which case they may produce the greatest bewilderment indeed. We love someone, but we also hate; we want to be loved deeply, but we are afraid of "chains." The song "Don't Fence Me In" states this common attitude. But these are the things which make fiction writing and reading interesting. The author is a sort of character detective, sleuthing out the configurations, patterns, and motives.

In conclusion let us admit that, for the reader who is familiar with psychological theory, this discussion is obvious and superficial. It is not, however, intended for the people who are already aware of these facts and approaches. It is for those who are unaware; and it claims to be only a hint of the treasures to be found in text-books, psychological case histories, and the writings of analysts. The reader is again warned that a little knowledge is dangerous; these excerpts and condensations of theory should serve only to stimulate interest in the psychological approach.

One thing is certain: characterization demands a great deal of insight. How one comes by that insight, whether by study of the science of psychology—and there are several different schools of thought—or by direct observation, does not, perhaps, greatly matter.

.11.

Social Comment in Fiction

W E have emphasized psychological subject-matter and have indicated types of social conflict. To let it stand at that, however, would be to give a one-sided view of fiction. Fiction writers have always been concerned with social comment; and especially in the last century, which has brought such vast social, economic, and political changes. During the first quarter of the century the outstanding writers were protesting against the growth of industrialism with its monopolies and standardizing influences. The progressive movement early in the century had its counterpart in a literary movement which voiced the protest against outworn traditions, economic inequalities, and world war. In the between-wars period, in which discontent and a sense of futility and despair grew with the growth of economic depression and of fascism, some of the outstanding writers were attempting to handle the social theme. Their contributions consisted of new emphasis in subject-matter and newly invented techniques.

Since Sherwood Anderson is one of the most significant members and a spokesman of a group that insisted upon a new realism and a greater sincerity, and since his short stories have for us today a real validity, we shall consider his theme of the warping effect which narrow, small-town life has upon the men and women groping for a richer and fuller experience.

Confused and baffled all his life by the complexities of

modern civilization, resenting business routines, seeing the death of creativeness in industrial society where the worker made only a tiny fragment of the finished product, Anderson voiced the mounting confusion of a protest that he shared with such writers as Theodore Dreiser, Sinclair Lewis, and the Chicago group of poets. Especially did he protest against Puritanical attitudes toward sex and against the "false truths" that get between people and isolate them from each other. Listen to him in the preface to *Winesburg, Ohio*, which he calls, "The Book of the Grotesque": [1]

All the men and women the writer had ever known had become grotesques.

The grotesques were not all horrible. Some were amusing, some almost beautiful, and one, a woman all drawn out of shape, hurt the old man by her grotesqueness.

Among the grotesques in Winesburg, Ohio, is Wing Biddlebaum whose story "is a story of hands."

Their restless activity, like unto the beating of the wings of an imprisoned bird, had given him his name. Some obscure poet of the town had thought of it. The hands alarmed their owner. He wanted to keep them hidden away and looked with amazement at the quiet inexpressive hands of other men who worked beside him in the fields, or passed, driving sleepy teams on country roads.

His story, so poetically and sympathetically narrated, is that of the sensitive, affectionate, outgoing young Pennsylvania school teacher. "He was one of those rare, little-understood men who rule by a power so gentle that it passes as a lovable weakness."

Wing was much loved by the boys of his school. But tragedy came when one half-witted boy "became enamoured" of him, imagined "unspeakable things," and went forth to tell his dreams as fact. "Strange hideous accusations fell from his loose-hung lips. Through the Pennsylvania town

[1] New York: The Viking Press, 1919.

went a shiver." Rumor grew and finally Wing was set upon by the saloon-keeper, beaten, and kicked. "I'll teach you to put your hands on my boy, you beast;" and the angry mob, threatening to lynch him, drove him out of town.

Thus it was that Wing became an outcast, "looking sixty at the age of forty" and always striving to conceal his hands. "Although he did not understand what had happened he felt that the hands must be to blame." Anderson finally leaves him in his lonely house by the ravine. He does not point his moral, but Wing Biddlebaum is clearly just as much a victim of mob psychology as is the negro in the lynching party.

The story "Mother" is that of a woman determined that her reporter son shall escape the blighting life that Winesburg has inflicted upon her. Mortally ill, Elizabeth Willard finally decides that she will kill her husband, who is determined to hold their son there. But her strength leaves her, and then the son comes in. "I'm going to get out of here," he said. "I don't know where I shall go or what I shall do but I am going away."

The woman in the chair waited and trembled. An impulse came to her. "I suppose you had better wake up," she said. "You think that? You will go to the city and make money, eh? It will be better for you, you think, to be a business man, to be brisk and smart and alive?" She waited and trembled.

The son shook his head. "I suppose I can't make you understand, but oh, I wish I could," he said earnestly. "I can't even talk to father about it. I don't try. There isn't any use. I don't know what I shall do. I just want to go away and look at people and think."

Silence fell upon the room where the boy and woman sat together. Again, as on the other evenings, they were embarrassed. After a time, the boy tried again to talk. "I suppose it won't be for a year or two but I've been thinking about it," he said, rising and going toward the door. "Something father said makes it sure that I shall have to go away." He fumbled with the door knob. In the room the silence became unbearable to the woman. She wanted to cry out with joy because of the words that had come from the lips of her son, but the expression of joy had become impossible to her. "I think you had better go out among the boys. You are too much indoors," she said. "I thought I would go for a little walk," replied the son stepping awkwardly out of the room and closing the door.

Over and over again Anderson repeats his protest: against the "truths" that men use against one another; against the frustrations and repressions that make people grotesque; against the *tabus* on sexual honesty and sexual experience which often result in "black loneliness" and a *hunger* for fellowship denied. He was interested, says Mr. Kazin, in

"sex as a disturbance in consciousness, the kind of disturbance that drove so many of his heroes out of the world of constraint; but once he had got them out of their houses, freed them from convention and repression, their liberation was on a plane with their usually simultaneous liberation from the world of business. It was their loneliness that gave them significance in Anderson's mind, the lies that they told themselves and each other to keep the desperate fictions of conventionality; and it was inevitably the shattering of that loneliness, the emergence out of that uneasy twilit darkness in which his characters always lived, that made their triumph and, in his best moments, Anderson's own." [2]

Anderson's sense of men's inarticulateness, revealed so clearly in the passage quoted from "Mother," was one of his finest literary assets, lifting his often subjective work into the universal. The inarticulateness was, he thought, the result of the crude, hypocritically "moral" environment that drove men farther and farther away from each other only to face walls of isolation from which there was no escape. Anderson's characters are, like Anderson himself, as his autobiographical novel *A Story Teller's Story* clearly shows, always trying to get away from what holds them fast.

In this book, so illuminating for people who wish to write fiction, Anderson tells about how he walked out of an advertising agency. He was determined to no longer concern himself with his "buying and selling. It may be all right for

[2] Alfred Kazin, *On Native Grounds*. New York: Reynal and Hitchcock, Inc., 1942.

others but for me it is poison. . . . I am going to wander about. I am going to sit with people, tell tales of people, what they are thinking, what they are feeling. The devil! It may even be that I am going forth in search of myself."

Anderson's search for himself is the search of many, if not all, creative artists; his reaction to *bourgeois* society is the reaction that Thomas Mann has written of in *Buddenbrooks*. It arises from a deep sense of alienation, of "separateness from the life about," which Anderson thought was common to all Americans. To him it explained the "everlasting get-together movements always going on among business men." Anderson wondered too about his own responsibility for his "lack of finesse" in expressing his thoughts and emotions; wondered how much "could be fairly blamed to the civilization" in which he lived. He wondered if "the giving of itself by an entire generation to mechanical things were really making men all impotent."

Perhaps Anderson's most important contribution to American literature was not so much his ideas about social influences as his revolt against traditional and patterned *forms*. He wanted a looseness of form that was more natural and more true to life itself. He was, of course, influenced by his friend Gertrude Stein. He maintained that there were no plot stories in life. In *A Story Teller's Story*[3] he speaks scornfully of "Poison Plot," and the artificial football story common to the slicks in which "one thought out a plot, as a football coach thought out a new formation that would advance the ball."

But life in the streets of a New England village wasn't like that. No short stories with clever endings—as in the magazines—happened in the streets of the town at all. Life went on and on and little illuminating human things happened. There was drama in the street and in the lives of the people in the street but it sprang directly out of the stuff of life itself.

[3] New York: The Viking Press, 1924.

Anderson's protest, then, was not only against the effects of standardization and mechanization of life itself, but also against the standardization and mechanization of fiction. In an era when the O. Henry plot with its surprise ending was every writer's model, Anderson brought forth the looser form which was based on fidelity to things as they are.

One has been walking in a street and has been much alive. What stories the faces in the streets tell! How significant the faces of the houses! The walls of the houses are brushed away by the force of the imagination and one sees and feels all of the life within. What a universal giving away of secrets! Everything is felt, everything known. Physical life within one's own body comes to an end of consciousness. The life outside oneself is all, everything.

A Story Teller's Story suggests innumerable ideas for short narratives; Anderson gives them away with a prodigal hand, these stories from the streets. He writes with the utmost frankness of his life as a rebellious creative artist, probing his own soul and motives, laughing at his own subterfuges and inconsistencies as a "word fellow"; loving words and the very physical tools of writing, pencils and white surfaces, loving the escape into the lives of others, loving and understanding his fellow men. This is indeed a stimulating and revealing book for the creative writer.

The protest against the evils of contemporary civilization was to be carried much further by the writers of the thirties, members of the "lost generation" who returned from World War I to a world they had made safe for democracy. Democracy was in a bad way they found, seeing the great depression with its unemployment, hunger, and dispossession; and looking at the rising nationalism, fascism, and war menace. These writers were tutored to the celebration of the little man and the description of the desolation and insecurity in which he lived.

Jean-Paul Sartre, writing in *The Atlantic Monthly*[4] for

[4] "American Novelists in French Eyes," *The Atlantic Monthly*.

August 1946, affirms: "The greatest literary development in France between 1929 and 1939 was the discovery of Faulkner, Dos Passos, Hemingway, Caldwell, Steinbeck." Indeed, he says, two thirds of the manuscripts which young French writers submit to his magazine "are written à la Caldwell, à la Hemingway, à la Dos Passos."

"These moralists who report on humanity," he adds, brought about "a veritable revolution in the art of telling a story."

The intellectual analysis which, for more than a century, had been the accepted method of developing character in fiction was no longer anything but an old mechanism badly adapted to the needs of the time. It was opposed to a psychology of synthesis which taught us that a psychological fact is an indivisible whole. It could not be used to depict a group of facts which present themselves as the ephemeral or permanent unity of a great number of perceptions.

Writing of Hemingway, he adds:

We learned from Hemingway to depict, without commentaries, without explanations, without moral judgments, the actions of our characters. The reader understands them because he sees them born and formed in a situation which has made them understandable to him.

And again, speaking of the trio, Hemingway, Faulkner, and Dos Passos, Sartre adds:

They have placed in our hands new and supple instruments, which allow us to approach subjects which heretofore we had no means of treating: the unconscious; sociological events; the true relation of the individual to society, present or past.

Steinbeck's *Grapes of Wrath* is the outstanding novel of economic and social comment written during the depression period. Dos Passos' *U.S.A.* is outstanding in that it reveals a much larger canvas, nothing less than a panorama of the whole United States. Hemingway's *Farewell to Arms* and his *For Whom the Bell Tolls* deal with the still broader topic of war. All three novels are based on concepts which the critics refer to as "collectivistic." They show the solidarity of men and the interrelationships of people living in an interdependent world which is at the same time often chaotic. These writers do not offer any naïve or oversimplified solutions for the problems which they see. They do not wind up, as the word "collectivistic" might imply to some readers, with communism. In fact Dos Passos and Hemingway, at least, expressly deny identification with communism, and Steinbeck's appeal seems to be largely that the oppressed shall use their brains and voices to raise a big shout for greater coöperation between human beings.

Steinbeck's *Grapes of Wrath*,[5] which we have referred to in our brief discussion of kinds of struggle, has a social importance that has been compared with that of *Uncle Tom's Cabin*. Its characters, the Joads, and its farmer group, the Okies, have names which are as symbolic for all of us as the name "Babbitt." The following discussion will serve, perhaps, to indicate what Steinbeck's theme was and what devices he used to produce his strong emotional impact.

First of all, we note that the author has used a sort of backdrop of explanation and description in short chapters interpolated between the various scenes. In other words, he has not left his characters to tell the whole story. We have noted heretofore and shall again, that, in *general*, present day techniques avoid exposition. Steinbeck, however, used the straight expository method and varied it within the short chapters between dramatized portions.

Steinbeck tells us that "the owners of the land came onto the land, or more often a spokesman came," and that "they came in closed cars," drove into the door yards, and "the tenant men stood beside the cars for a while, and then

[5] New York: The Viking Press, 1939.

squatted on their hams and found sticks with which to mark the dust."

In the open doors the women stood looking out, and behind them the children—corn-headed children, with wide eyes, one bare foot on top of the other bare foot, and the toes working. The women and the children watched their men talking to the owner men. They were silent.

Then he gives us his running commentary in which he uses with superb effectiveness a collective kind of thought of the farmers:

yes, they knew, God knows. If the dust only wouldn't fly. If the top would only stay on the soil, it might not be so bad . . .

.   .   .   .

The squatters nodded—they knew, God knew.

But it was too late, the owner men said. Men couldn't get enough produce to eat or pay taxes and had to borrow money at the bank. And the bank, often the distant holding company, lived on interests and profits. They couldn't wait.

The squatting men raised their eyes to understand. Can't we just hang on? Maybe the next year will be a good year.

But the men in cars grew impatient. (Note the realistic detail here, and the humor.)

Soft fingers began to tap the sill of the car window, and hard fingers tightened on the restless drawing sticks. . . . Dogs came sniffling near the owner cars and wetted on all four tires one after another. And chickens lay in the sunny dust and fluffed their feathers to get the cleansing dust down to the skin. In the little sties the pigs grunted inquiringly over the muddy remnants of the slops.

The squatting men looked down again. What do you want us to do? We can't take less share of the crop—we're half starved now. The kids are hungry all the time.

And then the owner men told them that they were going to have to get off the land and "the squatting men stood up angrily."

Grampa took up the land, and he had to kill the Indians and drive them away. And Pa was born here, and he killed weeds and snakes. Then a bad year came and he had to borrow a little money. . . . The bank owned the land then, but we stayed on and we got a little bit of what we raised.

The owner men replied:

We know that—all that. It's not us, it's the bank. A bank isn't like a man. Or an owner with fifty thousand acres, he isn't like a man either. That's the monster.

The bulldozer came and "the man sitting in the iron seat did not look like a man; gloved, goggled, rubber dust mask over nose and mouth, he was a part of the monster, a robot in the seat." And finally he crushed the house and drove off in his tractor.

And the Joad family are among the nameless tenants described in this passage with its oblique intermingling of exposition and colloquial talk. The Joads had to go. And lured by the lying pamphlets of the fruit growers, they joined the great trek west to California.

First we see them getting ready to leave, trying to pile all their most necessary belongings on an old broken down truck. Not counting the two dogs, there were fourteen of them without the preacher, Casy. Could they make it? Could they eat? Casy was very anxious to go too. Pa said:

"An' kin we feed a extra mouth?" Without turning his head he asked, "Kin we, Ma?"

Ma cleared her throat. "It ain't kin we? It's will we?" she said firmly. "As far as 'kin,' we can't do nothin', not go to California or nothin'; but as far as 'will', why, we'll do what we will. An' as far as 'will'—it's a long time our folks been here and east before, an' I never heerd tell of no Joads or no Hazlitts, neither, ever refusin' food an' shelter or a lift on the road to anybody that asked. They's been mean Joads, but never that mean."

In this speech of Ma's, we have the affirmation of the book: the human spirit is triumphant. This is Steinbeck's answer to the doctrine of economic determinism: the answer of the imperishable will that rises above vicissitudes and obstacle. Powerfully, as he shows the helplessness of the Joads before impersonal forces, so he also shows them as undefeated. Ma herself is goodness and affirmation in every act and thought. But it is the preacher, Casy, who pleads for the social application of the principles of Christianity; and it is the hot-headed Tom who thinks that the way out is organization. Tom and Casy are speaking about the pickers working for five cents a box. Casy wants Tom to get his father to tell the scabs to walk out. Tom says:

Think Pa's gonna give up his meat on account a other fellas? An Rosasharn oughta get milk. Think Ma's gonna wanta starve that baby jus' cause a bunch a fellas is yellin' outside a gate?

Casy says:

"This fella in jail, he says, 'Anyways, you do what you can. An', he says, 'the on'y thing you got to look at is that ever' time they's a step fo'ward, she may slip back a little, but she never slips clear back. You can prove that,' he says, 'an' that makes the whole thing right. An' that means they wasn't no waste even if it seemed like they was.'"

This philosophy of Casy's is, of course, the optimistic philosophy which believes that men have it in their power to overcome any obstacles. This is the faith which lies between the fatalistic concept that natural and social laws inevitably and inexorably determine man's destiny, and the old democratic idea of rugged individualism. The Steinbeck philosophy is a liberal middle-of-the-road philosophy, seeing the laws and tendencies, seeing man as a combination of frailty and strength, of evil and good, and yet believing in his power to gradually "step fo'ward."

Toward the end of the book, Steinbeck writes

In the souls of the people the grapes of wrath are filling and growing heavy, growing heavy for the vintage.

The "vintage" is, of course, a world in which men work together, using their collective will to exorcise the economic evils that are threatening their very existence. Steinbeck saw the disorganization of the period and was severe in his denunciation of the State which is all of us. His realism was not bitter because he saw in "the monster" only an impersonal menace that men could cope with if they used their brains. He sets before us no perfect hero; and no one remedy. He does not conceive of the struggle ahead as easy. That struggle is symbolized most perfectly by the wonderful passage early in the novel in which the turtle climbs an embankment. The animal has many set-backs; but it does, nevertheless, make some progress. It is patient, but determined, moving forward, slipping back, but going on, "its old, humorous eyes" looking ahead.

Dos Passos is not as optimistic about the destiny of man, which he shows on a much larger canvas than Steinbeck's and by means of new and startling techniques of narration. His novels tell the story not of any one group of characters, but of several characters that at first seem to have no relation to each other but often do enter directly or indirectly into each other's lives.

In the trilogy *U.S.A.*, he uses many new devices to accomplish his task of showing chaotic America, the "sprawling continent," painting his picture by means of the "newsreel," "The Camera Eye," the biographies of some twenty-five eminent persons, the fictionalized stories of a dozen characters, and an impersonal young job-seeker, balanced at the end by a similar picture of the young job-seeker holding up his thumb at the side of the road as the indifferent cars speed past. The effect is masterly in its realism, satire, political import, and atmospheric significance. At first sight the reader is tempted to feel, "Oh, I know all this" and to be repelled, perhaps, by the jumbled fragments of head-lines, the stream of consciousness techniques in the Camera Eye, and the

broken stories which at first seem to have no relation whatever to each other. But such judgment is mistaken, for this
trilogy is powerful, highly informative in a historical, satirical
sense, and (in a very few passages, it must be admitted)
moving. The contrasts in the lives depicted both biographi-
cally and in fiction are interesting and significant. While
the direct, unscenic narrative lacks the dramatic quality of
Hemingway's or Steinbeck's work, it nevertheless carries
conviction—partly because Dos Passos is, like Sinclair Lewis,
an investigator of the whole contemporary social scene. He
is pro-labor, and very much against all undemocratic tendencies, fiercely democratic in his feeling; admiring Debs and
Veblen, resentful of the Sacco and Vanzetti outrage; above
all, sympathetic with the man who cannot get work, the job-
less young man. But he is not communist; he has no use for a
central domination over the lives of individuals. He wants
the kind of democracy that politicians talk about and do
not mean to bring about.

One should know this book for its technical achievement,
if for nothing else. The newsreel is a most interesting device,
consisting as it does of scrappy headlines, large and small,
and bits of current talk and songs. Each newsreel is true to its
time and thus contributes to the sense of time passage from
year to year. These usually completely unrelated bits of
news about murder, suicide, divorce, calamity, politics, graft,
labor unions, strife, and French fashions, convey exactly, as
someone has pointed out, the feeling of hasty subway reading
of the papers unfolded about one. Above all, they provide a
feeling of the whole United States, that background of
stimuli in which and before which we all move from day to
day. In terms of setting—which is the feeling of the time
and place—the artistic accomplishment is unique and striking.

The other device, the Camera Eye, is equally brilliant. It

stems, of course from the stream of consciousness and, clearly, James Joyce. Here the unnamed consciousness reflects again the many impingements of environment, through the often chaotic paragraphs of words run together, sentences without capitals, and associative thought processes. Much of the Camera Eye evidently represents Dos Passos' own personal experience, his impressionistic reaction to the whirl and maelstrom of contemporary life. "Bits of reality in unusual combinations," as Professor Muller phrased it, "hard and metallic prose." And on the other hand, at times the style is poetic, full of cadence, image and symbolism.

The biographies are accurate, factual accounts of lives as diverse as those of Henry Ford, Eugene Debs, Isadora Duncan, and Woodrow Wilson. They give, for the most part, facts that many of us already know, but the juxtaposition of these facts is significant and highly ironic as we shall note in our next chapter. They constitute not only an impressive comment on American "greatness" and human life in general, but serve by virtue of their actuality in time and space to bring out again the validity of the fictional portrayals. These real lives are, in a way, evidence of the truth of the imagined lives.

And finally the characters whom Dos Passos has invented, the people who come and go, meet each other casually, share interests for a time, and part without much emotion, are significant in that they are, as is always pointed out in criticism, highly typical. Who has not known an Eleanor Stoddard, drifting up in the profession of interior decoration, going "arty," moving from Chicago to New York, where she finally "does" the office of the "tycoon," J. Ward Moorehouse, who is as authentic a promotor as the man who invented Mother's Day in order to sell carnations. J. Ward Moorehouse is the arch-type of success, a public relations "expert" who boasts that he can bring management and labor together, sells his services at high prices, flashes his ever blue-eyed smile to gain his ways, and would sell out his own mother. And Janey, the naïve stenographer is a beautifully accurate picture of the mousy little girl who is an audience, a slave, and a worshipper of the boss who can do no wrong. The reality of these people is very great in the typical sense; but so rapidly are their stories told, with so objective a biographical note, that as a rule they fail to move us one way or another. We do not care what happens to them. We cannot identify ourselves with them, and for that reason they seem more like mechanical figures than real people. Yet to say this is to be unfair to Mr. Dos Passos' remarkable gift of portraiture. It lies both in his keen observation of types and in his sense of the forces that make them what they are. He is definitely a social satirist as well as a political satirist. A journalist he undoubtedly is, as many commentators have pointed out; but he is a great deal more than a journalist. He is a philosopher and an artist. His contribution to the techniques of writing is memorable and suggestive in its richness to all writers of our time. His achievement as a novelist of society is magnificent.

Let us consider the device of his introductory paragraph which forecasts the novel to come. The reader will at once note that Dos Passos is, like John Steinbeck, interested in portraying a panorama of the *whole* U.S.A. in terms of the "speech of the people." [6]

U.S.A. is the slice of a continent. U.S.A. is a group of holding companies, some aggregations of trade unions, a set of laws bound in calf, a radio network, a chain of moving picture theatres, a column of stockquotations rubbed out and written in by a Western Union boy on a blackboard, a publiclibrary full of old newspapers and dogeared historybooks with protests scrawled on the margins in pencil. U.S.A. is the world's greatest rivervalley fringed with mountains and hills, U.S.A. is a set of bigmouthed officials with too many

___

[6] *U.S.A.* Reprinted by kind permission of the author.

bankaccounts. U.S.A. is a lot of men buried in their uniforms in Arlington cemetery. U.S.A. is the letters at the end of an address when you are away from home. But mostly U.S.A. is the speech of the people.

This introduction reflects Dos Passos' preoccupations, his sense of chaos, his eye for concreteness, his sly humor which is never bawdy in the way that Steinbeck's is—and his *feeling* about war. He is deeply involved in the diversities of American life, as well as the uniformities of selfish grasping "interests." He is the teacher, the man who reveals unflinchingly what he sees, who permits himself no fond illusions of panacea, no wishful thinking about human nature.

As Alfred Kazin says, Dos Passos "comes out with all his equations zero." "The conviction of tragedy that rises out of his work is the steady protest of a sensitive democratic conscience against the tyranny and the ugliness of society, against the failure of a complete human development under industrial capitalism. . . ." He does not separate the "I" from society. Kazin says, "Dos Passos certainly came closer to Socialism than most artists in his generation; yet it is significant that no novelist in America has written more somberly of the dangers to individual integrity in a centrally controlled society."

In his books, Dos Passos' despair for the individual is eloquently expressed in the final picture at the end of *U.S.A.* Here, "The young man waits at the edge of the concrete." The reader will see that he is *any young man* of the post-war depression. He is, like Steinbeck's nameless speakers, a sort of collective young man, symbolic of a "lost generation."

with one hand, he grips a rubbed suitcase of phony leather, the other hand almost making a fist, thumb up

that moves in ever so slight an arc when a car slithers past, a truck roars clatters; the wind of the cars passing ruffles his hair, slaps grit in his face.

Head swims, hunger has twisted his belly tight,

he has skinned a heel through the torn sock, feet ache in the broken shoes, under the threadbare suit carefully brushed off with the hand, the torn drawers have a crummy feel, the feel of having slept in your clothes; in the nostrils lingers the staleness of discouraged carcasses crowded into transient camp; the carbolic stench of the jail, on the taut cheeks the shamed flush from the boring eyes of cops and deputies, railroadbulls (they eat three squares a day, they are buttoned into wellmade clothes, they have wives to sleep with, kids to play with after supper, they work for the big men who buy their way, they stick their chests out with the sureness of power behind their backs). Git the hell out, scram. Know what's good for you, you'll make yourself scarce. Gittin' tough, eh? Think you kin take it, eh?

The punch in the jaw, the slam on the head with the nightstick, the wrist grabbed and twisted behind the back, the big knee brought up sharp into the crotch,

the walk out of town with sore feet to stand and wait at the edge of the hissing speeding string of cars where the reek of ether and lead and gas melts into the silent grassy smell of the earth.

Eyes, black with want, seek out the eyes of the drivers, a hitch, a hundred miles down the road.

Then Dos Passos gives a parenthesis in which he contrasts the lot of the hitch-hiker with that of the passengers flying overhead in the Douglas; and finally he comes back again to the young man on the side of the road whose "wants crawl over his skin like ants:"

went to school, books said opportunity, ads promised speed, own your home, shine bigger than your neighbor, the radiocrooner whispered girls, ghosts of platinum girls coaxed from the screen, millions in winnings were chalked up on the boards in the offices, paychecks were for hands willing to work, the cleared desk of an executive with three telephones on it;

waits with swimming head, needs knot the belly, idle hands numb, beside the speeding traffic.

A hundred miles down the road.

"There were many words that you could not stand to hear and finally only the names of places had glory," wrote Ernest Hemingway in *A Farewell to Arms*.[7] "Abstract words

7 New York: Charles Scribner's Sons, 1929.

like glory, honor, courage, or hallow were obscene words."
And so, in his famous account of the Caporetto retreat he
shows wind, snow, rain, mud, the wounded being carried
on men's backs—"wet to the skin and all were scared"—and
horses and men going to sleep in the traffic stand-stills. Avoiding elaboration, he leaves simple definite phraseology to
convey the impressions of war.

Now this avoidance of rhetoric, this effort to convey the
particular image, hard and clear, is based on the theory that
abstractions are ineffective. How sound this theory is one
recognizes when he considers the nature of experience: we
react first to real situations, whatever they are, in sensory
response to stimulus—stimulus to eyes, ears, nose, touch.
Emotions and thoughts then follow. What could be more
logical than to present in narrative, as far as possible, the
objects and forces which produced the original response in
the author? That is what the poets as well as the fiction
writers of the "imagist" school try to do. That is what
Hemingway has done, looking at war, reacting emotionally,
and reproducing what he saw, leaving the vividness of his
impression to produce the desired emotional reaction upon
the reader.

In *Farewell to Arms* he has also used variations of the
stream of consciousness method; for instance to show the
hero worn out, aware of a traffic tie-up. "It was a combination of horses and motor vehicles." Then he thinks about
the two virgins in his vehicle; and from them he drifts, one
does not know exactly when, into a dream state:

If there were no war we would probably all be in bed. In bed I
lay me down my head. Bed and board. Stiff as a board in bed.
Catherine was in bed now between the sheets, over her and under
her. Which side did she sleep on? Maybe she wasn't asleep. Maybe
she was lying thinking about us. Blow, blow, ye western wind.

Then he dreams of Catherine. His dream ends when the
procession starts again and his companion says: "You talked

out loud." And he answers, with beautiful unconscious humor: "I was having a dream in English."

Later we see, with the narrator, the halting and brief quizzing by stern subordinate officers, of a lieutenant colonel separated in the chaotic retreat from his men. The colonel merely answers: "Have you ever been in retreat?" Then, with almost no author elaboration, we next see him walking between the *carabinieri* to the river and the narrator adds, "I did not watch them shoot him but I heard the shots."

Hemingway seldom, if ever, talks about physical suffering. He *shows* it, usually in phraseology composed chiefly of nouns and verbs. He is sparing of adjectives and adverbs. In the story "In Another Country," the chief impact of the hospital scenes comes from our seeing the major "with the little hand like a baby's, being bounced on the machine"; the boy with the black silk handkerchief worn across his noseless face; the pale boy who "had lived a very long time with death"; and "the funerals starting from the courtyard."

We see brutality toward animals: mules with their fore-legs purposely broken, thrown into the bay to drown. In *For Whom the Bell Tolls* Robert Jordan saw the big gray horse hit by flying steel "sitting quietly down as though it were a horse in a circus. And then looking at the horse sitting there, he heard the sound the horse was making." This writing evokes vivid, direct images and also serves to give the feeling of comradeship between suffering men and animals. In addition it increases the tension because the hero is aware that his own immediately impending fate is going to be something like that of the horse. The impact is great. A lesser artist would have told us, perhaps, *how* the horse screamed. Hemingway leaves one to summon his own auditory memory and imagination of such horror.

Thus he has, to a certain extent, achieved that "new dimension" for which he worked. With misleading simplicity, he has loaded his writing so as to lead the reader to his own emotional interpretation of war. In both these war novels he has fused experience of facts, with love and philosophies by which soldiers have been able to endure what they must endure. He achieves this new dimension many times, synthesizing, drawing together facts and impressions into a powerful organic whole.

The frontispiece to *For Whom the Bell Tolls* [8] is taken from John Donne:

No man is an *Iland*, intire of it selfe; every man is a peece of the *Continent*, a part of the *maine*; if a *Clod* bee washed away by the *Sea, Europe* is the lesse, as well as if a *Promontorie* were, as well as if a *Mannor* of thy *friends* or of *thine owne* were; any mans *death* diminishes *me*, because I am involved in *Mankinde*; And therefore never send to know for whom the *bell* tolls; It tolls for *thee*.

This theme gives the novel its serious political purpose which Hollywood, most unfortunately, failed to reveal in the film; it states the philosophy which led Americans to volunteer for the defense of Spain against fascism.

Hemingway's theme is clear when we hear Robert Jordan and Anselmo talking. Robert hates to kill animals, but Anselmo has always lived by killing them. Still he has feeling for them. He is, in the following passage, talking in his thoroughly delightful way about his animal trophies.

"On the door of the church of my village was nailed the paw of a bear that I killed in the spring, finding him on a hillside in the snow, overturning a log with this same paw."

Then Anselmo adds that he cannot bear to take the lives of men. He rebels at the prospect of his appointed task of killing the bridge sentry. "To take the life of another is to me very grave. I will do it whenever necessary but I am not of the race of Pablo." Later, Anselmo worried about how he would "comport" himself, fearing his "tendency to run" from battle. And finally, having at last killed his sentry, he

[8] New York: Charles Scribner's Sons, 1940.

thinks as he runs with contorted face down the mountainside, "That gave thee too much emotion and thee ran blubbering down the bridge like a woman." But, reiterating the Donne theme, he consoles himself with the thought that the *Ingles* is still working under the bridge with the dynamite and that he himself is "one with all of the battle and with the Republic."

Robert Jordan hates the killing he has to do and must constantly defend it to himself and to his band of mountaineers. He also hates to die and knows that his death is almost certain. Perhaps he expresses one of the author's creeds when he thinks of his ability "not to ignore but to despise whatever bad ending there could be." He knew that "he himself was nothing, and he knew that death was nothing." But he is achingly conscious of his sacrifice when dawn comes on the day of the bridge-blowing: at the hour "when solid things darken and space lightens"; when the pine trunks are "hard and clear"; when the road is "shiny with a wisp of mist over it."

Today is only one day in all the days that will ever be. But what will happen in all the other days that ever come can depend on what you do today. It's been that way all this year. Its been that way so many times. All of this war has been that way. You are getting very pompous in the early morning, he told himself. Look what's coming now.

Thus Jordan looks at his last dawn, thinking of the things in nature which he has loved deeply. Over and over again the pine trees come into his consciousness; and they finally come most significantly, as we shall see in a moment.

Hemingway has fused in this scene eternal soldier values: love of nature and love of woman—this woman to be lived with for only three days; love enjoyed now for the last time. Maria had called it "La Gloria," and when she did so Jordan thought of all the glorious things that he had known and must soon leave forever.

Again the pine tree theme appears in the last scene of the novel, as Jordan lies alone awaiting the oncoming Germans. "He took a good long look at everything"; then he "touched the palm of his hand against the pine needles" and he touched "the bark of the pine trunk that he lay behind." The technique here is superb, truly that of a work of art.

But Hemingway never overdoes his poignancy. He relieves his narrative with the use of Spanish gypsy words, gypsy idiom, gypsy obscenity,—all serving to bring about reality and at the same time comic relief. The dialect is vivid and seems true to the way these people would speak. Each character is distinct from the others and can almost be recognized by his speech habits. And, as we have noted in Chapter 6, so skillfully are Spanish words woven into the talk with gesture and with rejoinder in English, that the reader is not troubled by his ignorance of the language: for instance, " '*No es nada*,' she said. 'A bridge is nothing.' " Very frequently the words and the obscenity which is so much in character and so true to the excitement of the moment have ironic impact.

This irony is characteristic of Hemingway's work. It is implicit in his habitual *understatement*. The vivid portrayals of the facts which he used as intermediary sketches to bring out the cold brutality of war and the bull ring, in *In Our Time*, have been quoted over and over again by critics. The passage about the paralyzed soldier who says to his dead buddy, "You and me we've made a separate peace," is typical of Hemingway's style and his ironic humor.

.12.

Irony and Affirmation

A CONTRADICTORY outcome of events as if in mockery of the promise and fitness of things is the larger meaning of irony which is revealed in the best literature, but first let us consider irony in its narrower aspect. The irony of the apt word or phrase is "a figure of speech in which the intended meaning is the opposite of that expressed by the words used." This irony appears very often in a story title. It conveys sarcastic comment. "Safe," "The Short, Happy Life of Francis Macomber," "The Conqueror," and "Something Jolly" are such titles. One finds them, very frequently, in a phrase coming near the end, frequently spoken by a character.

To begin with the irony of a phrase or small unit: when Stegner's father says to his little boy, "What detained you? You must not want to go very bad," he is using two kinds of irony. The first implies that the boy has important business, when he has, of course, nothing to do and has actually been dawdling to show his resentment; the second implies that the child, who is angry at being unable to go on the trip, does not now want to go.

There is irony in the father's question in Hemingway's "Indian Camp" when he asks Nick how he likes "being an interne"; and there is ironic *naïveté* in the boy's thought at the end of the story that he will never die.

Dorothy Parker is nearly always ironic. She puts ironic

words into Mr. Durant's mouth when he says about the dog, "You have a female around, and you know what happens." This is a double-edged irony, considering what happens to Mr. Durant when there is a female of the human species around. The monologist in "Lady with a Lamp" produces a strongly ironic effect when, having harassed the sick woman with her innuendoes for some time, she suddenly realizes that the patient is worse and calls to the maid, "Give Miss Morrison something to quiet her. I'm afraid she's got herself a little bit upset."

Gentle irony of the whole is implied in Katherine Mansfield's "Honeymoon," where the young couple are naïvely proud of seeming worldly wise, although they are, in reality, self-conscious and afraid of not doing the correct things. Irony is implied in "Bliss" when the heroine discovers that her husband is in love with another woman on this day which was to bring her and her husband to a state of bliss unknown before, especially when she goes over to the window and notes that the symbolic pear tree is "as lovely as ever and as full of flower and as still." Katherine Mansfield has used irony very extensively, especially in her character sketches, notably that of Mr. Peacock who dramatizes himself unrealistically.

Irony is implicit in the vast majority of endings when the hero either is reversed or comes to recognition of a truth which is the opposite of his previous conceptions. Two of the stories about little girls which we have discussed end ironically: the Van Duyn story ends with the formerly innocent child's dangerous guilt feeling and dislike of men; and the Patton story ends with the child's dangerous fear of confessing fear.

The irony at the core of human existence is strikingly brought out by Dos Passos in *U.S.A.* when he summarizes the lives of eminent Americans factually, revealing the inconsistencies and paradoxes. Andrew Carnegie, for instance, made his money in steel very basic in war, and then gave vast sums for the promotion of international peace. Henry Ford manned a fantastic ship to take pacifists to Europe to stop World War I and two years later was manufacturing munitions and "planning oneman tanks, and oneman submarines." Ford's Tin Lizzie was one of the great factors in the development of the automobile age and its accompanying good roads; but Ford went antiquarian in a big way and even "put back the old bad road" in front of his Wayside Inn "so that everything might be the way it used to be, in the days of horses and buggies." Many other important Americans whose lives are summarized by Dos Passos reversed themselves in one way or another. Dos Passos uses these summaries to reveal paradox in *known* lives, which enhances the paradox of the fictional lives recorded and of the panorama of modern life as a whole.

Sometimes fictional ironies are relatively limited and personal and sometimes they are broad and universal. But always they expose that dualism between man's vision of an ideal life and the reality of his actual life which is creation's great ironic joke.

The greatest fiction writer of our time, Thomas Mann, has written most ironically of all. Analyzing his own work in the "Joseph" series, in *The Atlantic Monthly* for February 1943, he characterizes it as "playful," written in "a stylized and bantering language, a contribution to the pseudo-exactness, very close to persiflage and at any rate to irony; for scientific treatment of wholly unscientific and legendary matters is pure irony." Mann's irony is wonderfully contrived in these novels which expand the few Biblical paragraphs into volumes. The beautiful Hebrew diction is, as he so illuminatingly points out, "not really the language of the author but of the work itself." It serves to give both an authentic flavor

of ancient times and a majesty of thought; the juxtaposition
of modern slang (it was not "any great shakes") in its turn,
brings the action down to date, universalizes it, and imposes
additional humor by virtue of its contrast. It also conveys
a sense of the eternal verities of human nature because it links
the present common man with the anointed Joseph of an-
tiquity.

In the "Prelude in the Upper Circles" of *Joseph the Pro-
vider*,[1] for instance, we learn that the members of the hier-
archy felt "a mild yet poignant satisfaction, an agreeable sly
sense of 'I told you so,' expressed in glances from under
lowered lashes and round little mouths discreetly drawn
down." The joke "to make anyone snigger" was that "the
very creature which if you like was nearer the image of the
Creator than any other brought evil with him into the
world." Man with "his biological tendencies" was a "constant
embarrassment to God."

> "The Angels," so ran the train of thought, "are created after Our
> image, but yet not fruitful. The beasts, on the other hand, lo, they
> are fruitful, but not after Our likeness. Let Us create man—an image
> of the angels, yet fruitful withal!"

Thus, Thomas Mann summarizes the age-old problem: the
conflict between man's ideal of himself as a very special kind
of spiritual creation and his knowledge that he is an animal,
made like other animals.

In Volume III Mann has shown Joseph as a very special
young man if ever there was one, "the chosen seed of Israel,"
dedicated to chastity, dallying with Mut, the wife of Potiphar,
his employer, who has elevated him to lofty position. Responding to Mut's flattering suggestions, playing with fire,
tempted, resisting, and again tempted, he has goaded her into
such a devastating fury that she has brought about his downfall, through especially ironic and amusing conduct. The Prel-

[1] Translated by H. T. Lowe-Porter. New York: Alfred A. Knopf, Inc., 1944.

ude to Volume IV, just quoted, pictures this "dashing and arrogant young darling, a dreamer of dreams, a scion of that stock which had hit on the idea of being a medium of self-knowledge to God," this Joseph, on his way to prison because he had "let love—as before he had hate—get entirely out of hand."

In these novels so intricately woven with anthropological lore, Jewish history, and modern analytical psychology, Mann sums up the many aspects of the doctrine of original sin which has inspired much of the greatest literature of our civilization. To his comment upon man's dualism he has brought a great deal of that "blythe scepticism" which he said in his essay "Freud and the Future," "unmasks all the schemes and subterfuges of our own souls." This unmasking becomes possible, Mann believes, to the writer who has "acquired the habit of regarding life as mythical and typical" and thus has gained a "curious heightening of his artistic temper, a new refreshment to his perceiving and shaping powers. . . ." He writes in his essay on Freud:[2]

What is gained is an insight into the higher truth depicted in the actual; a smiling knowledge of the eternal, the ever-being and authentic; a knowledge of the schema in which and according to which the supposed individual lives, unaware, in his naïve belief in himself as unique in space and time, of the extent to which his life is but formula and repetition and his path marked out for him by those who trod it before him.

A smiling knowledge of the eternal is, indeed, what one finds in really great writing. It is the product of a philosophic outlook which sees the universal tendency in the particular, which knows that man's role in the universe does not vary greatly, whatever his time or place.

Philo Buck has an interesting analysis of Shakespearean irony in his chapter "The Ironical Reply" in *The Golden Thread*.[3] He has pointed out the many ironic phrases as well

[2] *Freud, Goethe, Wagner.* New York: Alfred A. Knopf, Inc., 1937.
[3] New York: The Macmillan Co., 1931.

as the larger ironies in Shakespeare's greatest plays and asks what compensation Shakespeare found for tragedy: "Lear calling upon the heavens fittingly to celebrate his agony, Othello lashing himself into a passion of jealousy, yet by nature ironically the least liable to its tooth, exclaiming when about to strangle his wife, 'Iago, the pity of it, Iago.' Hamlet calm, yet with all ill about his heart, going bravely to his death, with passionate self-possession."—"Lear, Macbeth, Othello reveal their power through the magnificent sweep of poetic passion: Hamlet his through the very calmness of self-possession." And then Buck adds, "The issues of tragedy are great, for in it the irony that lies at the heart of life stands revealed."

Only great personality may dare the issue of tragedy, for only the great can enter the lists against the powers of the unknown. And it is the revelation of humanity put to the edge, reserving itself for the supreme test, and expending itself in magnificent failure, it is this that brings the gasp of admiration with the shudder of terror and the stretching appeal of pity.

And how does it come about that we are able not only to endure the spectacle of magnificent failure, but even to find in it alleviation and affirmation?

Through the centuries, students and critics of literature have drawn upon Aristotle's theories for the explanation of this phenomenon. Their interpretations of his words have been many and various and we can give only one or two that seem to have been most generally accepted. Parts of Aristotle's theory no longer seem applicable because they were based on the conventions of the Greek theatre which do not exist in our theatre; and, since they were purely theatrical conventions, they do not apply to other forms of narrative. Nevertheless, there are a few basic ideas which offer any writer food for thought and, often, the solution for his problems of conclusion. The ending of a story is, after all, of the utmost importance. Aristotle offers some relatively simple formulas which are yet sufficiently broad to be artistically sound and applicable and in no way formalizing or inhibiting of originality.

Aristotle wrote in the *Poetics* that the ideal tragic hero was, as we noted earlier, a man like ourselves, not too good, not too bad, a man whose downfall is brought about by "some great error or frailty" in character. A perfect tragedy, he thought, "should imitate actions which excite pity and fear, this being the distinctive mark of tragic imitation." The pity and fear aroused in the beholder effected, he believed, "the proper purgation of these emotions."

In the word "purgation" lies the key to what happens to the onlooker of the imitation of tragedy. Purgation, or *Katharsis* as Aristotle called it elsewhere, brings about certain emotional and intellectual reactions which are satisfying and more than satisfying. Let us see why.

If we take Aristotle's words, phrase by phrase their implications become clear. In watching a representation of the life of a man who is sufficiently like us that we can identify ourselves with him, we feel fear for his fate and pity for his sufferings. If he were all good or all bad, we could not make this identification and would remain aloof and unmoved: but if he is sufficiently "human," as we like to call it, we fear for and pity him, going out emotionally toward him, thinking, perhaps, "there but for the grace of God go I." We suffer with him and thus, the psychological theory goes, we get relief, vicarious relief which is not a possible result of our own personal suffering. In other words, we feel deeply about this hero, but we do not stay awake nights over his troubles. Instead we enjoy them. Enjoy them through some strange quirk in our natures. The cynic might say that we enjoy them because we unconsciously may want to commit some of the errors or crimes which he commits; and we find relief for our own guilt sense when *he* has to pay the penalty for sin. This, of course, is a very psychoanalytical explanation.

One of the chief traditional interpretations is the "pathological theory" in which tragedy is viewed as a "vent" for accumulated emotions; emotions to which we seldom yield expression, since we are socially trained to repress such expression. Butcher [4] points out that Aristotle was led to this theory, strangely enough, as is indicated in his *Politics*, by "observing the effect of certain melodies upon a form of religious ecstasy" in which patients "who have been subjected to this process, 'fall back,' to quote Aristotle's phrase, 'into their normal state, as if they had undergone a medical or purgative treatment.' The emotional result is a 'harmless joy.'"

It is natural and normal to crave a vent, especially when its source is an imitation of life in which the fate of the hero arises as Aristotle said, from "the inner structure of the piece." The inner structure is that unity upon which we have dwelt in an earlier chapter, implied in Aristotle's phrase "organic whole." Says Butcher in his commentary, "This inevitable sequence of cause and effect is the link that character forges as it expresses itself in action. . . . The fate that overtakes the hero is no alien thing, but his own self recoiling upon him for good and evil."

Now this idea of the *self recoiling* upon *itself* in tragedy is extremely important in modern thought. The flaw, Dr. A. C. Bradley has pointed out in *Shakespearean Tragedy*,[5] is

a marked one-sidedness, a predisposition in some particular direction; a total incapacity, in certain circumstances, of resisting the force which draws in this direction; a fatal tendency to identify the whole being with one interest, object, passion, or habit of mind. . . . It is

[4] S. H. Butcher, *Aristotle's Theory of Poetry and Fine Art.* London: Macmillan & Co.
[5] From A. C. Bradley, *Shakespearean Tragedy.* By permission of The Macmillan Company, publishers.

a fatal gift, but it carries with it a touch of greatness; and when there is joined to it nobility of mind, or genius, or immense force, we realize the full power and reach of the soul, and the conflict in which it engages acquires that magnitude which stirs not only sympathy and pity, but admiration, terror, and awe.

This theory is strikingly close to what Thomas Mann calls "the Schopenhauer-Freud perception that 'the giver of all given conditions resides in ourselves.' " It has tremendous implications for philosophy and it will bear considerable thought from any writer attempting serious work. It is, perhaps, an awareness of such a possibility that gives to so much of contemporary writing an emphasis upon abnormal and obsessive traits. There are, as we noted, three stories in the 1946 O. Henry Memorial Award collection dealing with insane characters, a very strange selection indeed.

Most writing does not go so far as to depict actual insanity, of course. It merely shows man as the victim of his own excessiveness. Serious writing is rarely concerned with external happenings having little or no relation to the actual character traits. Such writing has its place for those who desire mere entertainment, or for those romantics who crave the happy ending. But it is not worthy of our serious attention and has never been considered worthy. Aristotle himself scorned the "bad poets" who compose "show pieces for competition" and "stretch the plot beyond its capacity, and are often forced to break the natural continuity." The episodic plot is the worst, he said, "because the episodes or acts succeed one another without probable or necessary sequence."

This kind of plot, unreal and *contrived*, does not satisfy a really mature mind. If one is so constituted that he craves happy endings in literature, he will have to look elsewhere for it than in serious writing of the kind which we have been discussing in this book.

What kind of ending does the intelligently serious person accept? In general he accepts one of the two outcomes which Aristotle has discussed as suitable for tragic struggle: reversal or recognition, or a combination of the two.

"Reversal of the Situation," Aristotle said, "is a change by which action veers round to its opposite, subject always to our rule of probability or necessity. Thus in the Oedipus, the messenger comes to cheer Oedipus and free him from his alarms about his mother, but by revealing who he is, he produces the opposite effect." And recognition, Aristotle wrote, "is a change from ignorance to knowledge." The best form of recognition is "coincident with a Reversal of the Situation, as in the Oedipus."

The reader will remember that Oedipus, having been told that he would murder his father and marry his mother, went away into a strange country in order to avoid committing either of these crimes. But he did, after all, unwittingly do both things and when he became tragically aware of what he had done, he blinded himself.

Pity and fear resulting from the inner structure of the piece, as in the story of the Oedipus, will bring him who hears the tale told to thrill with horror and melt with pity.

Now we can rarely, if ever, think of even the best of contemporary writing as great tragedy; and we cannot, therefore, attempt to apply Aristotle's principles very closely. But it is interesting to note that a great many short stories depend for ending upon one or the other of these two devices and very frequently upon a combination of the two. Any good story brings one kind of recognition—the reader recognition of a truth. But Aristotle was talking about recognition by a character. We find such recognition in the story "Understand What I Mean?", where the narrator comes to see and to react violently against racial prejudice; in "Big

Blonde," when the heroine sees her plight clearly enough to try suicide and when she prays that since she must live, she can always have liquor; in "Main Currents of American Thought," where the hero becomes definitely aware of the fact that he is growing old chained to his mother, without having a chance to do what he wants; in "Flesh and Blood," where the soldier comes to see that he has not in reality been untrue to his wife.

Earlier, in discussing irony, we indicated the element of reversal in other stories discussed in this book. Reversal and recognition together carry a double impact. Sherwood Anderson's "I Want to Know Why" has such impact. The boy who has always loved horses and the men who train them is disillusioned when, after the beautiful race, he finds his hero in obviously shoddy feminine company. Innocent, the boy yet senses something wrong and is deeply disturbed. "How can people be that way? I want to know why."

Aristotle thought of reversal in terms of situation by which the action "veers round to its opposite, subject always to our rule of probability or necessity." But the principle of character reversal is also very sound and forms the basis of a great many character sketches, especially the satirical, as we have seen.

Writers casting about for ways in which to end a story would have less difficulty if they realized that something as simple as recognition is often enough, especially if the revelation is original or striking. There is little under the sun that is new; but interpretations can be new. The interpretation is the measure of the writer's quality and importance; it is his judgment and his comment upon life. What that judgment is depends upon his individual endowments: the clarity of his vision, the extent of his wisdom, the power and originality of his insight, the extent of his courage in facing and expressing truth.

Writing today puts a severe strain upon our powers of synthesis, for our civilization is changing rapidly and many old ideas and ideals have gone by the board. To reconcile one's concepts of biological, psychological, sociological, and philosophical truth with one's natural and instinctive idealism is for many sensitive people almost an impossible task. It has always presented a problem even in the days when the gods were thought to interfere in men's affairs to the extent of bringing their most cherished ideals and noble efforts to naught. Modern man, intellectual, rational, truth-seeking— and he has these qualities if he is modern in any real sense of the word—is at the same time emotional, often guided by instinctive wishes for a world nearer to his heart's desire. He craves something affirmative in which to believe. And the one belief that he ultimately clings to, regardless of his scientific training or his personal experience, is his belief in his fellow human beings. Man goes down before the forces of a mysterious and totally indifferent universe in which he is infinitesimal. The more highly developed he is, the more sensitive and idealistic, the greater seems his tragedy. Nevertheless the onlooker does find catharsis in the very magnificence of his failure. "The only real failure is the avoidance of truth and the acceptance of a lie." The great tragic hero is always magnificent and he brings catharsis in accordance with the degree of his magnificence.

But the little hero with whom most writers have to content themselves may also convey affirmation of life. His qualities of dignity, courage, and generosity bring their own kind of alleviation. Many good writers are both realistic and healing. Willa Cather's writings about the immigrants of the Nebraska farm lands have this fusion of realism and faith in humanity. Miss Cather is no sentimentalist. She is aware of the suffering and frustration in human life, but it does not make her bitter, for she sees at the same time the good, the humanly true, and the beautiful. Her Antonia has a hard life and an arid one by the superficial standards of complex city people. It is made up of extreme poverty, backbreaking work in the fields, and much self-sacrifice. But Antonia is never bitter, never defeated. She goes on working and finding her satisfaction and contentment in things that have always satisfied women who love nature and live close to her. The man who tells her story, in *My Antonia*, watching her with her large family of beautiful children, sees her as a "rich mine of life." Going with her over the farm he thinks that she reveals herself in many "immemorial attitudes." She is a symbol of adaptation and serenity. Life has "battered but not diminished her."

Miss Cather's portrait of Neighbor Rosicky in *Obscure Destinies* [6] is equally affirmative, revealing again her faith in a *rapport* with nature and the love of people for each other. Neighbor Rosicky is a thoroughly good man who knows how to meet death with the same grace with which he has met life. At the beginning of the story he is in the doctor's office receiving the news that his heart has given out. He takes the verdict calmly, "with an air of detachment, the easy manner of an onlooker and observer"; and then he places the doctor's fee "delicately behind the desk-telephone, looking the other way, as if this were an absent-minded gesture." After that he drives home, stopping at the grave-yard adjoining his land. The snow was falling over it, "a nice dry snow," and it "looked very pretty."

It was a nice graveyard, Rosicky reflected, sort of snug and home-like, not cramped or mournful,—a big sweep all around it. A man could lie down in the long grass and see the complete arch of the sky over him, hear the wagons go by; in the summer the mowing-machine rattled right up to the fence wire. And it was so near home. Over there across the cornstalks his own roof and windmill looked so good to him that he promised himself to mind the Doctor and take care of himself. He was awful fond of his place, he admitted. He wasn't anxious to leave it. And it was a comfort to think that

[6] New York: Alfred A. Knopf, Inc., 1932.

he would never have to go farther than the edge of his own hay-field. The snow, falling over his barnyard and the graveyard, seemed to draw things together like. And they were all old neighbours in the graveyard, most of them friends; there was nothing to feel awkward or embarrassed about.

He has had one worry: the restlessness of his son's young city-born wife and her aloofness from the family. But this worry is finally dissipated in a moving scene in which Rosicky has a heart attack and the girl helps him bear it. Suddenly she sees the beauty in the old man's character. "She had a sudden feeling that nobody in the world, not her mother, not Rudolph, or anyone, really loved her as much as old Rosicky did. . . . It was as if Rosicky had a special gift for loving people. . . ." And indeed he had! Like Antonia, he could not possibly qualify as a dramatic hero. However obscure, Rosicky is, nevertheless, heroic in his own quiet way and the quiet way is the way of most mortals, after all. He and Antonia have both made their own lives and made them worth living.

One does not have to be a sentimental romantic to feel the validity of these lives and of Miss Cather's outlook upon them. However deterministic one's philosophy, there is still something to believe in. That something is the worth-while-ness of man himself.

One sees this in the writings of the veterans of World War II. Those who actually fought came through with a humanism that the rest of us may well envy them. Their writings are surprisingly free from cant, as they are free of super-ficialities. They write sincerely about their experiences and about the heroism and comradeship of war, with an aware-ness of the solidarity of mankind. War, the grimmest of man's ironies against himself, has only served to deepen their faith in each other as members of the group that stood to-gether and met the test, and their faith is heartening.

Symbolism

THE best writing is that which conveys the most meaning and feeling, and has poetic quality. The poets have, of course, always known the power of reference, allusion, symbol, and metaphor. All words are by their very nature symbolic, being names for things or ideas or feelings, but the word "symbol" includes something beyond the concrete. We use it to imply likeness in objects that are different. We use the word "mother," for instance—to imply values of security: shelter in the womb and all through life; sustenance, food, in the womb and all through life; and love eternal and forgiving. The word "home" has similar connotations, which have nothing to do with four walls and a roof. Most people will respond to any appeal whatever which uses these two words directively. Most people will also respond to less common but still familiar symbols such as "dove," "snake," "lion," and "lamb." A great many people who would not understand many other literary symbols will respond to the symbols of religion and will understand much of the rich metaphor of the Bible. The study of symbols, their origins and connotations, is extremely interesting. It carries us back to the very earliest history of man.

The anthropologist and the student of folklore take us into much more interesting symbolism in their discussions of tribal religions and primitive customs, where we encounter fertility symbols, totems, and *tabus* which make us aware of the sources of many of our own cultural metaphors. The experimental psychologist carries us still further and we learn why it is that a red light, implying certain specific dangers, makes us automatically stop at the corner. The sociologist, with his study of the formation of public opinion and the mob mind, gives insight into the phenomenon of race pride and Ku Kluxism, that device by which men in mobs take "justice" into their own hands to "protect" the chastity of women from Negroes or to drive the "financially dominant and aggressive Jew" from their midst. Each of the three sciences makes its contribution to the study of the meaning of words, which has now come to be called *semantics*. The semanticist is able to point out to us how infantile most of our reactions are as soon as some orator or editor flings words of emotional judgment at us, arousing us by the use of "directive language." Directive language is language which, without appearing to do so, tells us how to react emotionally. The politician, the clergyman, the industrialist, the labor leader, the promoter of sales, even the teacher, use directive language. One presses the button on the word "mother" and the tears and sentimentality flow—in the right direction, of course, it may even be nationally, in the direction of carnations. One speaks of "The New Deal" and the direction taken by an emotional audience will depend upon the economic and political philosophy of that audience. To one audience the phrase implies a degree of security in food and shelter in a period of extreme depression in which lifelong savings vanished with falling banks, unemployment grew to staggering totals, and hunger and foreclosure were at hand. To another audience the phrase implies opposite things: confiscatory taxation, boon-doggling, men leaning on their rakes, and the ruin of individual initiative and free enterprise. Whether one's reaction is a "snarl" or a "purr" depends upon one's emotional configuration far more often than upon one's understanding of the economic theories and humanitarian social aims of the "professors" (another directive word) who "theorized" about matters that had best be left to "practical business men."

S. I. Hayakawa has written illuminatingly about why we snarl or purr in his *Language in Action*, an easily understood book about the implied meanings of the words which make Mr. Smith pound the table in fury as he reads his newspaper or listens to the radio. Mr. Hayakawa reminds his reader that to Mr. Smith *other* people often seem to be using words "trickily"; but Mr. Smith himself is quite unaware of his own emotional and tricky word-habits.

What has all this to do with fiction writing? It has a very great deal because the fiction writer must be conscious of what *happens* when he uses language. He must recognize that his aims can only be realized to their fullest if he is master of directive language. The poet has always understood this necessity and has chosen his words with the utmost care for their symbolic and metaphorical implications. The poet uses compressed language which intensifies meanings and experience. He gives us the qualities of things, the similarities, the differences, the likeness in things which are different and thus he enables us to see life in new ways. By using "the principle of the unhabitual" he at once shocks us into attention and enlarges our vision.

In E. A. Robinson's poem "The Man Against the Sky," the man symbolizes all men who go "mostly alone:" "Along one blind atomic pilgrimage whereon by crass chance billited we go because our brains and bones and cartilage will have it so." This and equally suggestive metaphors convey a view of life completely at the mercy of natural forces, in which man, "humbled" by death, can only look forward to a nothingness which is logically more desirable in itself. Robinson's philosophy is peculiarly appropriate to the atomic age which was to follow him.

Robinson Jeffers' poems dwell upon man's isolation from nature and his introverted preoccupation with himself. To him night, signifying death, is the "peace-bringer" and death itself is "no evil." Great is his disgust with man, from whom he retreats to "the quietness of stones," the "brave beauty of falcons," "the white gulls weaving a dance over blue water," the "wild sea-fragrance of the wind," the "cliffs of peninsular granite," the "beauty of the fountains of the sun."

> And life, the flicker of men and moths and
> the wolf on the hill,
> Though furious for continuance,
> passionately feeding, passionately
> Remaking itself upon its mates, remembers
> deep inward
> The calm mother, the quietness of the
> womb and the egg,
> The primal and the latter silences: dear
> Night it is memory
> Prophesies, prophecy that remembers, the
> charm of the dark.[1]

Ironic and Freudian this passage in praise of night and death! Powerful the terror, described in "Ante Mortem", of the end of life, when "the striped blossom insanity" may "spread lewd splendors and lightning terrors at the end of the forest", and intolerable pain "exile the monarch soul, set a sick monkey in the office."

We find powerful metaphor expressing ideas related to those of Robinson and Jeffers in Allen Tate's "Ode to the Confederate Dead," where he uses the blind crab as a symbol for man's "locked-in ego." The crab, he tells us in an essay about the rich but somewhat obscure poem, "is the first intimation of the nature of the moral conflict upon which

---

[1] From "Night" in *Roan Stallion, Tamar, and Other Poems*. New York: Random House, Inc., 1925.

the drama of the poem develops: the cut-offness of modern 'intellectual man' from the world." The crab has "mobility but no direction, energy but no purposeful world to use it in." And so his man seems "a jaguar" leaping Narcissus-like upon his own image in a pool.

The life-view is much the same in these poems. But the metaphors, and hence the suggested images and meanings, are dissimilar. The fiction writer can do no better than to study such writing if he wishes to enrich his work and extend his narrative references.

The following passages will serve to bring out some of the theory of multiple meanings which has entered into literary criticism of the past.

Writing of the many meanings in *The Divine Comedy*, Dante said,

The first meaning is the one obtained through the letter; the second is the one obtained through the things signified by the letter. The first is called literal, the second allegorical or moral or anagogical.

And again:

The subject of the whole work, then, taken merely in its literal sense, is simply the state of the souls after death, for from that subject comes the course of the whole work and with that it is occupied. But if the whole work is taken allegorically, the subject is man as by reason of meriting and demeriting through the freedom of the will he is liable to the rewarding and the punishing of justice.

And:

The end of the whole and the part can be multiplex, that is, near at hand and remote; but omitting all subtle investigation, one may say briefly that the end of the whole and the part is to remove those living in this life from a state of misery and to lead them to a state of happiness.

These quotations are taken from *Literary Criticism* [2] by Allan H. Gilbert, who made the translation. Mr. Gilbert also

[2] New York: American Book Company, 1940.

quotes from Boccaccio who, in "The Life of Dante," [3] wrote:

It is obvious that anything that is gained with fatigue seems sweeter than what is acquired without any effort. The plain truth, since it is quickly understood with little difficulty, delights us and passes from the mind. But, in order that it may be more pleasing, because acquired with labor, and therefore be better retained, the poets hide the truth beneath things apparently quite contrary to it. For that reason they produce fables, rather than some other covering, because their beauty attracts those whom neither philosophical demonstrations nor persuasions would have been able to allure.

The fiction writer should learn to look for the extended reference in important writings in order that he may become accustomed to thinking in this larger, more symbolic way; he should not yield to the temptation to cast aside the difficult, especially when qualified critics have pronounced upon its literary importance. In literature, as in painting and music, the plain statement, easily grasped, frequently will not bear further acquaintance. It soon becomes uninteresting and dull because it is thin.

Thinness is the defect most frequent in amateur writing, where authors may tell a story of some dramatic interest in itself but weak in its larger thematic and symbolic values. Thematic values arising from implied allegorical meanings lift fiction out of the realm of the literal and often merely realistic into the timeless and universal. The literal meaning should be clear, at least to a good reading intelligence, not loaded with the personal and subjective obscurities of a confused mind which others, however well trained, cannot understand. The wider meanings acquired only with labor will serve to make the literary experience satisfying to the more intelligent and philosophical. The practicality of Boccaccio's advice is evident. Tendencies of today are away from thinness and toward richness, as the stories in the O. Henry

[3] Translated by Charles G. Osgood in *Boccaccio on Poetry*. Princeton: Princeton University Press, 1930.

Memorial collection for 1946 to which we have referred earlier demonstrate.

Even characterization itself can have broad, implied meanings, concerned with man's place not only in society but also in the natural universe. Thomas Mann's novels, for instance, are profound chiefly in that they reveal man as the product of all the forces working upon him through inheritance that is both biological and anthropological. He reminds us that his Joseph series even uses style elements (Hebrew cadence in particular) to form "*one* stratum of its language which strangely fuses the archaic and the modern, the epical and analytical." He thought of his Joseph as a Faust and therefore as "a symbol of humanity," leading "from the original and simple, the typical and canonical," to "the involved, late." He thought of his task as a "mythical" one, and he believed that "to live in tradition means to live in the myth."

Modern man's tremendous range of knowledge lends itself magnificently to broad literary meaning. Never before in the history of the world has the author had so great a challenge to his insight into relationships and his powers of interpretation. The vision which enlarges the reader's sense of his place in this modern world and his awareness of its complicated relationships is characteristic of the great writers of our day. One of the greatest is, by common consent, T. S. Eliot. It is interesting to note how great is the metaphorical and symbolic range of his poem, which, at first thoughtless sight, might seem merely a characterization of a man.

"The Love Song of J. Alfred Prufrock" [4] is an example of multiple allusion that any fiction writer might well emulate. The name Prufrock itself implies an effeminate meticulousness which, combined with the "parted" name, J. Alfred,

---

[4] *The Collected Poems of T. S. Eliot.* New York: Harcourt, Brace and Co., Inc., 1936.

prepares us for the picture of a life spent wondering "Do I dare?" a life given to thought about "my morning coat, my collar mounting firmly to the chin, my necktie rich and modest, but asserted by a simple pin—" a life where

> In the room the women come and go
> Talking of Michelangelo.

This life is "measured out" with "coffee spoons"; a self-conscious life in which the speaker is "formulated, sprawling on a pin," accepting the role of an "easy tool, deferential, glad to be of use, polite, cautious, and meticulous."

> Shall I part my hair behind? Do I dare to eat a
>   peach?
> I shall wear white flannel trousers, and walk upon
>   the beach.

Prufrock has seen the mermaids, but he does not feel that "they will sing to me." Thus sterility of modern life, timidity in love and inability to participate in imaginative experience are implied. Modern man, "almost at times, the Fool," is subservient to his anxieties and the empty conventions of an unadventurous age.

The devices in Eliot are, as Elizabeth Drew says, "concrete images which do their work by their impact on the reader's *senses*, making him *feel* the force of the abstract ideas behind the passage." [5]

Such characterization is highest art. It suggests many possibilities to the fiction writer, possibilities for the enrichment of prose narrative by metaphor conveying many meanings at once. Now what others of our contemporary writers have any degree of this ability?

Implied comparison is dangerous and no comparison is

[5] Reprinted from *Directions in Modern Poetry* by Elizabeth Drew (with John L. Sweeney) by permission of W. W. Norton & Company, Inc. Copyright, 1940, by the publishers.

here implied. But let us begin with a writer who deserves more recognition than she has yet had, and then move on to Joyce and Proust.

Meridel LeSueur's "Annunciation" [6] is a very short narrative which contains many direct and implied meanings. It is really a narrative prose poem with the major theme of fertility imposed upon a minor theme of contrasting poverty and deprivation of several kinds. The pear-tree is, as it is in Katherine Mansfield's "Bliss," the symbol, but the metaphor here is much broader and deeper. The values are more dramatic and the emotional effect is more intense because more elemental ideas are projected. Miss LeSueur's heroine is pregnant, hungry, and lonely; her husband gets drunk, and he does not come home when he has no money. Living in a cheap rooming house, sitting on a porch in autumn and watching the tree, she writes on pieces of wrapping paper her thoughts about the child to be born, often addressing the child itself. She thinks of the wild, carrying young. "There is something wild about us too, something tender and wild about my having you as a child, about you crouching so secretly here. There is something very tender and wild about it. We, too, are at the mercy of many hunters."

The husband has wanted her to get rid of the child: "Everything I said only made him angry. So writing was a kind of conversation I carried on with myself and with the child."

The imagined fruitfulness of the tree extends to the life about her.

The many houses have become like an orchard blooming soundlessly. The many people have become like fruits to me, the young girl in the room alone before her mirror, the young man sleeping, the mother, all are shaking with their inward blossoming, shaken by the windy blooming, moving along a future curve.

[6] From *Salute to Spring* by Meridel LeSueur. New York: International Publishers, 1940.

She, like the tree, knows "the slow time of making." Finally she writes:

I sit here all the afternoon as if in its branches, midst the gentle and curving body of the tree. I have looked at it until it has become more familiar to me than Karl. It seems a strange thing that a tree might come to mean more to one than one's husband. It seems a shameful thing even. I am ashamed to think of it but it is so. I have sat here in the pale sun and the tree has spoken to me with its many tongued leaves, speaking through the afternoon of how to round a fruit. And I listen through the slow hours. I listen to the whisperings of the pear tree, speaking to me, speaking to me. How can I describe what is said by a pear tree? Karl did not speak to me so. No one spoke to me in any good speech.

The suggestive, poetic power of this story so rich—perhaps too rich, for it lacks restraint—in symbolism, is value sufficient in itself, but its narrative factual elements are also powerful and intensely moving. The story of a highly sensitive, imaginative woman, creative in the artistic as well as the life-giving sense, yoked to an insensitive, depression-ridden, and brutally neglectful man is told in understatement, almost as if the speaker were unaware of her situation, so absorbed is she in the richness of her experience of maternity. Yet there is stark isolation in the words, "No one spoke to me in any good speech."

"What distinguishes poetry from prose," writes Elizabeth Drew, "is precisely that the poet explores and exploits all the elements beyond that [the common logical basis], the elements lurking in the emotional and sensuous values of words. This means all the qualities of beauty, strangeness and power in rhythm and music, texture, color, oddness and subtle collisions." But why should not the fiction writer adopt these devices for his own?

Thomas Wolfe certainly drew upon Walt Whitman for much of his poetic method, just as he drew upon Joyce and through Joyce upon Freud for the dominant theme of the

young man in search of a father. James Joyce did use poetic
method and so did Proust. If the reader will turn back to the
quotations from *Ulysses* and *Remembrance of Things Past*
he will see the "elements lurking in the emotional and sensuous values of words" of prose narrative. In *Ulysses* he will
find texture, color, sensuousness, imagery, "subtle collisions";
for instance: "wasted body within its loose brown graveclothes giving off an odor of wax and rosewood," breath "a
faint odour of wetted ashes." These words give us the very
feeling of death and the corpse. Again, "a dull green mass of
liquid" for the bay, the "great sweet mother." And again,
the powerful image of "a bowl of white china" that "stood
beside her deathbed holding the green sluggish bile which she
had torn up from her rotting liver by fits of loud groaning
and vomiting." The words bring us not only the concreteness of sickness and decay, but the implications of "the rotting liver," the bile "torn up" in the wrench of vomiting.
Stephen's dream, partly, at least, the result of his guilty conscience, comes to him in very concrete images that appeal to
the senses of sight, sound, and even taste.

Again in the quotation beginning "Ineluctable modality of
the visible," Joyce names his "signatures of all things" and
goes from "seaspawn and sea wrack, the nearing tide, that
rusty boot," to colors—"snotgreen, bluesilver, rust." And
thence to bodies, a bald millionaire and finally a gate. This
very obscure passage is, of course, a direct representation of
the unguided stream of consciousness, the dream world of day
or night which is made up of objects and emotional tones combined in what seems at first an entirely irrational and unorganized welter. And again, for multiple suggestion in its
most uncensored, in the Freudian sense, we can take the passage from Molly Bloom's daydream. Here we find words de-
noting objects used clearly with a strong emotional bias,
enough to delight the semanticist: "that old faggot Mrs

Riordan," "greatest miser ever was." The nouns are used to call names, and her being "down on bathingsuits and lownecks of course nobody wanted her to wear" indicates Molly's daydream connecting the facts of Mrs. Riordan's attitudes as shown toward concrete objects and situations with her frustrations because "no man would look at her twice." The subconscious mind knows how to bring together the object and the emotional tone which it evokes in a given human being, evokes not only in one human being, but more likely than not, in most of us.

The passage quoted from Proust showing his reaction to his grandmother's voice on the telephone tells us directly of his awareness of the symbolism of the experience of a voice which he was hearing that afternoon "for the first time," because his grandmother gave way to an unaccustomed freedom in expressing her affections, an "outpouring of an affection" which she usually from principle "kept hidden." This "isolation of the voice was like a symbol, a presentation, a direct consequence of another isolation, that of my grandmother, separated, for the first time in my life, from myself." Finally, in his anguish he recalls how he felt when he lost her as a child and knows that he will feel it again "on the day when we speak to those who can no longer reply." Proust has enlarged the reader's experience here by investing the telephone conversation with symbolic meanings of separation and death. He writes on several levels—emotional, analytical, philosophic.

He brings the same powers to his descriptions of his feelings upon looking at "the twin steeples of Martinville, on which the setting sun was playing."

In ascertaining and noting the shape of their spires, the changes of aspect, the sunny warmth of their surfaces, I felt that I was not penetrating to the full depth of my impression, that something more lay behind that mobility, that luminosity, something which they seemed at once to contain and conceal.[7]

These spires associated with the walks near Combray, were to return to Proust again as an important part of "the life of the mind."

But it is pre-eminently as the deepest layer of my mental soil, as firm sites on which I still may build, that I regard the Méséglise and Guermantes 'ways.' . . . And yet, because there is an element of individuality in places, when I am seized with a desire to see again the 'Guermantes way,' it would not be satisfied were I led to the banks of a river in which were lilies as fair, or even fairer than those in the Vivonne, any more than on my return home in the evening, at the hour when there awakened in me that anguish which, later on in life, transfers itself to the passion of love, and may even become its inseparable companion, I should have wished for any strange mother to come in and say good night to me, though she were far more beautiful and more intelligent than my own.

The reader must know *Remembrance of Things Past* in order either to appreciate fully Proust's analytic discussion here of the role of sensory experience in memory and "the life of the mind" or to respond to the wealth of associations brought up. He must know that the whole of the man's life was conditioned by his intense desire for his mother's caresses, which are vividly associated in his memory with the scenery at Combray and the two "ways" (walks) which he took as a little boy. The "anguish" which was to grip him later whenever he felt the passion of love was the inevitable result of his inability to free himself from his early infantile desires for his mother who often deprived him of the caresses he longed for. Proust has written a truly Freudian passage here, one that is characteristic of the poetic quality of his imagination. His writing is far too intricate an orchestration to be susceptible to brief quotation that in any way does it justice. Unless one knows the whole symphony with its interwoven themes, he will fail to appreciate the extended meanings of most of the passages. Much of the effect arises from the powerful symbolic overtones, repeated over and over again. Interestingly enough, too, even the close reader does not comprehend the magnificent whole until he has reached the concluding volume in which Proust explains the structure and his working out of his study of "the form of Time," which he wanted to make "continually perceptible in a transcription of human life necessarily very different from that conveyed to us by our deceptive senses."

Modern studies of consciousness have a great deal to do with today's interest in the depths of human nature, of which Freud speaks in his *New Introductory Lectures on Psycho-Analysis*, as "a new found land, which has been reclaimed from the regions of Folklore and Mysticism."

The writers of today draw more and more upon this new found land just as do the painters. Surrealism, based on irrationality rather than rationality, on the subconscious rather than the conscious, on the illogical rather than the logical, is the extreme development of the symbolist tendencies of Proust and Joyce. Dream-like juxtapositions, rather than strictly logical exposition or narration, no longer seem as strange to us as they did even a few years ago. We are learning to look, too, for the more obscure symbolisms and meanings. It is not surprising, therefore, to find in *The Kenyon Review* such an astonishing and provocative story as "Innocents" by M. P. Hutchins. That this story with all its psychoanalytical implications should be later given a place in the O. Henry Memorial collection for 1946 is a portent for the future. It reminds one of Edmund Wilson's statement in *Axel's Castle*[8] about the Symbolists: "They break down the walls of

[8] New York: Charles Scribner's Sons, 1931.

the present and wake us to the hope and exaltation of the untried, unsuspected possibilities of human thought and art." Speaking again, of Yeats, Valéry, Joyce, and Proust, Wilson says:

These books revealed new discoveries, artistic, metaphysical, psychological: they mapped the labyrinths of human consciousness, as they seemed never to have been mapped before, they made one conceive the world in a new way.

Few of us are innovators but it is heartening to think that we live in a period when literary as well as psychological and scientific boundaries are being constantly extended. Literature has lagged somewhat behind painting in freeing itself from the traditional and realistic bonds, and it may be a long time before most of us are willing to pore over highly symbolic and surrealistic writing in order to try to understand its intention. But it seems that we should conclude our study of contemporary fiction and its techniques with a recognition of the fact that there may remain still more "new found lands" and "new ways" for those who have sensitivity, imagination, and courage.

Bibliography

Theory, Criticism, Technique

Anderson, Sherwood. *A Story Teller's Story*. New York: The Viking Press, 1924.

Aristotle. *Theory of Poetry and Fine Art*, translation and commentary by S. H. Butcher. New York: The Macmillan Co., 1932.

Beach, Joseph Warren. *American Fiction 1920–1940*. New York: The Macmillan Co., 1942.

———. *The Twentieth Century Novel*. New York: D. Appleton-Century Co., 1932.

Bradley, A. C. *Shakespearean Tragedy*. New York: The Macmillan Co., 1930.

Buck, Philo M. *The Golden Thread*. New York: The Macmillan Co., 1931.

Burke, Kenneth. *The Philosophy of Literary Form*. Baton Rouge: Louisiana State University Press, 1941.

Dewey, John. *Art as Experience*. New York: G. P. Putnam's Sons, 1934.

Drew, Elizabeth and Sweeney, John L. *Directions in Modern Poetry*. New York: W. W. Norton & Co., Inc., 1940.

Freud, Sigmund. *New Introductory Lectures on Psycho-Analysis*. New York: W. W. Norton & Co., Inc., 1933.

Gilbert, Allan H. *Literary Criticism*. New York: American Book Company, 1940.

Hoffman, Frederick J. *Freudianism and the Literary Mind*. Baton Rouge: Louisiana State University Press, 1945.

Horney, Karen. *The Neurotic Personality of Our Time*. New York: W. W. Norton & Co., Inc., 1937.

———. *Self-Analysis*. New York: W. W. Norton & Co., Inc., 1942.

James, Henry. *The Art of the Novel*, Introduction by R. P. Blackmur. New York: Charles Scribner's Sons, 1934.

Kazin, Alfred. *On Native Grounds.* New York: Reynal and Hitch-
    cock, Inc., 1942.
Krutch, Joseph Wood. *The Modern Temper.* New York: Harcourt,
    Brace and Co., Inc., 1929.
Maier, N. R. F. and Reninger, H. W. *A Psychological Approach to
    Literary Criticism.* New York: D. Appleton-Century Co.,
    1933.
Mann, Thomas. *Freud, Goethe, Wagner,* translated by H. T. Lowe-
    Porter. New York: Alfred A. Knopf, Inc., 1937.
Mansfield, Katherine. *Journal,* edited by John Middleton Murry.
    New York: Alfred A. Knopf, Inc., 1927.
——. *Letters* (2 vols.), edited by John Middleton Murry. New
    York: Alfred A. Knopf, Inc., 1929.
——. *Scrapbook,* edited by John Middleton Murry. New York:
    Alfred A. Knopf, Inc., 1940.
Menninger, Karl and Menninger, J. L. *Love Against Hate.* New
    York: Harcourt, Brace and Co., Inc., 1942.
Mirrielees, Edith R. *The Story Writer.* Boston: Little, Brown and
    Co., 1939.
——. *Writing the Short Story.* Doubleday and Co., Inc., 1929.
Muller, Herbert. *Modern Fiction.* New York: Funk and Wagnalls
    Co., 1937.

Richards, I. A. *Principles of Literary Criticism.* New York: Har-
    court, Brace and Co., Inc., 1925.

Stein, Gertrude. *The Autobiography of Alice B. Toklas.* New York:
    Random House, Inc., 1933.

Tate, Allen. *Reactionary Essays on Poetry and Ideas.* New York:
    Charles Scribner's Sons, 1936.

Wharton, Edith. *The Writing of Fiction.* New York: Charles
    Scribner's Sons, 1925.
Wilson, Edmund. *Axel's Castle.* New York: Charles Scribner's Sons,
    1931.

Zabel, Morton D. *Literary Opinion in America.* New York: Harper
    and Brothers, 1937.

Short Story Collections

Anderson, Sherwood. *The Triumph of the Egg.* New York: The
    Viking Press, 1921.
——. *Winesburg, Ohio.* New York: The Viking Press, 1919.

Best American Short Stories, published yearly; Martha Foley, editor. Boston: Houghton Mifflin Co.

Boccaccio. *The Decameron*.

Caldwell, Erskine. *Kneel to the Rising Sun*. New York: The Viking Press, 1935.

Cather, Willa. *Obscure Destinies*. New York: Alfred A. Knopf, Inc., 1932.

Conrad, Joseph. *Youth*. New York: Doubleday and Co., Inc., 1903.

Hemingway, Ernest. *In Our Time*. New York: Charles Scribner's Sons, 1930.

——. *Men Without Women*. New York: Charles Scribner's Sons, 1927.

——. *Winner Take Nothing*. New York: Charles Scribner's Sons, 1933.

James, Henry. *The Great Short Novels of Henry James*, Philip Rhav, editor. New York: Dial Press, Inc., 1944.

Johnson, Josephine. *Winter Orchard and Other Stories*. New York: Simon and Schuster, Inc., 1935.

Joyce, James. *Dubliners*. New York: The Modern Library, 1926.

Lawrence, D. H. *Lovely Lady*. New York: The Viking Press, 1933.

LeSueur, Meridel. *Salute to Spring*. New York: International Publishers, 1940.

Mann, Thomas. *Stories of Three Decades*, translated by H. T. Lowe-Porter. New York: Alfred A. Knopf, Inc., 1936.

Mansfield, Katherine. *The Garden Party*. New York: Alfred A. Knopf, Inc., 1923.

——. *Bliss*. New York: Alfred A. Knopf, Inc., 1923.

——. *The Doves' Nest*. New York: Alfred A. Knopf, Inc., 1923.

Modern American Short Stories, Bennett Cerf, editor. Cleveland: The World Publishing Co., 1945.

New Yorker, The. Short Stories from The New Yorker. New York: Simon and Schuster, Inc., 1942.

O. Henry Memorial Award Prize Stories, published yearly; Herschel Brickell, editor. New York: Doubleday and Co., Inc.

O'Hara, John. *Pipe Night*. New York: Duell, Sloan and Pearce, Inc., 1945.

Parker, Dorothy. *After Such Pleasures*. New York: The Viking Press, 1933.

——. *Laments for the Living*. New York: The Viking Press, 1930.

Porter, Katherine Anne. *Flowering Judas and Other Stories*. New York: Harcourt, Brace and Co., 1935.

———. *The Leaning Tower*. New York: Harcourt, Brace and Co., 1944.

Saroyan, William. *The Daring Young Man on the Flying Trapeze*. New York: Random House, Inc., 1934.

———. *Little Children*. New York: Harcourt, Brace and Co., Inc., 1937.

Scott-Moncrieff, C. K., editor. *Marcel Proust: an English tribute, by Joseph Conrad, and others*. New York: Boni and Liveright, 1923.

Shaw, Irwin. *Sailor off the Bremen*. New York: Random House, Inc., 1939.

Steele, Wilbur Daniel. *Urkey Island*. New York: Harcourt, Brace and Co., Inc., 1926.

Stein, Gertrude. *Three Lives*. New York: The Modern Library, 1933.

Steinbeck, John. *Tortilla Flat*. New York: The Viking Press, 1935.

Stephens, James. *Etched in Moonlight*. New York: The Macmillan Co., 1928.

Suckow, Ruth. *Iowa Interiors*. New York: Alfred A. Knopf, Inc., 1926.

Tchekov, Anton. *The Stories of Anton Tchekov*. New York: The Modern Library, 1932.

Welty, Eudora. *A Curtain of Green*. New York: Doubleday and Co., Inc., 1941.

Index